A THEOLOGY PRIMER

A
Theology
Primer

ROBERT CUMMINGS NEVILLE

STATE UNIVERSITY OF NEW YORK PRESS

Cover by Beth Neville and Naomi Neville

Symbols illustrated on cover adapted from windows
at Marsh Chapel, Boston University

Published by
State University of New York Press, Albany

Printed in the United States of America

Production by Marilyn Semerad
Marketing by Dana E. Yanulavich

For information, address State University of New York Press,
State University Plaza, Albany, N.Y., 12246

Library of Congress Cataloging-in-Publication Data

Neville, Robert C.
    A theology primer / Robert Cummings Neville.
       p.   cm.
    Includes bibliographical references and index.
    ISBN 0-7914-0849-3 — ISBN 0-7914-0850-7 (pbk.)
    1. Theology, Doctrinal—Introductions.   I. Title.
BT65.N48   1991
230—dc20   90-19636
                                             CIP

10 9 8 7 6 5 4 3 2 1

Dedicated to Thomas J. J. Altizer
Mentor and Reluctant Church Theologian

Contents

Preface

This book aims to provide a text in Christian theology for introductory courses in seminaries, for advanced undergraduate courses, for rigorous adult education, and for individual study. It supposes that students would not have studied theology seriously before, or if so, only with regard to selected topics. What is attempted here is a review of a systematic selection of theological issues aimed to prepare students for further study in depth. Whereas no previous serious study of theology is presupposed, this text assumes that students have been introduced to basic philosophic ideas about God and related matters, or will acquire that introduction in passing while dealing with the theological issues. The distinction between theology and philosophy, like that between theology and the study of scripture, hymnody, and liturgy, is by no means hard and fast.

The approach to theology in the *Primer* reflects the author's Protestantism; discerning readers will note that the themes are organized with a Wesleyan bent, although other traditions are discussed far more often than that one. In American theology at the present time, the Protestant and Roman Catholic academic discussions are united, and most of what is argued here will be as acceptable to Roman Catholics as to Protestants. The *Primer* does not treat several important Roman Catholic themes, however, such as the infallibility of the Pope and saints. Because of Wesley's interest in the Cappadocian theologians, the *Primer* takes a position rather close to that of Orthodoxy in many respects, especially concerning sanctification. The style of thought here, however, is not particularly close to that of current Orthodox theology. Despite the inevitable particularity of the *Primer's* standpoint, it aims to address the concerns of Christians in all communions worldwide; at least it is explicitly vulnerable to all.

   The format of this *Theology Primer* is to provide a brief discussion of major doctrines in systematic connection, treating each doctrine or cluster of doctrines in a section of a chapter. The discussion will attempt to present a coherent and plausible, if ultimately flawed, theological position. Other positions or approaches will sometimes be sketched in order to prepare the reader for an alternative angle of vision; as a primer, however, the present discussion does not go into elaborate comparative argument. The position taken here is unique in several respects, and thus does not pretend to represent a bland consensus. Three unusual points of emphasis or doctrine should be noted.

   In the first place, the *Theology Primer* presents the doctrine of creation as the pivotal notion for understanding both God and the human condition. I am deeply grateful to the State University of New York Press for reprinting, in 1992, my *God the Creator*; originally published in 1968, that book set out my argument for God as creator *ex nihilo* with exhausting detail, and readers wishing to inquire beyond the "primer" level can consult that text. Central to the doctrine of creation is a contemporary theory of the Logos according to which it consists of four elements, each irreducible to the others but of necessity mutually ingredient in any created thing: order, components to be ordered, the particular actuality of things, and the value or valuable coordination of things. This Logos theory was not present in *God the Creator*; but see Neville, 1989: chap. 6, 1991, chap. 1. The elaboration of the implications of these elements provides the opportunities for expressing the basic orientations, respectively, of the traditional theologies of God as orderer and lawgiver, of the feminist theologies of God as Mother of the conditions and connections of life, of the existentialist theologies of God as ground of existence and challenge to authenticity, and of the soteriological theologies of sanctification, social liberation, and restoration of the covenant. This fourfold theory of the Logos is elaborated not only with regard to creation and the human condition, but also with regard to the characterization of the covenant, of sin, of salvation, of spiritual life, and of the Church. The organization of the *Primer* according to the idea of the Logos perhaps is oversystematic and surely oversimplifies some extremely complex doctrines; yet it provides a unifying principle for thinking through a great many related issues.

   The second unique feature of the *Primer's* position is that it employs a peculiar notion of covenant to interpret the created status of human beings and their relation to nature and to the social institutions constituting their environment. Covenant is understood here not as an agreement (perhaps one-sided) between God and already created human beings, but rather as a capstone condition of the created status of humanity as such: Adam was not a full human being without Eve, without the conventions involved in naming the animals, without purposeful work, and without an obligation to acknowledge the responsibilities and limits of the human place. The text for this theory of covenant is thus the second creation story in Genesis, not the covenant with Noah, Abraham, Moses, or David, although each of those illustrates essential components of covenant. By emphasizing the fact that the covenant binds people not only to God and each other but to the rest of nature and to the institutions of life, the position taken here integrates the concerns of ecological theology and social justice. It embraces ecological theology without overly romanticizing nature-mysticism. It embraces social critique without the Marxist reduction of institutional injustice to power relations among classes of people, sketching instead the roles of people in institutions that carry value and disvalue, institutions which for justice require either support or amendment.

Perhaps the most unusual point about the position taken in this *Primer* is that, although aimed to present Christian theology in the language, traditions, and cultic practices of global Christianity, the position has been developed out of reflections that respect the theological positions of all religions and of the secular world. Thus many of the arguments for the specific theses defended here cannot be expressed except in discussion with Judaism about Messiahship or with Buddhism about Enlightenment, or with Confucianism about spiritual perfection. Those extended discussions are beyond the scope of the *Primer*. The theology here also arises from an appreciation of the vitality of Christian traditions other than the European and North American tradition that has seemed "classic" until recently. Although the classic positions clearly inform the *Primer's* position, positively or negatively, they are not the only ones to do so.

The general outline of topics—God and creation, the human condition, sin, salvation, and spiritual life in the world and religious community—is typical of Christian systematic theology from Thomas Aquinas in the thirteenth century down to Paul Tillich in the twentieth. Therefore, even if the *Primer's* position is internally confused, or conceptually mistaken, or too advanced toward religions other than Christianity or toward the secular world, or incompatible with yet other profound truths within the Christian or other traditions, this should show up in an examination chapter by chapter. Despite the variety of its sources, the *Primer* claims that its doctrines express orthodox traditions of Christianity as well as truths of which other religions should take account. Making that claim, the *Primer* makes its position vulnerable to criticism and invites correction.

The doctrines do not come out of the blue, but from a long historical process. Rather than duplicate or summarize the work of historians of theology, each chapter of the *Primer* ends with citations of classic and contemporary texts that students should regard as historical background for the discussion at hand. That they serve as background does not mean they necessarily support the position of the *Primer*; on the contrary, the *Primer* often takes the cited texts as positions to be rejected. Where this is not made explicit, the reader who compares both sides will see the disparity immediately. The *Primer* can be understood without this background, but its underlying strategies and rhetorical choices will seem a bit arbitrary without understanding the background in relation to which the position here is taken up.

A prefatory word is needed about the relation of the writing to the intended audience. In *The Analogical Imagination* (1981: chs. 1–2), David Tracy distinguishes three kinds of theology: fundamental, systematic, and practical. Practical theologies are those associated with movements of social change, and their audience is the participants in the movement. Fundamental theologies are those that ask the basic questions in a wholly pluralistic and perhaps secular context with little or no regard for communities of faith, and their audience is mainly the academy. Systematic theologies are those oriented to the self-understanding and guidance of "communities of faith." The *Theology Primer* is aimed at the audience to which Tracy assigns systematic theology, and the language of the *Primer* reflects that. Nevertheless, the commitment to publicity of theological argument subjects the *Primer* to criteria appropriate to fundamental theology, even if the non-Christian world is treated only in abbreviation. At bottom, the *Primer* rejects Tracy's distinction between fundamental and systematic theology. Fundamental theology is far more dependent on a positive experiential vivification of various traditional symbols and cultic practices than his distinction suggests; thus it cannot do without embracing communities of faith, perhaps all of them. On the other hand, no single community of faith, especially theologically acute Christians, would want a theology that is only the language game of Christians; theology for one's community should be true as well, insofar as truth is an issue in theology. Therefore, theology needs to embrace without clear separation both the public rigor of fundamental theology and the cultic particularity of the various religious faiths.

A central conviction permeating this text and repeated with perhaps boring frequency is that theology is a public discipline, addressed to anyone who has an interest to engage the issues. As such, theology is not particularly Christian but rather a discipline seeking either a universal language or a habit of dialogue among many languages. Yet theology is also the discipline that critically examines the language and symbols of particular traditions, and the tradition at stake here is the Christian. The

Primer is written expressly for Christians and others who are interested in Christianity. Many of the points could be expressed in the terms of non-Christian religions, and others would illustrate serious differences between Christianity and the other religions; yet neither kind of discussion is undertaken at length here. An explicitly public theology would have to relate to the other religions in ways the *Primer* relates only to Christianity. The *Primer* is thus just an introduction to fully public theology, a place to begin.

Having found stressed here as elsewhere my convictions about the public character of theology, the reader might wonder whether there is any personal and private passion motivating the theology. At least, several friends have suggested that I 'fess up to such. Three points are important in the history of my own piety for the theological position taken here. When I was fourteen, my high school English teacher remarked to me, "You know, Bob, God is not in time." I knew instantly what that meant, and also that it was not an ordinary kind of thought. Moreover, I knew then that thinking that kind of thought was what I was for, although it took some years to identify it as philosophical theology. Then, when I was in graduate school attempting to write a dissertation on Duns Scotus' theory of divine creation, one evening I suddenly understood the logic of the causal asymmetry represented by the idea of creation *ex nihilo*. That has been my topic ever after. Finally, early in our marriage my wife and I had a daughter, Gwendolyn, whose birth was celebrated by the congregation of St. Stephen's United Methodist Church in the Bronx, all of whose people stood up as a corporate God-parent at her baptism; she lived but four months and then the congregation wiped our tears, the living fingertips of the ancient and encompassing Body of Christ. So my theology is intended to understand two private things: the eternity in her short life, a speck in the eternity of God's creation, and the eternity in the historic Body of Christ reaching from the Mount of Ascension to the Bronx in 1966.

The occasion for writing this *Primer* was my obligation to teach the basic Christian doctrine course in the Boston University School of Theology. That course is an integral part of a new Master of Divinity curriculum designed by the whole faculty for the education of current and future parish ministers. For the first time I have had to think in a systematic way about what Christian ministers ought to know about theology on an elementary level. For putting these things together I am indebted to the whole faculty but especially to John Berthrong, Anthony Campbell, John Cartwright, Linda Clark, Katheryn Darr, Merle Jordan, Dana Robert, Simon Parker, Paul Sampley, and John Ward. Jon Westling taught me that nothing is more important for theological education than theology. As for the theology itself I am deeply grateful for conversations with Horace Allen, Ray Hart, Peter Manchester, Harold Oliver, Jennifer Rike, and William Sullivan.

A draft of the *Primer* was used in the Christian doctrine course in the spring of 1990, and I thank the students in that class for their patience as well as critical suggestions. Several people have given helpful editorial comments, among them Robert Morrison, Curtis Daugaard, and Sean Recroft. Daugaard was the Teaching Assistant for the course, and valiantly explained the text's obscurities to me. As my graduate assistant, Recroft gave extensive comments on organization of the second draft, prepared bibliographies, helped with correlating assignments to chapters, and oversaw the production process; as my friend he has tried to keep me from the more egregious theological errors to which I'm prone. I owe thanks as usual to Jay Schulkin, my closest conversation partner save for Beth Neville who declines to be thanked in print except for her cover for the book. I want to pay special tribute to Marilyn Semerad, Production Editor at State University of New York Press; this is the seventh book of mine whose editing and manufacture she has overseen, and she is at work on the eighth. Beth Neville, who designs the covers, joins me in thanks. Ms. Semerad is responsible for all production details except typos, for which the author retains responsibility as sole proofreader and creative spelling genius. William Eastman, my publisher, deserves credit as well as thanks for understanding that theology is public discourse, and therefore fit for a university press, even while it aims to be faithful to religious practice.

John Cobb once said of Thomas J. J. Altizer that he was the most God-intoxicated theologian on the contemporary scene, and for ten years as his colleague at Stony Brook I learned how true that is. Although I learned many academic things from Altizer, including how Christian theology is based in world religions and the importance of history within Christianity, his mightiest lesson has been the seriousness of theology. He may not recognize much of himself in this *Primer*, especially because it is Church theology which he rejects as apologetics. Yet his radical, anti-apologetical theology is at root a genuinely conservative Church theology. The orienting theme of the *Primer* is the articulation of an identity for Christianity in a context where the usual resources of identity have been frittered away. This concern for Christian identity is pure Altizer, and I dedicate this book to him to express my gratitude.

Biblical quotations are taken from the New Revised Standard Version Bible, copyright 1989, by the Division of Christian Education of the National Council of the Churches of Christ in the United States of America. Among other reasons, this translation is selected for its sensitivity to inclusive language.

How To Use This Book

The book, of course, may be used any way the reader pleases. If the *Primer* is for a class, or for a group's or an individual's serious study, it might be advisable to supplement it with additional materials. At the end of each chapter is a bibliography of "Readings in Key Texts." The key texts are thirteen important books. The books, singly or in varying combinations, might serve as collateral readings for a course, according to the interests of the teacher and the time allotted. They can be organized to provide an historical background from antiquity onward, to provide a contemporary set of options, or to provide a set of the teacher's favorite theological heroes and villains. Of course a teacher might choose very different texts as collateral reading.

The key texts cited are the following; they can be acquired in any edition, for instance those listed in the Bibliography at the end of this volume.

Aquinas, St. Thomas. *Summa Contra Gentiles: On the Truth of the Catholic Faith.*

—*Summa Theologica*, in Pegis, 1945.

Barth, Karl. *Credo.*

Calvin, John. *The Institutes of the Christian Religion.*

Cobb, John B., Jr., and David Ray Griffin. *Process Theology: An Introductory Exposition.*

Ferm, Deane William, editor. *Third World Liberation Theologies: A Reader.*

Hildegard of Bingen. *Scivias.*

Luther, Martin. *Three Treatises.*

Rahner, Karl. *Foundations of Christian Faith.*

Ruether, Rosemary Radford. *Sexism and God-Talk: Toward a Feminist Theology.*

Schleiermacher, Friedrich. *The Christian Faith.*

Tillich, Paul. *Systematic Theology.* In three volumes.

No one could assign all the key texts for a one-semester course, although a group or person studying Christian doctrine for an indefinite period might want to work through all of them. The readings from the key texts suggested here are long, usually whole essays or book sections, and teachers will want to modify them for the emphasis of the particular class. There are many instances in which the key text assigned to a particular chapter here could with equal reason be assigned to another chapter; again, the emphases in the context in which the *Primer* is read should determine relevance. The *Primer* does not make a point of commenting on the key texts, except where relevant to the independent argument of the *Primer*; substitution of other key texts would thus not lead to unclarity here.

The five most systematic authors of key texts, Thomas Aquinas, John Calvin, Karl Rahner, Friedrich Schleiermacher, and Paul Tillich, are represented with selections for each chapter of the *Primer*. Aquinas, however, is not represented by a single book, but by selections from both the *Summa Contra Gentiles* and the *Summa Theologica*; neither of these books is comprehensive enough to be represented in all chapters. Augustine could be represented in all chapters if one were to supplement the *Confessions* with *The City of God*. The books by Barth and by Cobb and Griffin are systematic and are cited here in their entirety, but they do not break down their discussions into as many groupings as needed to match the *Primer's* structure. The books by Ferm (an anthology), Hildegard of Bingen, Martin Luther, and Rosemary Radford Ruether do not have a systematic structure, although their orientation is systematic; they are cited only at the chapters which deal with topics they address.

To match the readings in the key texts to the topics of the *Primer*, it is necessary often to take them out of the order in which they appear in the key texts. Thus, in several instances passages occurring earlier in the original will be cited later here. In all instances, the introductory material and major orienting selections are given here first. But the reader might want to look through each of the key texts from beginning to end in order to understand its scheme.

History of theology is, of course, an indispensable part of theological inquiry. A student would be well advised to acquire and frequently consult Bernhard Lohse's *A Short History of Christian Doctrine from the First Century to the Present*, or some other up-to-date outline. A truly magnificent large history is Jaroslav Pelikan's *The Christian Tradition: A History of the Development of Doctrine*. For beginning students Van A. Harvey's *A Handbook of Theological Terms* might be very helpful; advanced students will still find it intriguing.

Because many readers come to theology with assumptions that the real action is in liberation and feminist theologies—topics discussed throughout the *Primer*—special selections from the Bibliography have been culled for the appendices, brief bibliographies of liberation and feminist theologies, respectively. The feminist bibliography includes not only books of theological critique but also historical and anthropological studies of the Earth Mother and other elements of the feminine in religion.

Introduction

> Since in its essence the church is a theological reality having to do
> with God's redemptive shaping of human community, the task of
> ministry is profoundly theological. Above all else, the minister is a
> theologian, and the theological purpose of ministry—to enable the
> church to be church—should infuse and transform everything the
> minister does, whether in pastoral care, liturgy and preaching, in-
> stitutional management, education, or social mission. The church is
> indeed a "treasure in earthen vessels." It is all too easy for the
> minister to become preoccupied with the vessel, to forget that the
> treasure must infuse and transform the vessel. The treasure without
> the vessel is dissipated in formless ways; the vessel without the
> treasure is merely an empty container. In order for the minister to be
> a theologian, to recognize the treasure and know how to work with
> it, she or he must engage in an ongoing process of theological reflec-
> tion and study. Nothing should be more central to the work of
> ministry, yet nothing is more commonly neglected.
> —Peter C. Hodgson, *Revisioning the Church*

This book addresses a need for an introductory text for adults
engaged in serious study of systematic theology in the Christian tradition. Its chapters treat sequentially most of the major doctrines of Christian theology, especially those that have analogues or alternatives in
other religious traditions or that stand opposed to assumptions
characteristic of the nonreligious, secular world. Further, these doctrines
are systematically related to one another, and the relations are unfolded
as the argument proceeds. Although there doubtless are omissions that
will seem important to one scholar or another, the result is a fairly
systematic exposition of central problems of Christian theology.

A particular system is presented to address these problems and,
although it provides an initial orientation, the reader is invited to explore

its alternatives and disagree. At the minimum, two results are to be sought. First, the topics introduced here are those any Christian should address in order to have a faith comparable in sophistication to an excellent liberal arts education in other subjects, a faith that can be articulated with the same degree of subtlety as is desirable in knowledge of the sciences, politics, and belles lettres. Second, although expressed most often in terms of the contemporary debates, the topics here articulate central parts of the Christian traditions and thus provide a crucial connection between current thought around the world and the past of Christian theological inquiry.

The discussions here make no supposition about the reader's faith community or lack thereof. Jews, Muslims, Buddhists, secularists, and technocrats can learn about Christian theology here if they are interested. Christians can use this text to find an overall, systematic orientation and review of doctrine.

Designed specifically for a first-semester theology course for divinity school students, it is also appropriate for adult Christian education classes and for individuals prepared to begin rigorous theological inquiry. Although the book does not presuppose advanced preparation in theology, it does presuppose a number of other items.

1. It assumes that the reader is motivated to learn theology. The motivation may well arise from an interest in a particular theological question. Or it may stem from the realization that theology is instrumentally necessary for the intelligent fulfillment of a special ministry. It might arise from the need to articulate Christian identity, either on the part of the faithful or from the curiosity of another perspective. But along the way, it assumes that the reader's curiosity will be piqued by the intrinsic interest of the topics. There are at least three dimensions to this interest. How do Christians attempt to understand divine matters? How does this relate to other attempts to understand them? And, what is the truth about divine matters, insofar as this can be determined, either parochially or collectively?

2. It assumes that theological understanding must be systematic at certain points, and that the introductory level is one such point. Many theological topics have obvious connections with others, such as the bearing of the nature of God or the nature of divine action in salvation. More interesting is the frequent lack of obvious connection, where theological inquiry must discover something otherwise obscured, such as the bearing of divine presence in history on church organization. There are many concrete senses of "system" in theology, some of which are discussed in chapter 2, one of which is exhibited in the text, and others of which are given in the collateral readings suggested.

The very project of systematic theology is not without controversy today, however. Two theological developments have formed in our time that appear on the surface to be inimical to systematic thinking. One is the movement, mainly among academics, to express the Christian message in story or narrative form rather than in the form of concepts.[1] Narrative theology itself rests upon a broader interest in narrative in literary studies (e.g. Alter, 1981). An elementary motivation for this movement is general discouragement about the viability of abstract conceptual thought. A related motivation is that the compelling quality of stories might overcome the modern or secular distrust of religious language. The problems of abstraction will be discussed at length in the first two chapters.[2] The point about the compelling quality of story is very well taken. Nevertheless, as David Tracy has shown (1987: ch. 1), a story needs to be told from all perspectives, and still is ambiguous. The story of the Christianization of Europe from the standpoint of the Druids has an unexpected feel to it; the story of the development of Christian ministry from the perspective of women is quite different from the same story told by men; the story of Jesus understood by Rabbi Hillel is not the same as that told by Luke. As concepts need stories to attain conviction, stories need justifiable concepts to provide orientation and context. Furthermore, both stories and concepts have histories in which elements of the other are deeply related. Systematic theology is important for providing orientation and context for religious stories, as chapter 1 shall argue.

The second movement casting doubt on the usefulness of systematic theology is the family of liberation theologies, including most especially many feminist theologies. Often nonacademic, liberation theologies arise from particular struggles, are preoccupied with the issues that come to focus in the elements of the struggle, and are suspicious both of the traditional forms of systematic theology and the content of that theology itself which is so closely associated with the structures from which liberation is sought. By contrast with systematic theologies, many liberation theologies attempt to express themselves in narrative form or in the language of the social sciences.

In her fine book, *Transforming Grace: Christian Tradition and Women's Experience* (1988: pp. 7–8), Anne E. Carr makes an astute distinction that locates the genre of the systematic theology of this *Primer*. Writing specifically of the women's movement, she says:

> Both logically and chronologically, its first task is *critique of the past.* Like parts of liberation theology with which it is allied, feminist theology has criticized aspects of the Christian tradition that denigrate women. . . .

Second on the agenda of feminist theology is the *recovery of the lost history of women* in the Christian tradition. Work in this area has made it clear that women exercised significant leadership within almost all the Christian traditions and historical periods: as genuine apostles in the earliest Christian communities; as scholars and foundresses in patristic and medieval times; as social archivist organizers in Catholic Reformation religious communities; as preachers in Quaker, sectarian, and evangelical circles; as religious and social reformers in nineteenth-century America. . . .

A third aspect of feminist theology is *revisioning Christian categories* in ways that take seriously the equality and the experience of women. This broad rubric includes reformulations of the doctrine of God (no longer conceived in purely masculine images and concepts); of understandings of Jesus Christ (in ways that emphasize his humanity rather than his maleness); of the church, its ministry, and its ritual (as a community of equal partnership rather than one of male dominance. [Italics in the original.]

The *Primer* is clearly a work of the third stage, revisioning Christian categories.

In particular, the *Primer* attempts to incorporate the major insights of feminist theology, liberation theologies, and the history of the dialogue between Christianity and other world religions, including many of the major positions of the other religions themselves. For instance, regarding the doctrine of God, chapters 3 and 4 will argue that the male aspect of the Sky God, who brings order and morality to creation, needs to be balanced over against the equally important female aspect of the Earth Mother, who constitutes the round of natural forces a bit oblivious to the scale of human order, a feminine type of the weaver of the conditions for human community rather than the order of the community itself. Earth Mother and Sky God are but two of four equally important, irreducible, and quasi-independent aspects of God-in-creation, as expressed in the doctrine of the Logos. This quatrapartite analysis of the presence of God is carried through the doctrines of the human condition, sin, and redemption. Therefore, in a systematic way of reconstituting Christian categories, the *Primer* returns the Goddess to the temple along with Yahweh. At the present time, I believe, no other systematic theology attempts to reconstitute Christian categories so as to incorporate major feminist concerns as thoroughly as the *Primer's.*

Precisely because a reconstruction of categories is called for, including a profoundly systematic reinterpretation of the traditional Christian language, much of the rhetoric of the first two stages of liberation theology must be eliminated as belonging to the very cultural mind-set to be overcome. There is very little rhetoric in the *Primer,* for instance, of the "power," "empowerment," "oppression," "victim," and "woundedness" sort. These words all arose in early modernity when the models of physics were being employed to express everything, and the human sphere was translated into the language of mechanisms and power vectors. People, especially women, were conceived to be passive bodies to be acted upon by others and to move with mere inertia, to be pushed out of the way and cut open as objects (Bordo, 1987). This "modern" rhetoric expresses and is controlled by the very cultural evil feminism aims to attack, and, whereas it might serve to express the pain felt within the unjust culture, it cannot serve to express a superior "revisioning of Christian categories."

Because some students might come to the *Primer* in introductory theology without experiencing the first two stages in liberation theology, or without awareness of other religions, attention should be called to what is presupposed to some extent here as experiential and intellectual background. For the first stage in feminist theology, people might want to consult Daly (1973, 1984) or Ruether (1983); for the second stage Elisabeth Schussler Fiorenza (1984, 1985) or Mollenkott (1988). Both stages for Third World liberation theologies are expressed in Ferm (1986). Daniel L. Migliore (1980) presents an insightful transition from the second to the third stage for liberation theology in general. For students needing an elementary introduction to world religions, Huston Smith (1958) is still the most accessible; Chan (1963) and Radhakrishnan and Moore (1957) provide basic texts of Asian religions. In the *Primer*, non-Christian world religions will not be discussed in much depth, and knowledge of the first two stages of liberation, including feminist, theology will be assumed. That the *Primer* responds to these movements, of course, does not mean that it accepts them in all their manifestations; they are internally highly diverse. The *Primer* is not the place to provide critical assessments of liberation theologies or other world religions, however.

3. This book assumes a commitment to theological study deep enough to justify an investment in collateral reading, either through the purchase of other books or through taking the trouble to use a library. In addition, the text here will not be used to its best purpose unless the reader begins to ask whether it is on the right track, whether its arguments are cogent, whether its assumptions are reasonable, and whether it is worth believing so far as it goes. What would it mean to develop a contrary theology, in part or whole? What other assumptions ought to be made? What *is* the truth about the divine matters discussed? Although attempting to be historically connected with the Christian faith, and accurate in representation, this book is not a sociological study of what (some) Christians think about divine matters. Rather it is an attempt to express what is worth believing about divine matters, of

relevance to Christians and anyone else prepared to enter into consideration of the Christian approach.

The plot of the book is to provide a systematic exposition of a specific version of the doctrines listed, anticipating the later chapters in the earlier, restating the earlier points in later discussions. At its narrowest, the argument here is the particular theology of the author, expressed in outline form; others may accept the argument on its own terms, or re-express it in other terms, arising from other traditions and responsive to other problematics. Still other Christians and Christian theologians might find little point of contact here.

For the last seventy-five years, much European and American Protestant theology (and more recently Roman Catholic theology) has taken its rise from the problems of commentary on scripture. By contrast, the approach here comes to theology from philosophy. The author has been assured by some theologians, particularly neo-orthodox theologians, that this cannot be theology at all, but only philosophy. It helps to remember that Augustine, Boethius, Anselm, Aquinas, Scotus, Calvin, Schleiermacher, and Tillich, to name only a few of the giants, came to theology through philosophy, and that many of them extended their work to scriptural commentary. The peculiar contemporary advantage of philosophy as the theological entry point is that it allows contact with other religious theological traditions, and with the assumptions of secularity. If theology is not to be mere confession of what some Christians believe, but an inquiry into what is worth believing about divine matters, engagement with the approaches of other theological traditions is intrinsic to the enterprise.

The positive argument of each chapter is relatively brief, but does put forth a doctrine or set of doctrines. This approach is preferable to at least two alternatives. One might be tempted to aim at presenting the core answers on which all Christians agree.[3] The core of common theological agreement is an illusion, however. Even the choice of topics reflects a particular theological perspective. This already biases the alleged core of common agreement, even if one can gerrymander the problems to find apparent unanimity. Furthermore, the presentation of a "common core" has the consequence in intellectual politics of marginalizing and probably delegitimating those positions falling outside the core. That is dogmatism at its worst. Another alternative is to present a comprehensive review of all major (and maybe minor) theological positions.[4] In principle, this might be desirable. But it would still be selective, would be severely limited in the interest of manageable length, and would fail to provide a focused attempt to define Christian theological identity, relative to which one might agree or disagree. The review of possible options is rather a matter for history of theology, and is pursued with far more accuracy, objectivity, and thoroughness by means of that approach.

The systematic approach here will proceed according to the following outline.

The first chapter introduces the idea of theology, giving definitions of crucial terms appropriate to the kind of theology practised here, and raising the question of truth in theology. At this stage, of course, the discussion is preliminary and aimed more to orient the reader than to present a doctrine of theological method. The second chapter, however, takes up the topic of revelation, about which the reader doubtless has opinions already formed. The uses of scripture, tradition, reason, and experience as revelational sources for theology are discussed and related to the question of authority. Revelation is also related to salvation and spiritual life, including church life, as well as to theology; these other focal points for revelation are discussed in subsequent chapters, though usually under the terminology of grace rather than revelation. These first two chapters constitute a prologue to theology proper, as defined in chapter 1.

Chapters 3 and 4 are about God. The former introduces the question of God as a peculiar problem for the modern age, arguing that science has taught culture to view the world as bounded with closure, and God is either within or without the bounds of closure. After noting some alternatives, it is argued that God should be conceived most generally as the creator of everything determinate; determinateness is the defining closure of the world. All less general and determinate conceptions or symbols of God, such as being a personal agent or as loving, refer to characteristics that are the result of the creation itself, characters God has in relation to the created world. Chapter 4 specifies the general conception of God as creator to explicitly Christian themes. First, the doctrine of the Trinity is explained in terms of creation, preparatory to the more Christological discussion in chapter 12. Then the doctrine of eternity and time is introduced with reference to the divine life and preparatory to later discussions of eternal life. The doctrine of the Logos is then introduced as consisting of four irreducible notions: order, components to be ordered, the actual mixture of components and their order, and the value or orientation to God of the creation. The elements of the Logos are explained as defining families of symbols relating to religions generally as well as to Christianity.

Chapter 5 presents the doctrine of the normative creation of human beings, the ideal human condition. That ideal, constitutive of what it means to be human, is interpreted in terms of the idea of covenant, and the rest of the system is thus a covenant theology. The ideals defining the covenant are ideals for order (that is, righteousness), ideals for acknowledging the components (that is, piety), ideals for authenticity regarding historical particularity (that is, faith), and ideals for the religious path to achieve value relative to creation (that is, hope). The fourfold elements of the Logos are thus normative for human life as created.

Chapter 6, on sin, discusses the breakdown or perversion of righteousness, piety, faith, and hope on both the personal and social levels. People cannot live without righteousness, piety, faith, and hope being normative ideals, however much they fail them; they can only be immoral, impious, alienated and despairing. This is a way of understanding that people are created by means of and always with the Logos. Human sin cannot escape divine love.

Chapter 7 contrasts the freedom native to human beings with the bondage that results from sin. The topic of human freedom versus divine control is explored. Chapter 8 begins the exposition of divine love with a theory of justification and freedom, Acknowledgment of God's love is shown to be the key to recognition of one's own sinfulness, repentance, the development of faith, and commitment to the path of sanctification. The principal, though not only, form of God's love, for Christians, is in Jesus Christ.

Whereas chapters 7 and 8 focus on sin and its remedy in the heart, chapter 9 draws out the implication of this for society and social structures. The covenant is redescribed in social terms relating to contemporary social justice movements. Salvation, it is argued, consists both in justification (God's act) and in sanctification (for which people are mainly responsible). Sanctification is both personal and social, and these two sides cannot be separated except in abstraction.

Chapter 10 is about sanctification itself, in personal and social aspects. Personal sanctification is developed with respect to spirit, mind, and heart, whereas sanctification as social justice is interpreted in terms of the restoration of the covenant, so far as that can be restored.

Chapters 11 and 12 present the doctrine of the Christ, arguing that both historical and metaphysical Christologies are necessary to account for the roles of Jesus Christ in Christian thinking and practice. The former introduces the notion of the cultic community of disciples of Jesus, preparatory to the discussion of the Christian Church in chapter 13. Both the teachings and works of Jesus are presented in classifications deriving from the Logos-forms of righteousness, piety, faith, and hope. The distinction between disciples of Jesus and followers of other paths governed by expressions of the Logos in other religions is drawn and explored. The twelfth chapter develops a formal Logos-Christology, arguing that the historical reality of Jesus Christ in fact incarnated the Logos. This discussion requires the explicit introduction of the notion of the

Holy Spirit that is operative throughout most of the doctrines discussed in the *Primer*. The Christian doctrine of history is discussed in connection with the doctrines of eternity and time.

Chapter 13 relates the doctrines of the Christ and the Holy Spirit to the Church. It presents a theory of the sacraments, focusing on baptism and the eucharist, and then interprets the Church in terms of mission, teaching, preaching, and action. The discussion concludes with a treatment of the relativity of certain senses of truth to life within the Christian Church, in connection with parallel cultic expressions of truth in other traditions, and the claims of all to truth in a deeper sense.

1

The Nature of Theology

Theology is the conceptualization of the assumptions and assertions about divine matters that are made, can be made, and ought to be made in order to know as much of the truth as possible.

There are many components of this definition that require attention, here and in the chapters that follow.

I. DIVINE MATTERS

The subject matter of theology, as evident from the name deriving from the Greek roots for "God" (*theos*) and "discourse" (*logos*), is the nature of the divine and those things that are to be understood in relation to the divine. Thus the principal topic is God or, in religions such as Buddhism that reject the appropriateness of the idea of God for divine matters, whatever is indicated by the ideas that exclude that of God. The divine bears upon many other topics in addition, that are thus also theological. These include the world insofar as it is contingent or dependent upon the divine, the nature of human life and society insofar as they receive their ground, meaning, and goal in relation to the divine, and the problems of human life that are of ultimate significance and whose resolutions are understood as salvation, personal or social perfection, or transcendent enlightenment. Both individuals and society are to be analyzed theologically insofar as they require understanding in relation to the divine. The same may be true of history, of institutions, of culture in the sense of arts and letters, all of which may be understood non-theologically on their own terms but which also require interpretation in terms of their relation to the divine.[1] Most especially theology studies religious institutions such as churches, musical and liturgical traditions, and the traditions of theology itself on which the divine has special bearing.

The term "divine matters" is used in order to indicate the need for a kind of conditional neutrality with regard to the idea of God and its alternatives. No theologian from any tradition would disagree with the assertion that every category or name for the divine is finally inadequate to say all that can be said about the topic.[2] Theological ideas can be true and valid but still too vague, too narrow, too limited to a set of parochial assumptions, too confined to a family of metaphors, to exhaust the truth. Most theologians would agree that the root of the problem is that the divine is infinite and any system of representing the divine is finite, however appropriate the finite representations might be within the assumptions of their approach. It is better to think of theology as studying "divine matters" rather than simply "God" because there may be more differences than meet the eye between the Indian Hindu idea of Brahman, for instance, and the Christian notion of God; there may be more connections than meet the eye, on the other hand, between the Christian notion of God and the Confucian idea of Principle of Heaven. In either case, the Hindu and Confucian ideas are alternatives to the traditional Christian idea, at least upon initial reflection, and theology is interested in understanding the issues between them. If Confucian Principle is an alternative to the Christian God as a representation of divine matters, it is a theological topic. Thinkers in the Confucian and Hindu traditions who would find themselves puzzled and challenged by Christian theology are thus also theologians.[3]

Much of contemporary secular culture rejects the validity of the whole topic of divine matters, and thus would seem to offer nothing for theological reflection. But precisely so far as secular culture rejects the topic, it is living from assumptions or making assertions that are theological alternatives to religious traditions, even if those counter-divine elements are rather thin. Furthermore, there are elements within secular culture that are functional equivalents of theological assumptions about the world and human life. For instance, if it is thought that the world is not contingent or dependent in any way on the divine but rather on a big bang, that belief is an alternative to religious understanding and hence theological (or countertheological). Religious life for human beings has been characterized by Paul Tillich (1951, pt. I, B, 4), an important twentieth century Protestant Christian theologian, as the pursuit of an ultimate concern, the concern you would give up last when push comes to shove. A proper religion, he argued, has God as the ultimate concern; but most people are idolatrous in pursuing money, security, ego aggrandizement, or other merely finite objects. In Tillich's view, Marxism thus registers as a religion because it defines an ultimate concern for society and organizes institutions and movements in pursuit of this concern; its commitment to progress, for example, and to the derivation of the meaning of individuals' life from participation in the movement toward progress, is a variation on Jewish, Christian, and Muslim ideas about sacred history, despite the theoretical atheism of Marxist philosophy.

The phrase "divine matters" reflects a Western theistic origin. But any other phrase seeking neutrality would also have a particular origin; no language with a level of abstraction required to transcend all historical conditioning, such as mathematics, has the richness to express theologically interesting ideas. Therefore, the best that can be done is to generalize from some rich tradition and attempt to control for the biases introduced. The context here is theology, aiming at the truth for everyone and thus in indefinitely open dialogue, as practised at least by Christians. Hence the theistic root is appropriate for a term that explicitly neutralizes itself with regard to the question of whether the divine is best represented as an individual (the usual meaning of theological theism).

II. THEOLOGICAL ASSUMPTIONS AND ASSERTIONS

Theology does not launch itself from nowhere to know about divine matters, but begins by attempting to understand how those matters are and have been represented. Sometimes representations of the divine are explicitly formulated as beliefs expressed in assertions. But more often, and historically at the motivating source of theology, those representations are contained in social practices directed to this or that end but assuming things about divine matters. Religious liturgies, to take but one example, preceded theological attempts to explain the references in the texts, songs, gestures, and ritual acts. The ancient Christian baptismal liturgy, for instance, was a ceremony to give individuals a new identity as members of the Christian community. But some of the things the individuals said and did during the ceremony represented God to be a certain way, Jesus to have a special relation both to God and to themselves, and the Holy Spirit to be performing a concommitant action with the ritual. The Apostles' Creed originated as a baptismal formula. Christians can agree or disagree with the creed insofar as they give it a theological interpretation. Regardless of theological agreement, they can recite it as part of contemporary liturgy to affirm continuity with the ancient practice of the performance of inducting members into a new identity in the Christian community. Following contemporary philosophic usage (Searle, 1969), we can speak of the "performatory" use of theologically important representations in distinction from their "assertive" use. The performatory use assumes the appropriateness of the representation while using it in the performance of some activity.

Theology thus needs to examine the assumptions in the symbols and symbolic actions of religious and social practices (Long, 1986). Verbal symbols are the easiest to identify, and many people think that their analysis exhausts the field. But some other symbols are explicit in being symbols, such as a cross or Star of David, or gestures such as making the sign of the cross at the mention of the Trinity, or *davening*, the Jewish practice of swaying in a bow while reciting certain prayers. In addition there are symbols that might not be recognized as such, for instance looking "up" to find God, or special piety toward ancestors in excess of their particular merit. Religious institutions and practices are fraught with assumptions expressed in many ways. We can discern theologically interesting assumptions about whole ancient societies, however, by determining how they buried their dead or decorated their pots; we can discern contemporary theological assumptions by analyzing popular entertainments, or the budgeting priorities of governments.

Because there never has been a completely fresh beginning for theology, there have always been explicitly formulated religious beliefs. Often these have been framed in stories, histories, laws, and poetry, rather than descriptive propositions. But they are no less representative of divine matters for all that, and intended to be so in various critical ways. Theologians have to beware of a preoccupation with the history of highly refined theology rather than with a broad range of assertive representations; it is so easy to pick up where previous theologians left off rather than with the beliefs of multifarious communities. All assertive representations, like all assumptions about the divine, are of theological interest.

Sometimes it is thought that theology must assume that its major claims are true, and therefore should not stoop to argue for them. Such theological authoritarianism is the source of dogmatism on the part of some theologians and of derision on the part of critics. There is a confusion in this way of thinking. It is one thing to assume that this or that is true, such that when the assumption is pointed out the question can be asked as to whether it is really true. Assumptions like this run throughout all life. It is quite another thing to hold a set of beliefs and then assert their truth by claiming that they have to be assumed, or that they are supposed to be assumed if one is a Christian (or Jew, Buddhist, etc.). The latter posture implicitly calls the assumption into question at the very point where it attempts to forestall questioning and inquiry.

In fact, assumptions should be interpreted in relation to ongoing life and practice. There are representations of the world that are assumed in any structured activity; sometimes these have been previously analyzed and approved, and sometimes the activity in fact is the analysis of them. Sometimes the assumptions are unrecognized. Sometimes they are false and misleading. The function of reflection is not usually to invent representations from whole cloth but to correct those involved in living activity; it is in its role of guide that thinking formulates assumptions in clear representations and asks whether they are worthy of assertion. There is never a position from which theology can simply rest with an assumption if someone has reason to question it, as the discussion of truth below shall argue.

III. THEOLOGICAL CONCEPTUALIZATION

Perhaps the most important part of the definition of theology is that it is the disciplined intellectual work of fashioning clear concepts by virtue of which the various assumed and asserted representations can be understood, coordinated, criticized, and assessed for expression of the truth. Furthermore, theological concepts are needed to frame the large issues of theological truth, issues that are not completely addressed in the more concrete representations of most practice and religious belief.

In the Christian Bible, for instance, God is called a rock, a warrior, and the King of Israel who preceded Saul (I Samuel 8), a spirit, love itself, a father, judge, and redeemer; and creator of all the world including rocks, warriors, kings, spirits, love, parents, judges, and redeemers. How do these fit together? By what concept of God can we understand God to be all these things, in some sense or other, in the right context, and without generalizing one symbol to the point that it contradicts the others? This is not just a conceptual puzzle: many people find it practically hard to reconcile the loving creator whom Jesus said we should regard as we would our father with the God of vengeance and judgment, with the warrior and Lord. Christian theology, in contrast to non-Christian forms of Jewish theological reflection, had to explain how a creator God committed to Israel could be associated with an alleged Messiah who was crucified and then was more popular with gentiles than with Jews. Paul's letters are filled with attempts to wrestle with these issues. The dialogues of Justin Martyr, a Christian living a generation or two after Paul, were explicit in attempting to answer these questions by explaining the Christian assertions in terms of assumptions of Greek philosophy.

A theological concept is very abstract, relative to most symbols in practice and popular belief (abstractions in some of the popularly recited creeds are exceptions). Often, the root ideas or metaphors for theological concepts come from philosophy, especially from metaphysics.[4] The early Christians made imaginative use of Greek philosophy, and also Roman philosophy and law, to frame their concepts. It is a mistake to exaggerate the difference between the Hebrew and Greek roots of Christianity, however, claiming that theology in its abstractions comes only from the latter. The greatest abstraction is that God is the creator of absolutely everything, such that there is no human conceptual standpoint from which we can apply rules to understand or judge creation. Isaiah and Job are the classic texts to illustrate the invention of the abstractions required to express divine creation. Greek philosophy did not move beyond far more finite conceptions of God until after the encounter with Jewish and Christian assumptions and assertions. Whereas European Christianity continued for nearly two thousand years to develop the original first- and second-century mixture of Greek, Roman, and Hebrew theological concepts, this mixture was but a way station for those forms of Christianity that early on spread to Africa, India, China, and farther, long before the sixteenth-century European missions around the globe.

Considered in itself, a theological concept is a rule for integrating other representations, including other abstractly theological representations.[5] By virtue of the rule, it is possible to see how those other representations relate. Particularly, it is possible to see in which context a certain representation has meaning and might be true, and how that meaning and truth are threatened if the representation is taken out of context. In historical perspective, this allows us to see how, for instance, the Hebrews would look upon God as King and Lord as they were attempting to establish themselves as a nation amongst other peoples: God appeared with political metaphors in a crucially political context. Isaiah, however, argued that God is not just King of Israel; by virtue of being creator of the whole world, God is Lord of all nations. Thus when Jesus revived the theological language of the Kingdom of God, it did not mean Israel's nationhood over against the Romans, but rather a normative way in which creatures respond to each other in light of their relation to the creator. For Jesus, the metaphors expressing divine kingship had little to do with a mighty warrior fighting the enemies of Israel (the Lord of Hosts: "host" means army), but rather with the way a loving parent judges and chastens children. For Jesus, the end of history, the eschaton, was not a matter of military and political victory or defeat for Israel, but of the end of the whole creation. A Christian theological concept of God needs to be able to represent how God could be represented properly one way in one context, another way in another. What is true of the concept of God is true of theological concepts of sin, salvation, grace, divine presence and absence in individuals and in religious communities, and a variety of other topics.

Part of theology is the exploration and elaboration of concrete representations. As such, it is like a critical extension of a metaphor. But underlying such thematic development is a model of *how* the representation can be stretched, and that model needs to be formulated in order to know how *far* the metaphor can be stretched. The relatively abstract theological idea of God as creator of the universe is a kind of control on the extension of metaphors of God as warrior king, fecund mother, and loving father, since kings, mothers, and fathers are obviously part of the created universe. Kings and fathers are analogies for understanding God, and the abstract concept of divine creator prevents those analogies from being taken too literally. Some theologians have argued that analogies allow us to make logically binding inferences about the nature of the divine. This is a difficult case to defend, however, because we would not know that something is only an analogy unless we had some non-analogical concept to mark the limitation. Nonetheless, analogies are very important for the invention and development of new abstractions, and sometimes cease to be analogies by breaking into two clearly different concepts, for instance God as creator of everything and a potter as creator of some crockery.[6]

The function of theological conceptualizations is not just to manage the variety of symbolic references to divine matters but to allow divine matters to be relevant to the understanding of our own situation. We are, after all, concerned principally with the truth about divine matters, not just with the ways they have been represented. Therefore, we can observe the distinction between theological assertions that *are* made, *can be* made, and *ought to be* made.

IV. TRUTH AND THE MODES OF THEOLOGICAL ASSERTION

Theology emerges from the concrete activities of a society that represent divine matters, and thus is always grounded in practices and discourse to be empirically grasped. That is, theology requires erudition about the representations contained in social life, especially in the religious institutions of social life. Insofar as a particular theological program arises out of a living religion, it has that social life as its very context. Yet even a living tradition has outlived something of its past, and part of theology is a recovery of old symbols, or current symbols that once meant something different, or contexts of representing the divine that no longer obtain. Further, theology in living traditions needs to take an interest in other traditions, for they either reinforce or present an alternative to one's own representations. There is no logical limit to the alternatives to which one might pay attention. So the realm theology needs to survey includes the whole of world religions and secular rejections of them, insofar as these practically can be brought into discourse. Saint Paul coped with a variety of Jewish sects, Hellenistic religions, and the Roman traditions of philosophy and law. Thomas Aquinas developed a theology out of the encounter of his Neo-Platonic forebears with Aristotelian and Islamic theology. The current ecumenical dialogue among world religions constitutes the survey base for contemporary theology. Furthermore, because theology cannot limit its survey only to abstractly formulated theology, but must include representations in many concrete forms, it must incorporate the discipline of history of religions into its practice. Any given theological effort or discussion, of course, will be practically limited. A Christian theologian might deal exclusively with representations that have historical significance within Christianity. But the background for that work either will include the representations of the alternatives to Christian representations or it will leave the work with nothing to say about whether its representations are true or false relative to the alternatives.

In addition to critical reflection on theologically significant representations in religious and secular life, and on the history of theology, it is incumbent on theologians to use speculative imagination to frame yet more alternative conceptions. The first and most obvious reason for this is that we are always lacking adequate theological conceptions. The great religious traditions, including Christianity, are still deeply engaged in reformulating their theological representations in light of their encounter with one another. There have been many periods in which great minds have wrestled with the implications of that encounter. Matteo Ricci, for instance, a sixteenth-century Christian missionary to China, struggled to determine whether the Confucian veneration of ancestors is compatible with the Christian exclusive ultimate devotion to God (Ricci concluded yes, the Roman Catholic church, no). Our own is a time when all the religions are brought into dialogue by an integrated world economy, and interfaith dialogue is itself a cultural institution whose discourse is creating a new set of theological representations. In addition, most world religions, not only Christianity, have become convinced that their literate theological heritage has been parochially bound to certain social classes, and to the male gender; theology is in ferment to determine how its representations are biased by those social limitations and to correct them.

A second reason for speculative theology, for imaginative construction departing from received representations, is the need to bring together the representations from various domains of theology, to see how they bear upon one another, and to determine whether they are complementary, coherent, contradictory, or essentially irrelevant. This is the need for system, and many theologies have a form that attempts to present theological topics in categories that are systematically connected. Aquinas's *Summa Theologica*, Calvin's *Institutes of the Christian*

Religion, Schleiermacher's *The Christian Faith*, and Tillich's *Systematic Theology* are examples of systems, each with a different and yet effective form for systematizing. The chief advantage of system in theology (and philosophy), after the obvious virtue of allowing things to be seen in one view, is that it is a hedge against dogmatism (in the bad sense of that term, meaning unsupported opinion urged as unquestionable truth). System allows theologians, indeed requires them, to come at issues from as many sides as possible, minimizing the danger of the common error of taking a partial truth for more than it is worth.

The final and only serious purpose of theology is to know the truth about divine matters. That purpose is not adequately served by interpreting the major representations of divine things and systematizing them. Theologians must also ask whether they are true, in what senses, and in what contexts. There are many performatory uses of representations that assume their truth, roughly speaking, but that do not assert them. A good example is reciting a creed in order to maintain liturgical continuity with an ancient baptismal tradition, without much regard for whether the creed's assertions are true. But when someone asks whether the creed is a valid statement of Christian doctrine, theologians should be able to give a response that respects the truth of the matter. If it is important for the creed to be good doctrine as well as in historic liturgical continuity, then it is important for theology to be able to assess its truth accurately. The temptation to fudge the truth because of the liturgical continuity does a disservice to the community as well as to the truth.

The question of the nature of theological truth is a part of theology itself, comprised within the subdiscipline of philosophy of religion. In general, truth is a correspondence of our representations to that which they represent. Or, as Thomas Aquinas put it, truth is an adequation of our intellect to the object. A contemporary way of describing truth is to say that it is the carryover into the interpreter's experience of the value in the things interpreted, as qualified by the special limitations of the interpreter's physical being, culture, symbol systems, and purposes (Neville, 1989: chap. 3).

In the particular case of theological truth, the issue is complicated because the divine is not an object like any other object. It does not have a form that the mind can represent, though of course its connections with things are formed and representable. Furthermore, most religions agree with the theistic claim that the divine is infinite, and therefore finitely representable only in extremely limited ways, ways that are false to the infinite properly considered. Put in theistic terms, it is far easier to represent what God does in, to, and for the finite world than what God is apart from the world. Another way of making the same point is that we can represent God's revelation about which there is finite truth, although perhaps not God's essence. In terms of other religions, we can represent the qualities Brahman has relative to the world, or the embodiment of Principle, but not what divinity is in itself. The higher-level point just made, about what can and cannot be represented, can itself be represented, and it is from this that we derive what we know about transcendence as such. Concerning the other divine matters, those having to do with the bearing of various dimensions of the world on divinity, the question of truth is more straightforward: the issue is to identify what the divine bearing is. These issues will be explored concretely in chapters to follow.

To ascertain the truth of a representation or system of representations is to approach the matter critically. "Critical" derives from a Greek root meaning judgment as in a law court. The critical process consists in giving arguments against the adequacy of a representation, defending the representation, amending it in light of what is learned, and in general making the best case that can be made. Often the best case is a negative one, arguing that the set of theological assertions one is defending is less limited and misleading than alternatives. Although some theologians have sought to provide absolutely clear and irrefutable arguments, most now agree to a humbler assessment of what they have shown. What constitutes a good case for a theological assertion depends on the kinds of assertion involved, the ready alternatives, the reasons for questioning, and the practical uses to which the assertion might be put. There is no rigid rule defining a good case.

Readings in Key Texts: (Please see "How To Use This Book" for the complete titles of the books cited here.)

1. Aquinas, *SCG*, Book 1, chaps. 1–5.
2. Aquinas, *ST*, I-I, ques. 1, arts. 1–7.
3. Augustine, *Conf.*, Book 1.
4. Barth, *Credo*, chap. 1.
5. Calvin, *Inst.*, Book 1, chaps. 1–5.
6. Cobb and Griffin, *PT*, chap. 2.
7. Ferm, *TWLT*, chap. 27 (by Balusuriya).
8. Hildegard, *Sci.*, "Declaration;" Book 1, Vision 1.
9. Luther, no reading.
10. Rahner, *Found.*, "Introduction."
11. Ruether, *Sexism*, chap. 2.
12. Schleiermacher, *CF*, pp. 3–93.
13. Tillich, *Sys.*, Vol. 1, "Introduction;" Vol. 2, "Introduction."

2

Revelation: Sources and Uses of Theology

I. AUTHORITY IN THEOLOGY

The question of the sources of theology deals with the same topic that has sometimes been addressed by the question of authority. Is there any way of making a case by citing a source that simply settles the issue? European Christianity was greatly challenged by the rise of modern science and by new, reasonably objective, ways of interpreting its history and institutions. Scriptures were read as ancient documents, church history as a matter of politics and social development, church institutions as a subject for sociological classification, religious faith as a matter of psychology, and theology itself as an example of the development and defense of an ideology serving the maintenance and interest of particular communities rather than as an attempt to get at the truth about divine matters.

Under the pressure of this challenge, European and American religious communities built up the absoluteness of claims for authority and then split with regard to the acceptance or rejection of strict authority as religiously relevant. Roughly speaking, this was the origin of the split between left and right, liberal and conservative, that characterizes the European-American religious situation throughout the twentieth century. On the liberal side, Jewish leaders founded Reform Judaism out of a concern for the scientific study of Judaism; at the same time (the 1820s and 1830s), liberal Protestant thinkers unfolded the objective hermeneutical approach to the Bible and ancient world, and associated their communities with "progressive" social movements. Roman Catholic thinkers were more cautious about the abandonment of

11

authority, but by the end of the nineteenth century the modernist movement had largely done so. On the conservative side, Orthodox Judaism underwent a resurgence as a recovery of the authoritative Jewish way of life in the face of liberalizing secular tendencies resulting from the opening of the ghettos. Cardinal John Henry Newman led many Anglicans and Protestants back to Rome, precisely to find an absolute, question-settling authority, and joined Roman Catholics in the movement that led to the proclamation of papal infallibility toward the end of the nineteenth century. Other Protestants sought absolute authority in scripture, laying the groundwork for the fundamentalist movement at the beginning of the twentieth century, while others developed a more charismatic appeal to the authority of the Holy Spirit, the roots of Pentecostalism. The religious left and right fundamentally disagree over authority—not over "which authority," but over the question whether authority in any strict sense is valid or religiously helpful. The right requires some strict authority, the left does without authority even when attempting to give it a place.[1] To describe the topic of this section as "sources of theology" is to side mainly with the left. There are several reasons for doing so.

First, there are many authorities. They sometimes are in conflict, but even when they are not they differ in the nuancing and weight of issues. David Tracy, one of our most important theologians who has written extensively on method, distinguishes (1975: chap. 3 and *passim*) between "Christian texts" and "common human experience and language." His distinction reflects somewhat Paul Tillich's distinction between religious "answers" and cultural "questions" as used in Tillich's "method of correlation"; that method will be discussed in connection with revelation in section 4 below. To Tracy's two sources should be added at least two more. In addition to "Christian texts" or scriptures (in a broad sense) should be added the importance of tradition itself. And in addition to "common human experience and language" should be added critical and synthesizing reason, reason that can transform experience and language. At least scripture, tradition, reason, and the experience of individuals and groups need to be acknowledged, and surely even these four can be subdivided significantly and yet other important sources for theology added. There are many instances in which the truth of the theological issue at hand depends on contributions from the scriptures, traditions, experience, and reason of other, non-Christian, religions, and the multiplicity of potential authorities is vastly increased.

Where these are in conflict, one must "make a case" for the best authority, and the "case" decides the issue without itself being an authority.[2] Even within alleged authorities, for instance scripture, there are conflicting conclusions that require interpretation, and the interpretation is not always more scripture.

Second, authorities in the religious sense are not supposed to be judges at the end of the process whose deliverance itself decides the issue, as the Supreme Court decides the meaning and application of the law: the law requires what the Supreme Court says in the end. Rather, the alleged authorities are at the beginning of an argument; that is what is meant by "authority," a premise whose conclusions are true because of the standing of the premise. But the initial authorities always require interpretation, even to assert their standing as trustworthy premises. Given their need of interpretation, and the fact they exist within a network of interpretations, the alleged authorities realistically function as sources rather than as judges. The case for an authority's deliverance must be made by interpretation, which is not authoritative in the strict sense. None of this is to suggest that what some have alleged to be authoritative in the strict sense, and are now rejected from that role, are not important and perhaps indispensable sources of theology.

Third, one can understand neither the history of theology nor grasp the richness of one's own theological situation without taking into account the plurality of sources once alleged to be authoritative; taking them all into account, at least scripture, tradition, reason, and experience, allows each to be a critical interpreter and appraiser of the others. This point, like the last, acknowledges the forward-looking direction of argument: an argument is not good because of some uncriticizable beginning point, but because it is able to balance out consideration and settle matters at the end of inquiry. Furthermore, an end to inquiry is only provisional; new considerations arise causing a reconsideration even after it seems everything was settled. This has happened throughout the history of theology, just as it does in everyday life.

To abandon strict authority in theology is not to say that important and conclusive opinions cannot be arrived at. A carefully developed argument might indeed take into account all relevant considerations, and no concrete challenge to reconsider might be possible. Even in the case of good argument, however, it must be acknowledged that theology is always potentially vulnerable. Therefore the distinction between open inquiry in theology and the firm commitments of religious faith and cultic practice must be observed. To commit oneself to the congregation of Christians, to faithfully observe the sacraments, and to devote oneself to discipleship to Jesus are all possible while recognizing the fallibility of theology. The same may be said for participation in other religious traditions.

A supporter of strict authority can reject all of these arguments. Such a rejection would claim that only alleged authorities consistent with one another could be authoritative, that those authorities do not require interpretation or, if so, supply it themselves, and that religious life is sufficiently narrow as not to require acknowledgment of such a plurality of potential authorities. Protestant fundamentalism and pre-Vatican II Roman Catholicism often have been explicit in making these points. Yet because each of the rejections involves excluding something that seems so worthy on the face of it, those rejections have not been persuasive in public debate where multiple sets of presuppositions are addressed. What has happened most often is that the argument over authority has shifted from considering the alleged authorities, such as scripture, to a hidden authority that attempts to set the limits as to what counts as a presupposition for inquiry. Indeed, sometimes the argument takes the form of claiming that those theologians who acknowledge no authority in the strict sense, but only sources for theology, themselves are adopting the canons of secular argument as authorities. Thus it seems as if authority is something that can be adopted at will. If the liberals can adopt secular argument as authoritative, the conservatives say, the conservatives can adopt the councils, the Pope, or the Bible as authoritative, because authority is a matter of will. The opposite is the case, however. Authority in the strict sense is precisely that which is not subject to will but which has its standing on its own. A real authority commands respect, and is not established by the voluntary bestowing of status. The argument that the recognition of authority is a matter of presupposition, or voluntary choice, at best amounts to saying that the will by itself is the only authority. Although much of liberalism, like religious conservativism, has emphasized the importance of will, liberalism has not looked to will to settle intellectual arguments. Rather, it has looked to argument itself.

The liberal point is perhaps best summed up in the contemporary movement called "hermeneutics," which means the art of interpretation. Any argument, whatever its form, is an interpretation. It is justified when a further argument or interpretation can make a case for its being justified. When that further argument is called into question, yet another argument must be given, and so on until the serious questions have been answered. Theologians know that the issues that seem settled today can be called into question tomorrow.[3] The logic of interpretation, each step criticizing its predecessors and in turn subject to revision if called for, has come to define the very meaning of publicity (as characterized by Toulmin, 1958, for example).

Sometimes the logic of interpretation has been carried to great extremes, as when it is argued that the only test or measure of an interpretation is yet a further interpretation. If this were so, then interpretation would be endless before it could assert anything, and theological affirmation would be impossible. This view of interpretation is sometimes called idealism because it amounts to saying that only the interpretations, not their objects in the world (or in the divine), are real. Against this view a preferable approach points out that interpretation always takes place within the context of ongoing life, and it serves to monitor and correct our engagements with each other, with the rest of the world, and with God. Interpretation is a corrective in the face of living questions. When the *living* questions have been answered religious life is seriously and energetically engaged; the only reason to return to further critical interpretation is if a new vital question is uncovered. Thus there is a pragmatic limit to further interpretation required to justify a theological claim, and the burden of proof in criticism of the claim falls back on the critic.[4]

II. SCRIPTURE, TRADITION, REASON, EXPERIENCE

If the sources of theology are all subject to interpretation, then it is necessary to spell out how they stand in the practice of interpretation itself. Hermeneutics, the art of interpretation, supposes what has come to be called the "hermeneutical circle," which aims to connect the interpreter and the original text. Since the rise of historical consciousness in the modern period, we recognize that the cultural world in which a text, the Bible say, was written is different from our own cultural world. Not only was the language different, but the whole social context. How do we get at the ancient world to analyze it? We always carry our own presuppositions into the analysis. The hermeneutical circle moves back and forth between the text as we possess it in our own time and the text in its own original cultural context. The more we know about the ancient world, the more we can interpret the original meaning of the text. But that in turn alerts us to our own presuppositions that are different from those of the text's original world. With the new consciousness of our own angle of vision, we go back once again to the original context with new insight, which in turn reveals more about us, on around and around.

There appear to be at least four essential moments in the hermeneutical circle. The text, or scripture, to be interpreted, the historical tradition connecting the text to the interpreter, the experience of the interpreter and of the world of the text, and the process of reasoning about how these fit together. If we are interpreting a tradition, or someone else's experience, or the nature of reason as involved in a particular argument, that is to take the object of interpretation to be a text itself, connected with other texts, traditional elements, experience, and reason. Instead of any of these four being an infallible starting point for theology, each is an essential moment in the elucidation, interpretation, and criticism of any of them, and of the theological problems for which we might appeal to scripture, tradition, experience, and reason.

Scripture is to be understood in primary and secondary senses. The primary sense is a central text, such as the Torah in Judaism, the Bible in Christianity, and the Koran in Islam. The secondary sense includes the writings that interpret the central text or that express the community's normative life in reference to the text. Secondary texts include hymns, creeds, imaginative interpretive literature, and theology itself. Secondary texts can have many different kinds and degrees of importance, from sources that simply must be taken into account to those that might or might not be helpful.

Tradition refers to that in the life of a community which is taken to be determinative of what is normative. How to distinguish primary and secondary scripture, indeed what role scripture is to have in the religious life, is a function of the normative processes of tradition. The relative weight of primary scriptures versus church councils is different in Roman Catholicism from what it is in Protestantism. In Protestantism, some groups emphasize the Christ and the bindingness of the Bible whereas others emphasize the Holy Spirit and the bindingness of contemporary experience. The relative role of scripture is a function of tradition. Of course, arguments about what the tradition says are often settled by appeal to scripture or reason or experience. This use of tradition as a source for theology is related to, but not simply identical with, the concrete use of tradition in liturgy and church life.

Neither tradition nor scripture can be interpreted apart from reason. Some thinkers go so far as to say that reason is nothing more than making a case for one's theological or practical religious assertions, and that therefore reason is the true authority. But aside from consistency and imagination, reason has little character of its own to be authoritative in any strict sense. A case can be successful because it persuasively appeals to scripture, to a part of tradition, or to a particular class of experiences. Reason is a most conspicuous source for theology when it makes connections that bring to bear considerations that otherwise would be ignored.

Experience is an important source for theology, and for criticizing scripture, tradition, and reason, because it provides the ground for relevance in theological assertions. Although theology is unwise to confine itself to the needs of a particular domain of experience, it has no ground for determining in what respects theological assertions need interpretation except by appeal to experience. Some experiences, such as the need for some kind of order in a religious community, or the cultivation of individual spiritual life, or the prophetic critique of society in the name of divine justice, are fairly universal. Others, such as the experience of women, or poor people, or, in a given national tradition, the minorities, are special and add perspectives lacking from general experience. When theological movements based on scripture, tradition, reason, and old experience fail to address the particular experience of individuals, experience becomes the critic of scripture, tradition, and reason.

Although it has not been uncommon in the history of Christian and other theologies for experience to attain a kind of dominance over the other sources of theology, ours is a time when it has achieved a unique and special kind of dominance. Ordinarily, its importance has been observed in connection with a rise of a pietistic movement such as the Anabaptist or Wesleyan movements in Christianity, or the practice of Pure Land Buddhism. In contemporary Christian theology, however, experience has suddenly come to be an especially important source for theology because many people feel that both the dominant theological traditions and the dominant methods of theological reasoning are parochial and limited to white, male, European theology. In the face of this parochialism, the experience of poor people, women, and those from non-European cultures needs to be heard. There is a truly extraordinary expansion of the experience thought to be a relevant source for theology in the contemporary scene. Perhaps the time is premature to determine whether those hitherto neglected experiences will decisively alter the reading of scripture, of the tradition, and of reason. The cases for a new look at scripture and tradition seem far stronger than those for wholly new approaches to reason, but the dialogue is far from over. Because of the hermeneutical circle, the cases for the decisive importance of newly articulated experiences have to be made in the process of the critical review of reason, tradition, and scripture, each altering somewhat as they receive new layers of interpretation and mutual criticism.

A middle ground in the debate between left and right in the matter of authority and sources for theology perhaps lies in the following consideration. In his early work, Karl Barth (1921) attempted to draw a contrast between religion as the work of human culture and God's revelatory and transformative work; he advocated that Christians reject religion in that sense and accept the divine initiative. But this is a difficult contrast to maintain, if it is not downright false. Hardly a religious tradition fails to claim, in its ancient sources, that its forms and understanding derive from divinity. Furthermore, if one maintains a strong doctrine of divine creation, or immanence of Principle in things, or Brahman in *atman*, or Buddhist Emptiness in the Form of the changing world, then in some sense the divine is in all things. Everything that happens does so because of divine as well as finite causes. Indeed, the theological problem is not to bridge the gap between human and divine initiative, but to understand enough separation so as to exempt the divine from the perversions of the creaturely situation. Most often, this takes the form of showing that God is not responsible for evil, although this problematic might exhibit too narrow a view of God. For a person convinced of the sovereignty of God as creator, *whatever* is done in theology is an expression of divine creation, and must therefore have some appropriateness. For a faithful theologian, it is impossible to get things so wrong that no truth is served and correction impossible. The theological task is to weigh the sources and provide the corrections.

III. USES OF THEOLOGY

Discussion of theology's sources is incomplete without reference to the uses to which theology is rightly put.

The most important use has already been spelled out, namely, to obtain the knowledge of the truth in divine matters so far as that can be determined. If this use is ever compromised or sacrificed in the pursuit of theology for other purposes, those purposes are themselves perverted.

A secondary use of theology, perhaps primary in the order of motivation for many people, is for the guidance of corporate and individual religious life. Our lives individually and collectively are based upon habits of action, which in turn are based on beliefs. Theology is the critic of beliefs in religion. Whenever doubt arises concerning the appropriateness of our religious actions or beliefs, theology is called for.

Another use of theology is to understand religious identity, either one's own, or one's group's, or someone else's. *How* one is religious or unreligious is perhaps the most important part of personal or social identity. It colors all other aspects of identity and, as shall be argued below, is fundamental to human existence as such. Theology is the intellectual part of coming to terms with identity, putting off identity, taking it on, and reacting to it. Human beings differ from most other species by having a representation of their identity through time, a representation of their career, as itself a component in identity to which a person reacts. The peculiarly human elements of identity, such as one's moral value, one's sense of place and time, of contribution to public and private life, and of relations with other persons, come from relating oneself to one's life and times as represented. This relation to oneself as having a life is religious, and requires theology for understanding. Referring to the temporal and historical elements of life as it does, that expression is peculiarly Western; an East Asian would speak of relating to one's given and acquired roles as represented. The point, however, is that theology is the cognitive approach to identity. The issue is the role of understanding in creating that element of identity that comes from relating oneself to one's representation of oneself. A similar remark could be made about group self-definition and identity. Religious people find it hard to avoid theology, even when they are anti-intellectual. The issue is not avoiding theology, but finding good theology.

A fourth use for theology is as a form of worship. Knowing divine matters is a kind of incorporation of them. Because truth is the carryover of value from the object interpreted into the interpreter, theology is a way of human divinization, if that expression may be used without sacrilege.[5] Worship can be practised in many forms, most of them not directly representational. But theology itself can be an act of worship, and through that a transformation of the character of an individual or group. The point can be made negatively. A person or group that does not attend to theology is infected with representations of the divine that are needlessly crude, mushy, misleading, and perverse. The heart may be more important in the long run than the mind, supposing them to be distinguishable. But a heart with a stupid or crooked mind will find its good intentions dissipated in banalities.

These several uses of theology take on a special cumulative urgency in the case of Christian ministry. The quotation from Peter C. Hodgson at the head of the Introduction above sums up the need of the church for theology, for deep, ongoing theological reflection. The church needs theology for truth, for guidance, for identity, and for worship. Too often the church forgets the theological essence that makes it church rather than a welfare agency, a psychotherapy clinic, a social club, or an aesthetic experience. Hodgson says immediately prior to the passage quoted above:

> The fundamental purpose of ministry is to guide and serve the process of ecclesial formation, ecclesial preservation, and ecclesial mission—that is, to enable the church to *realize* its ecclesial essence, to be a community of faith, hope, and love, a sign and sacrament of the kingdom of God. (1988: 98)

Even if ministers have no personal interest in theological truth (may the Lord preserve us!), no personal need for guidance, for the critical establishment of personal identity, or a personal need for theologically informed worship, the church in which they minister does.

IV. REVELATION

The Christian doctrine of revelation, like that in any of the other religious traditions that claim revealed truths, has often been misunderstood in the modern period to be a problem of knowledge, of epistemology. Insofar as revelation is thought to be just a special miraculous form of knowledge, it is confused with the problem of strict authority. And because such authority has not been able to sustain itself as a viable notion for much of the Christian community, or for much of most other religious communities, the idea of revelation has come to be dismissed as childish, authoritarian, or as a subterfuge for defending inherited positions that contemporary experience shows to be false. Yet this is a false identification of revelation. Revelation is not a special kind of knowledge, but a special kind of learning.

Revelation is knowledge about divine matters acquired in ways that transcend the ordinary ways of learning that can be passed on from generation to generation. Even when a revelation is something that occurred in the past and its expression passed down by scripture or tradition, for it to be received as revelation by the new generation means something more than the ordinary appropriation of past texts and traditions. Revelation is a kind of learning that puts persons and communities in touch with the divine, that engages them with the divine in transforming cognitive ways.

Paul Tillich (1951: part 1) was on target when he characterized theology as a method of correlation. On the one hand are the questions raised by and in human culture about the ultimate issues of existence. On the other are the answers from the divine as expressed in the symbols, statements, visions, and practices of religion. There can be failure on both sides; culture can fail to raise ultimate questions and the religious expressions of the divine can fail to convey anything. The active work of theology consists in bringing both to vitality insofar as is possible for human endeavor. As Tillich put it:

> Theology formulates the questions implied in human existence, and theology formulates the answers implied in divine self-manifestation under the guidance of the questions implied in human existence. This is a circle which drives man to a point where question and answer are not separated. This point, however, is not a moment in time. It belongs to man's essential being, to the unity of his finitude with the infinity in which he was created . . . and from which he is separated. . . . A symptom of both the essential unity and the existential separation of finite man from his infinity is his ability to ask about the infinite to which he belongs: the fact that he must ask about it indicates that he is separated from it. (1951: 61)

Revelation is not a divine answer in itself, but a divine address received by people with a culture to receive it. The religious dimension of culture is not just secular thinking about the divine, but culture as addressed by the divine. There are at least four kinds of revelatory learning.

The first is the revelatory power in religious symbols. The fact that a symbol has historically been religious, or is about divine matters, does not make it revelatory. The revelation comes in the functioning of the symbol to engage people with the divine. At one point in the Christian tradition the symbol of blood sacrifice had revelatory power; for most people today, blood sacrifice is associated with abuse of animals or wastage of food, and hence does not connect with the divine. Some liberal theologians claim that almost none of the traditional Christian symbols have revelatory power today, except perhaps those associated with ethics. Others say that symbols such as those of creation, covenant, cross, and resurrection are just as powerful today as ever, given new interpretations and received in significant circumstances; the *Primer* will develop some of these symbols.

The second kind of revelation consists of persons, events or special situations the interpretation of which creates special engagements with the divine that transform the interpreting community. The exodus from Egypt, the founding of the Davidic state, or the life of Jesus Christ with the formation of the early Christian community are examples. The revelatory power of such events is registered and responded to even when there is ambiguity in or over interpretation of the events themselves. There are four gospel stories of Jesus plus Paul's accounts, and also liturgical and creedal traditions, none in complete consistency with the others; yet the revelatory power of what they express comes through to many people and has come through in radically variant situations. The point in the events is not whether any particular account of them is authoritative in the strict sense, or is even defensible in the sense that a final case can be made for it. The point is that the events in at least some of their interpretations transform human life to be in better accord with the divine by engaging life with the divine.

A special class within the second kind of revelation deserves to be singled out, namely, the persons whose life or self-presentation functions to mediate the divine. These are the saints, those individuals whose character or acts are persuasive witnesses to the truth of larger claims about divinity. Saints are often unnoteworthy in most respects, ordinary people without classy jobs. But they exhibit humility under stress, or love without measure, or self-effacing leadership that makes good the central religious claims to some who meet them. Surely, Christianity would not long be persuasive if there were no saints in whose lives the central figure of crucifixion and resurrection is a living analogy. All the crooks, the weaksouled and selfish people, the pompous hypocrites, and the genuine villains that have acted with acceptable representations of Christianity are set aside as fakes by the presence of one truly Christ-like person. Corrupt people are to be expected in great numbers; the existence of one truly holy and just person is a revelation proving the truth of religion to those who have eyes to see and ears to hear.

The third kind of revelation is the peculiar kind of interpretive event or activity by which a person or people relates certain symbols to their own situation so as to engage the divine in a transformative way. Liberation theology's reappropriation of symbols of the exodus and demand for justice, for instance, in special forms that are related to contemporary experience are current examples of revelatory interpretation. This is a point where contemporary experience is a focal point for revelation. Such an experiential revelation is not reducible to either the viability of the symbols or the intrinsic significance of events, but rather is a divinizing of contemporary experience so that it bears a revelatory message. In Christian theology this kind of revelation is particularly associated with the ongoing work of the Holy Spirit. It has to do with finding the divine in the authentic appropriation of symbols that particularize our own lives as subjects of revelation.

The fourth kind of revelation is not a symbol, event, or self-reflexive interpretive experience as such, but a life process of finding the divine. Whether for individuals on a spiritual path or for communities seeking their destiny, the career itself reveals the divine in such a way as to center and give deep meaning. A person, for instance, on a spiritual path with profound attainments might well be a revelatory event for someone else, for instance a community, but this is not the fourth kind of revelation per se. The fourth kind is the making of the person divine in part, what the Eastern Orthodox Christians call "divinization." The divine does not so much appear to such a person but in the person. This is perhaps the profoundest kind of revelation.

Although theology obviously is based on the first three senses of revelation, it is just as truly indebted to the fourth kind. Theology, relative to the fourth kind, is itself a kind of spiritual practice. Of course it is difficult to make the revelatory elements of theology in this sense public. Surely, those who are not themselves engaged in this difficult spiritual path will find it hard to access the revelatory evidences in the life of a person or community. But experience has shown that deeply spiritual people can communicate with each other in theologically sophisticated and profound ways difficult for others to assess. What is true for individuals is true by analogy for communities. Israel at times was itself a revelatory community in this fourth sense of revelation. Its self-interpretation has been profoundly moving for other communities with similar deep revelatory dynamics, for instance the early Puritans.

The fact of revelation, in any of these four senses or in others, is not the same as the identification of a particular symbol, event, experience, or path as truly revelatory. The identification is always a theological matter subject to debate and correction. After two thousand years of Christian theology, we can be confident that any claim for revelation will provoke quibbles if not controversy. This is not to imply that, because a claim is controversial, it is false. Revelation is a fact: it either happens, with consequent transformation of people to set them better in relation to the divine, or it does not. Some people argue that ours is a time when God seems largely absent, when nothing is revelatory; others have found striking revelatory elements in common life and culture. Few can doubt that the negative revelations in the World Wars about hypocritical Christian peacemaking, or in the recovery of women's experience, or in the demands of the world's very poor for justice, are truly revelatory, even if they do not relate us better to the divine. At least they question some false relations to the divine.

The Christian traditions claim that their symbols have saving potency, that their central events reveal both human nature and divine purpose, that their ongoing traditions have cast revelatory light on situation after situation, and that their disciplines have the power to allow the divine to appear significantly in the lives of individuals and communities. The proper interpretation and assessment of these claims is one of the crucial tasks for theology, especially in its roles for ministry.

Readings in Key Texts:

1. Aquinas, *SCG*, Book 1, chaps. 6–9.
2. Aquinas, *ST*, I–I, ques. 1, arts. 8–10; ques. 2.
3. Augustine, *Conf.*, Book 12, chaps. 18–32.
4. Barth, *Credo*, "Appendix."
5. Calvin, *Inst.*, Book 1, chaps. 6–10.
6. Cobb and Griffin, no reading.
7. Ferm, *TWLT*, chap. 6 (by Segundo), chap. 25 (by Song).
8. Hildegard, no reading.
9. Luther, no reading.
10. Rahner, *Found.*, chap. 1 (here or with chap. 5 below).
11. Ruether, *Sexism*, chap. 1.
12. Schleiermacher, *CF*, pp. 94–128, 591–611.
13. Tillich, *Sys.*, Vol. 1, pt. 1.

God the Creator

I. GOD THE PROBLEM

For most people who turn to theology, the chief problem is whether there is a God. The question has meant many quite different things, only some of which will be addressed in this chapter. Sometimes the question has meant, Is there a benevolent God who saves us (or, more particularly, saves me)? This version of the question will be postponed to the Christological and sanctification chapters below. Other times the question has meant, Is there a special omniscient, omnipotent, all-good being, among the beings of the universe, which some thinkers now call the object of the "traditional concept" of God? This question will be dealt with in the present chapter, and be shown to be misleading and religiously unimportant. At other times, and perhaps as an underlying motif in the other versions, the question has meant, Does reality include anything to which the vast array of symbols of the divine can be referred, each in its own context, so as to make critical sense of the uses of those symbols in religious life? This last version has become the central theological question of the modern period (see Kaufman, 1968, 1972, 1981).

Among the more important symbols of the divine are God as agent of the creation of the world; God as source of the covenant binding people to each other, to the realm of nature, to their institutions, and to their creator; God as lover of justice, protector of the weak and oppressed, and judge and executioner of the wicked; God as redeemer and savior; God as the goal and fulfillment of mystical longings; God as the principle of order, the source of the component stuff of the world, the ground of individual actual being, and the telos of destiny; the underlying self of the universe, the Tao that cannot be named, the non-being from which springs the Great Ultimate, and the divine presence in finite things that partake of the uncanny holy. This is but a preliminary list of symbols for the divine taken from the large, general systems of religion. Significant epiphanies are more usually quite specific. The question of God is how to understand these, each in its own sense and place.

For purposes of theological discussion, "modernity" can be defined precisely.[1] It is that culture whose basic senses of the world have closure. "Closure" is a mathematical notion that defines a set of things as limited to certain specifiable properties and distinguished from things that might have contradictory properties. A closed set might be infinite internally, as the set of even numbers, 2, 4, 6, . . . , but still have closure with respect to the odd numbers, 1, 3, 5, . . . , which constitute a different closed set.

With the invention of mathematical physics during the European Renaissance, physical reality came to be conceived with closure in the following way. A physical thing is something measurable with a standard measure, for instance a yardstick, a miles-per-hour rate of speed, or a pounds-per-volume density, that is the same under the same conditions wherever it is applied; laws of nature are then the constant relations among the things as standardly measured. A yardstick is the same at home as on the moon, on the sun, or in the far-off galaxies, given standard conditions such as frames of reference for relative motion. With this cultural conception we can conceive of the universe as a vast integrated machine of standard measurable parts. We might still debate just what the measures are, and whether the universe is infinite or finite in extent. Regardless of these open questions, the universe is conceived to have closure in the sense that it can be understood completely without reference to anything outside the system of standard measures.

Correlatively, the modern period conceived mind to have closure in the sense that mathematical reasoning is taken to be the paradigm case of understanding. Human beings are conceived to be like machines with a natural momentum or inertia that defines their inbuilt good, and practical reasoning is like mathematical puzzle solving in that it attempts to determine how to achieve those inbuilt goods amidst the conditions of the environment. Because the outstanding successes of modern science show that it is true at least in some sphere, the whole of Western culture has become modernized, and makes the closure assumptions even when it employs rhetoric from a cultural consciousness that lacks closure. Furthermore, because of the spread of science, every society in the world has become affected to one degree or another by the modern consciousness of closure.

The theological question regarding closure is whether the divine is closed in or closed out. For historical cultures that did not regard the universe with closure, the universe could be populated with just about anything someone has a locally plausible reason to believe in, with magical principles, Heavenly Principles, spirits, angels, demons, gods, and The One God, or Buddha-mind, the Tao, heavenly realms for reincarnation, or whatever. The unclosed universe has no principle that gives it unity and hence exclusiveness. Ancient thinkers such as the pre-Socratics attempted to find scientific closure by suggesting a basic stuff of the universe, for instance water or air in varying degrees of condensation and rarefaction; but those notions did not pan out scientifically: standard measure is the key. Once there is a standard measure, the question of God, or of any of the alternatives to God in other religions, is whether divinity fits in or is excluded.

Christian thinkers in early European modernity, holding fast to the view that God is a spirit and not material in the sense of being subject to standard measures, developed the deist theology (Klaaren, 1977). According to deism, God created the world as a vast machine with closure, set it going, and left it wholly to its own devices. Out of piety the deist can still refer and defer to God. But there is nothing within the closure of the universe that requires reference to God, and the world can be conceived as a complete secular whole. The deity's creation of the world is not causation as understood by the standard measures, and hence is not intelligible in secular terms. If one asserts, as a matter of miracle, that God does interfere in the world after it is created, then miracle is understood as some kind of breaking of natural law. The deist theology, while consistent in that God and the world are conceived not to contradict one another, was incoherent in the sense that God and the world are conceived to have nothing to do with one another, except for an occasional miracle that offends science. Being functionally irrelevant to life and scientific understanding, the divine side of deism was quietly forgotten and modern secularism resulted.

Other Western theologians understood that the divine cannot be separated from the affairs of the world if the religious life of people is to be maintained. They then took certain aspects of the principles of closure and expanded them to represent God as within the universe but not entirely of it. Idealists (Hegel, 1807, 1832; Royce, 1899, 1913) and personalists (Bowne, 1882; Knudson, 1927; Brightman, 1940), for instance, took the characteristics of mind, argued that measure is to be understood in terms of mind, not vice-versa, and urged that God is infinite or perfect mind.[2] Mind is thus a kind of superclosure. The idealist move has not been overwhelmingly persuasive, however, because it seems that mind might be understood within the limits of standard measure, and need not make reference to perfection or infinity. Process theologians (Whitehead, 1929; Hartshorne, 1948; Cobb, 1965; Cobb and Griffin, 1976) have developed a deeply original theory of causation according to which standard measure is derivative from elementary creativity, not the other way around, so that God can be conceived as a creative entity sovereign over but not subject to standard measure. The metaphysical boldness of process theology is extremely promising, though it is not yet clear that it is metaphysically successful or that it serves to make sense of the needed array of symbols of the divine employed in religious life (Cobb, 1965, 1967, 1975, 1982; Griffin, 1973; Cobb and Griffin, 1976; Neville, 1980; Ogden, 1973).

The problem of God is thus to develop conceptions of the divine that provide interpretations for the various symbolic representations in religious life and at the same time cope with the conception of the universe as having closure. The apparent irrelevance of older conceptions of God stems from the fact they do not address the modern dilemma caused by the culture of closure. Western theisms are no more in jeopardy from the culture of closure than other religious traditions. The many forms of Hinduism, most forms of Buddhism, Confucianism, and Taoism, all are challenged by the closure of the secular world. Whereas there are many things we might learn from one another, the solution to this problem is not one of them. None of the traditional religions or their theologies contains a ready-made representation of the divine that bridges the fence of cultural closure.

Nevertheless, any culture, including the secular, must represent its most general assumptions about the world, and hence has a theology or anti-theology. Because the question of the very applicability of the idea of God, or divinity more generally, has been raised by the closure principles in secularism, the relation of God to nature, and to society as a part of nature, is an elementary step in theology. One might be tempted to think the contrary, to suppose that because our conceptions of nature seem to exclude divine questions, God is to be found only in History, as supernaturally revealed. This has been an underlying suggestion in much evangelical and neo-orthodox theology in the twentieth century (although those movements were motivated by far more complex conditions than the attempt to add divinity to science from the outside). Yet any representation of God as acting in history, or within persons, must suppose some causal manner by which God is present. For all its emphasis on the historical activity of Yahweh, the Bible was perfectly clear in its assumptions (different assumptions at different times) about God and natural forces. Therefore, the groundwork for a conception of God adequate to the variety of symbols orienting religious life can be found first in a metaphysics of God and nature.

II. THE PRIMACY OF DIVINE CREATION

The idea that God is creator of the universe developed slowly in the Hebrew Bible. By the time of the composition of the Book of Job, God was conceived to be the creator of the entire realm of nature, including national and historical destinies; moreover, the manner and standpoint of divine creation was declared to be so disanalogous with human creating that the moral questions that are sensibly asked of human creation simply became inappropriate in God's case. This is perhaps the first clear instance of a distinction between ontological and cosmological senses of causation (see Neville, 1968; 1978: chap. 5). Cosmological causation takes place *within* the created world, and illustrates the laws and measures defining closure within the world. Ontological causation is God's creating of the world as such, and it is different from the cosmological. The New Testament expressed the same idea, embellished with categories from Hellenistic thought, such as the Logos through whom all things are created and asserted to be incarnate in Jesus. Subsequent speculations among the fathers of the Church expressed the idea of divine creation in ever more detailed and abstract ways.

For reasons discussed in the previous section, the conception of the world as having closure requires a new look at conceptions of God. Specifically, it provides the challenge to reconceive divine creation, or creation *ex nihilo* (out of nothing). Far from it being the case that ontological creation is discredited in the modern world, we are now in a position to appreciate its true power and generality (Neville, 1968). The early development of the idea was hindered by a lack of a true sense of the bounds of the world supposed to be created: The social order and welfare of the Hebrew people? The fertility of their lands? The political economy of the Near East nations? The seas, the dry lands, and the visible heavens? The order rationalizing chaos, but not the chaotic stuff? Divine creation cannot be understood sharply without a sense of closure for the world created.

The hypothesis to be put forward technically in the next sections is that divinity is best understood as the creating of the world *ex nihilo*. This is the root notion. If the world is the sort of thing a rational agent would create, the creating can be ascribed to a creator who is a rational agent. Or if the world is the sort of thing that manifests some principle, the creator might not be conceived as an individual agent but as a principle. Yet in all instances of filling in the character of the divine from the character of the created world, the creator has no characteristics except those deriving from the world with its closure in connection with creation. All characters are created, even the characteristics of being creator, whatever they are. Science can thus say what it finds to be true about the nature and regularities of the world; whatever is, is created. Whatever accrues to the creator in the creating is a function of what is created. This sounds very abstract. But its abstractness is what allows the conception of creation *ex nihilo* to be the frame within which various symbols of divinity find their application and limits. As abstract, it has little religious power, little force as a symbol conveying the divine to engagement with human life. Its power—the power to connect and place the symbols that are indeed spiritually vital—is theoretical.

III. DETERMINATENESS AS THE CHARACTER
OF THE CREATED WORLD

Modernity suggests that the world is what it is by virtue of having measure. To avoid undue narrowness by attempting to identify the latest theory of measure, the idea of closure can be generalized in the following way (Neville, 1989). The world consists of things that are determinate. "Determinateness" is thus the universal character of everything in the world; the world has closure in the sense that everything with determinateness is in it, and whatever is outside it is not determinate, at least not in the ordinary sense of determinateness. That a thing is determinate does not mean it is wholly determinate: the future is not wholly determinate, for instance, although it is what it is at least by being future to something in its past.

To analyze creation, then, is to begin with an analysis of determinateness. In the European High Middle Ages determinateness was analyzed with theories of "transcendentals," concepts such as unity, being, goodness, and so forth that are thought to inhere in each determinate thing. In this *Primer*, determinateness will be analyzed on two levels. On the metaphysical level, determinateness consists in harmony, involving essential and conditional features; this will be analyzed here. On the cosmological level, determinateness consists in realizations of what will later be explained as the four aspects of the Logos: pattern, components, actuality, and value. For the purpose of the present discussion, the analysis of determinateness is necessitated by a need to understand divine creation: the world has closure as the set of all things with determinateness.

Each determinate thing is what it is by having features of its own (essential features) and features relating it to other things by virtue of which it is different from them (conditional features). The distinction between conditional and essential features is a functional one. That is, conditional features are those a thing has by virtue of which it is related to, different from, and thereby connected with, the other things with respect to which it is determinate. Red, for instance, is determinate with respect to being a color and also with respect to being different from yellow and blue (among other things). Those features that put it into the class of colors, and order it with respect to other colors, are among its conditional features. Redness per se, however, is among its essential features, and it is by virtue of that essential quality that red occupies a place as a color and occupies the place among the other colors that it does. The function of essential features is to order the conditional features so that the thing has a nature or place of its own. Without essential features, a thing would be nothing more than the sum of other things that intersect in it; and there would be no point of intersection, nothing but the other things without a medium for intersection. Without the conditional features, on the other hand, a thing would be no different from anything else—difference requires connection and relation; red would be neither a color nor not a color, neither the same as nor different from yellow and blue. A thing cannot be a thing without being something rather than something else, and something rather than nothing. So a thing must have conditional features that connect it with other things and essential features by virtue of which it orders its conditional features and establishes its own nature.

A thing is a harmony of its essential and conditional features. "Harmony" is not an innocent notion, and it does not always convey that a thing is good or as good as it should be. A harmony is simply the togetherness, the coherence, the integral juxtaposition of the thing's features; the features harmonize because it is their own determinate character to do so. A harmony thus is not some inclusive higher entity that integrates its primary features according to its own determinate character. If a harmony would have to be that, then we would always be seeking some higher entity to give determinateness to lower entities, until we got to some tiptop entity that has nothing different from itself with respect to which it could be determinate. Some kinds of mystical idealisms suppose that harmony is always some higher thing and that two things cannot be related unless included within something else; this theory sometimes expresses itself with the claim that all relations are internal to some inclusive thing that comprehends the terms of the relations. The "inclusive higher entity" view of harmony overemphasizes unity and cannot recognize real diversity, or real relations between two or more things that are not wholly included in higher things. Things have essential features not included in their conditional relations with other things.

Nor should harmony be interpreted solely as the unity of a thing's own nature apart from its conditional features. Atomism makes this mistake, believing that things are what they are regardless of other things, and are connected only by extrinsic factors such as relative place in an external spatio-temporal field. Yet things would not be different from one another at all unless they had some conditional features that connect them. A thing wholly by itself is not different from any other thing, and thus is not determinate, not a thing, not even different from nothing at all.

To say that a thing is a harmony of essential and conditional features, and that each of these features is also a harmony with its own components, and so with the components on down and around, is to take up a particular stance toward individuality, relationship, and existence. To be a thing is to have both essential and conditional features, and hence to have an intrinsic own identity and a relational conditioned identity. A thing is no more its essential components than its conditional ones, nor vice versa. Both conditional and essential features are necessary. "Essential" does not mean better or more important than conditional. Things are what they are by virtue of their relations as much as by virtue of their essential properties by which they take their own stand in the world. This has enormous practical implications for basic conceptions of human nature, the necessary connections of people with one another and with nature and God.[3]

Each thing in the world, in this conception, "measures" other things with respect to itself and one another insofar as they are determinately related and, wherever it is possible to distinguish things as being different in some respect or other, that "respect of difference" is the standard in terms of which they are measured as different or the same. We do not need to say that the world is a totality, only that everything in the world is determinate with respect to at least some other things. Whatever science discovers about the determinate characteristics of the world illustrates the hypothesis that to be a thing is to be determinate. Much else is determinate that science will probably never discover, and things that are determinate in some respects might be indeterminate in others. But nothing science discovers needs to be denied in this definition of world. The world as knowable by science has closure so far as science goes.

If the defining feature of the world is that everything in it is determinate, then divine creation is the creation of everything determinate, including all those kinds of causation that are determinate. This is a far more general conception of divine creation than that of the creator of the heavens, dry land, and seas. Furthermore, it is necessarily extremely abstract, because it entails that even the determinate aspects of God *as creator* are created.

By itself, the hypothesis that God is creator of everything determinate does not have much religious significance. By itself, the conception does not say that the created world contains people, that they have religious problems such as sin and suffering, and that the divine creation includes anything that addresses those religious problems. None of those or like religious matters can be derived from the abstract conception of God as creator of everything determinate. Each needs to be established and understood on the basis of particular analyses and experiences of the human condition.

Just as the abstract conception allows for any determinate world that science might discover, it allows for any religious situation that theology might discover. Other sources than the abstract conception of divine creation are needed to make it religiously relevant. And insofar as accounts of the religious situation differ, we cannot choose among them on the basis of appealing to the abstract notion of creation *ex nihilo*. What we can do with that abstract conception, however, is to use it to understand how the various determinate aspects of the religous situation relate to one another. It is the abstract frame for a conception of God that can be spirit, a warrior, loving, vengeful, parental, and trinitarian.

IV. GOD AS CREATOR *EX NIHILO*

Although by itself the hypothesis that God is creator of everything determinate does not say anything specific about God, the hypothesis does say that whatever the determinate world consists in, God is creator of it, and whatever divine creating involves, God is or does that. By itself, in fact, the hypothesis probably should not call the creator "God," where that carries Western theistic connotations. By itself, the hypothesis merely asserts that the realm of determinate things is consequent upon a ground: the Brahman of Hinduism, the Tao of Taoism, the Heavenly Principle of Neo-Confucianism, and the Emptiness, Nirvana, and Buddha-mind of Mahayana Buddhism all illustrate some version or other of the ground-consequent relation, just as well as does the theistic God of Judaism, Christianity, and Islam. One must look further to the kind of world that is created to determine whether to employ metaphors of Mind, Principle, Force, Person, or something else to explicate the meaning of divine creation. Religious traditions offer a plethora of options for interpreting what the creating of the world involves. The *Primer* focuses on the Christian options.

The language of creation itself, of course, is of Western origin and carries connotations of an agent who creates. Mind, Principle, and Force are not exactly agents, although they are, in their respective traditions, conceived to be that upon which the manifest world depends (Neville, 1982: chap. 6). The focus in Christian theology is to determine how the idea of creation *ex nihilo* serves to provide an interpretive referent for the God of the Bible and the Christian tradition, learning as much as possible, of course, from other religions.

A secularist might object to this consideration of God as creator by pointing out the fact that the realm of determinate things, with closure as determinate, does not make internal reference to a creator. Rather, the secularist would argue, we can get along by making reference to the determinate world and explain it by its first principles, which are also determinate and part of the world. Not only secularists but also process theologians argue this way (Cobb, Ford, and Hartshorne, 1980). There are at least two lines of answer to this argument that respect the integrity of the modern notion of closure but maintain the transcendence of divine creativity.

The first argument calls for a reflection on why we say something needs explanation in the first place. The general principle is that something needs explanation if it has an arbitrary order; by "arbitrary" is meant that the order is determinately what it is but could have been different. The course of temporal affairs is explained, point by point, by showing how a complex, determinate state of affairs could have been different except for the fact that various causes external to the state make it what it is.[4] But what about the laws of nature and other principles, such as those characterizing consistency and intelligibility? Are they to be explained? They themselves are determinately what they are; otherwise they would not determine or explain anything else. If what they are is determinate, they are determinately different from some other principles, and as a whole are different from a state of affairs in which nothing is determinate and they do not exist. Therefore, we need to find something that explains why there are these determinate laws and principles, and not others or none. Of course, we cannot consistently imagine a state of affairs in which things are contradictory or other than themselves. But then, our capacity to imagine is contingent and, by itself, arbitrary, as shown by this very point. The simplest rule of explanation is to say that any determinate thing, complexly related to other things with respect to which it is determinate, is to be explained by the decisions that made it to be what it is rather than something else. Most of those decisions are to be found in antecedent states of affairs, such as those that brought us to where we are now and prevent us from being on the other side of the world in two minutes. But some of the decisions are the kind that determine the large-scale structures of the universe that are illustrated in everything else, structures such as intelligibility, consistency, space-time existence, and a myriad other metaphysical considerations. Divine creation is the determining of those large-scale structures as well as all the things governed by them that determine one another. To object that only principles explain, rather than the decisive *making* of things, is to miss the point: principles are not ultimate explanations but themselves need explanation. Expressed religiously, even the most elementary structures of the universe declare both their contingency and their maker.

A second line of argument arises from a more precise consideration of the nature of determinate things. It was remarked above that a determinate thing has two kinds of features, essential ones of its own and conditional ones that relate it to other things with respect to which it is determinate. A thing is a harmony of these two kinds of features. Perhaps it is possible to understand the conditional features by finding cosmological acts of causation by which one determinate thing affects another. But it is not possible to understand how the essential features of different things can be together if the only kind of togetherness is conditional, constituted by determinate cosmological causation. For things would not have conditional features unless they simultaneously had their essential features. Because a thing is not its conditional features alone but a harmony of those with essential features, the precondition for things being together so that their essential features can condition one another is that things be together with both their essential and conditional features. Therefore the mutual conditioning of things by one another presupposes that they are in a context of mutual relevance in which their essential features are together nonconditionally. This is an *ontological* context of mutual relevance, not a cosmological one (see Neville, 1992: chap. 1).

The ontological context cannot be one more determinate thing, because determinateness is the very question at issue. Therefore we can say that things can be together ontologically by virtue of being created that way.[5] The creation of things as together, essence to essence, is not mere cosmological, intraworldly, creativity, but the ontological creation of their very determinateness. This is an abstract metaphysical way of saying that things cannot be together with genuinely other things, related to them but different, except insofar as they are jointly elements of the divine act of creation. They are together insofar as they are jointly created. Furthermore, their mutual conditioning of one another is subsidiary to their being together ontologically; their existence as creatures is the ground of their causal relations with one another.

To return to the secularists' point, even the world of determinate things cannot be thoroughly understood without taking into account its radical contingency. Therefore it must be conceived to be created by a creative act that is not itself part of the determinate world. The closure of the world itself depends on ontological divine creation.

The point about ontological contingency is still a far cry from a religiously interesting characterization of God. But it does point up the sense of contingency so close to the heart of mystics in the Christian and other traditions. Friedrich Schleiermacher (1830), one of the greatest Christian theologians, argued that the feeling of radical dependence is the root of all theology. The argument here has not dealt with dependency as a matter of feeling. But it finds reinforcement in that sense of religious experience. The next chapter shall continue the development of the religious significance of creation *ex nihilo*.

Readings in Key Texts:

1. Aquinas *SCG*, Book 1, chaps. 10–25.
2. Aquinas, *ST*, I-I, ques. 3–16, 25–26.

3. Augustine, *Conf.*, Book 12, chaps. 1–17.
4. Barth, *Credo*, chaps. 3, 16.
5. Calvin, *Inst.*, Book 1, chaps. 11–12, 14.
6. Cobb and Griffin, *PT*, chap. 1.
7. Ferm, no reading.
8. Hildegard, no reading.
9. Luther, no reading.
10. Rahner, *Found.*, chap. 2, sections 1–3.
11. Ruether, *Sexism*, chap. 3.
12. Schleiermacher, *CF*, pp. 131–156, 170–193.
13. Tillich, *Sys.*, Vol. 1, pt. 2, Sect. 1.

God As Trinity

I. THE TRINITARIAN CHARACTER OF DIVINE CREATION

The Christian doctrine of the Trinity arose in the first two centuries of the Church as a way of making sense of certain strong beliefs at the heart of the new Christian way, and the controversies in the definition of the Trinity continued at least into the fifth century.[1] At the beginning of Christian theology in the first century, there were some abstract notions, such as the Wisdom or Logos, that were presupposed and used. The initial theological interest was not the metaphysics of Trinitarian relations, however, but the concern to connect Jesus and the Holy Spirit to the God of the Jewish tradition. In some sense or other, or in several senses, both were thought to be divine; this was affirmed in spite of the strict anti-idolatry emphasis in the contemporary sects of Judaism, an emphasis that made it hard to imagine anyone or anything except Yahweh as being divine. The very practical problems of understanding the relations of Jesus and the Holy Spirit to God forced the theoretical issues that called in the abstract metaphysical categories in terms of which the doctrine of the Trinity is expressed.

Jesus, of course, had worshipped and taught about Yahweh, the God of the Torah and the Jewish people. Though perhaps not alone among his contemporaries in thinking of God as Father, that was the peculiar focus of Jesus' theology that became central in the Christian community. The image of "father" connotes, first, that God is creator and source of the world, especially of all people, and that God nurtures, cares about, loves, disciplines, provides for, and rescues from trouble the world's peoples who are considered children of God. The centrality of the father image shifts attention away from God as warrior, courtroom judge, and king; even though Jesus made heavy use of the images of the "kingdom of God" and the "kingdom of heaven," the head of the kingdom was a father, not royalty. The early Christians thus called God "Father" with these connotations in mind. That the term has a sexist ring now, and had the side effect through nearly two thousand years of ascribing masculine characteristics to God, should not detract from the new anti-warrior emphasis early Christians found in the use of the term.

Jesus himself was regarded as not merely human from very early in the Christian movement. Mark, for instance, began his gospel, "The beginning of the good news of Jesus Christ, the Son of God." Aside from the obvious reference to a special sonship to God, "Christ" seems to be used almost like a last name, a surname. This marks a distinct development in the notion of messiah or Christ. Whereas before "messiah" had meant a person annointed to provide a special rescue or support for the people of Israel—Saul, David, and Cyrus the Great were all called "messiahs" in the Hebrew Bible—the Christians thought of Jesus as messiah in an expanded sense. Not only the people of Israel but all the peoples of the Earth are in need of salvation. Furthermore, they need to be rescued not from the Philisitines or the Babylonians, but from the consequences of their own pervasive sin. So messiahship for Christians was not merely a matter of political and spiritual leadership but also the cosmic drama of rescuing humankind from the bondage of evil, often personified in the devil and demonic minions. For this drama, Jesus was understood to be the very Word of God through which the world was created in the first place, as in the prologue of the Gospel of John. John also, in his account of the Last Supper, stressed Jesus's various forms of unity with God the Father. Jesus was thus conceived to be both fully human, the lineal descendent of David, and the first-born of the family of the saved (Romans 8:29). Does this make Jesus a second God? Or are there levels of divinity, with the Father at the top and Jesus on a lower level? The doctrine of the Trinity was developed to address these questions, relating God as the Father and Jesus as the Son.

In addition to the Father and the Son, the Holy Spirit was recognized early to be divine in a special way. The principal reference was Jesus' promise to send the Spirit as a substitute for himself (John 14:26), and this Spirit was experienced by the assembled disciples at Pentecost and in worship across the Christian communities thereafter. The Spirit was identified with the spirit of prophecy in the Hebrew Bible and also with the Spirit of God present in things insofar as they are creatures. The Holy Spirit was conceived to be God active, making a difference in the world, indeed, making the world. Most of all, the Spirit was interpreted to be the experienced presence of God, confirming and disconfirming interpretations of events of the Christian life. The Holy Spirit is God present in prayer, indeed, the one who creates praying in us (Romans

8:26–27: "Likewise the Spirit helps us in our weakness; for we do not know how to pray as we ought, but that very Spirit intercedes with sighs too deep for words. And God, who searches the heart, knows what is the mind of the Spirit, because the Spirit intercedes for the saints according to the will of God"). With these beliefs, the early Christians needed a way of conceiving the Spirit's relation to the Father and Son.

Whatever the concepts underlying the doctrine of the Trinity, Father, Son, and Spirit were the names, almost proper names, of the divine persons, names arising from the history of the development of the Christian conception of divinity. The masculinity of at least the first two, Father and Son, is offensive to many people because it seems to describe God as masculine. But the description of the Persons of the Trinity is far more complicated than anything having to do with gender, and the names of the persons may be preferable to inclusive language that attempts to name through generalized descriptions, for instance Creator, Redeemer, Sustainer. The ancient Church discovered that the unity of the Trinity, if the differences among the persons be acknowledged, requires that the "action" of any one person is at the same time the action of the other two; hence a description according to different functions threatens the unity of the Trinity.

In order to understand the relations among the Father, Son, and Spirit, the early Church turned to the philosophic categories of Greek and Roman philosophy. These were not immediately useful, but were reconstructed in the process of being applied to the Christians' problems. Although it is possible today to see and appreciate how those categories were used, we must employ contemporary philosophical categories for our own use.[2] What follows is an attempt to employ contemporary categories, those introduced in connection with the theory of creation *ex nihilo*, to spell out how we might best understand God, Christ, and the Spirit.

Before proceeding to spell out how the abstract conception of God as creator is specified by the concrete epiphanies in the Christian tradition, a peculiar characteristic of that abstract conception should be pointed out, namely, its own Trinitarian character. In the act of divine creation, three elements are necessarily involved: God as source of everything determinate, God as the product or end point of the creative act, and God as the creative activity itself. These shall be explained shortly. Notice that the abstract model is not the specific Christian Trinity. The Christian Trinity includes, as its second person or member, the Christ Jesus who is both wholly divine in one sense and wholly human in another; the abstract model is vague with respect to the specific character of the terminus of the creative act. Furthermore, in the Christian conception the universe is not simply the terminus of the divine creative act, although it is that surely enough; it also has an integrity of its own over against God, or over against its creative status, so that it can be fallen or sinful. The explication of the abstract Trinitarian character of divine creation remains vague with respect to how Christians (and Buddhists, Hindus, Moslems, etc.) articulate specific versions of the Trinitarian relations. Chapter 5 will begin the Christian specification by analyzing the traits of the human condition as developed in the Christian tradition.

As to the abstract Trinitarian character of divine creation, the most important key to understanding the concept is the asymmetry in the idea of creation. Within the flow of ordinary events, causation might be viewed as a rearrangement of previously given elements. But divine creation is the making of the determinate things as such, not out of something else but, as the traditional phrase goes, "out of nothing." Ontological creation is the sheer bringing into positive being of the determinate things. (Actually, a good argument can be made that even ordinary causation involves a little bit of positive novelty, in that there are new arrangements and even new features over and above what was given before. A painting cannot be predicted on the basis of the paints, canvas, and the artist's prior ideas and talents: the artist's creative capacities emerge and evolve in the exercise of the prior capacities on the materials.) Some people say that such sheer creation is impossible because nothing can come from nothing (it sounds better in Latin: *ex nihilo nihil fit*). That is the question at issue, however, not a principle to resolve the issue, and it cannot be presupposed. If there is genuine creation and novelty in the world, then something does come from nothing by an ontologically creative act.

In the asymmetry of the act of ontological creation, the source of the act is indeterminate because all determinateness is the result of the act (Neville, 1992: chap 4). Insofar as God is conceived, therefore, as abstracted from the Trinitarian source-product-act relation, God is utterly indeterminate and unknowable. We cannot say that there is a potentiality in God to create the world apart from creation, because that potentiality would either be determinate (hence created) or vacuous (and different in no way from utter lack of potentiality). Nor can we say, apart from creation, that God is knowing, good, powerful or any of the other things there has been reason to say of God from a religious perspective. Apart from creation, God is indistinguishable from nothing.

But of course there *is* the universe and God *is not* apart from creation. Because of the asymmetry in creation, the universe is wholly dependent on being created; it is thus wholly dependent on God as source. God as source creates the world, having no determinate need to do so but strictly and purely out of divine self-constituting grace. The universe is wholly dependent for its existence as a set of determinate things on God as source. That God is source is itself a function of the world's being created.

From the perspective of the movement of our spiritual reflection, we can begin with the contingency of some striking parts of the world, move to their dependency on the source, and then note that the source would be wholly indeterminate apart from the creative activity that makes it creator.[3] The relation of the source to the product is itself a determinate product of creation. As the mystics have known, in the transcendence of the spirit God appears finally as the Nothing from which the world is a free creation.

II. TIME AND ETERNITY

The world has the integrity of its own closure as determinate. Nevertheless, it exists only in being created. Many of its things are spatial and temporal, yet space and time are among the things created. There is no medium in which God creates and from which the creative activity can depart, leaving the things. Rather, things exist because of the immediate presence of God creating them. The created things themselves might do things that pervert authentic responses to the fact of being created, as humans do when they sin; and there might be elements of the created order such as suffering that are intrinsically perverse in their part of the universe. Yet there is nothing that is not an expression of the creative act after the fashion of its own determinate character. Even in the manifestations of sin and suffering there shines a glory of the creating God to those who have eyes to see and ears to hear, without minimizing the awful truth of the sin and suffering. The glory of the creative presence is specific to the determinate characters of the things created.

Implicit in the discussion of both source and product of creation is the creative act itself. None of the three can be conceived without the others. The determinate character of the act, of course, is the world created; the act is not a medium with a character of its own, for that character would be either determinate, hence created, or vacuous. The power in the act is the source creating. The act is the source creating and the world being created.

The kind of unity the act has depends on the character of the world created. If the world has the kind of unity analogous to what we would expect of a personal agent, the act is like a personal act. If the world's unity is far more scattered, or is of a radically different sort, the act would be characterized differently. Whatever the kind of unity in the divine ontological creative act, it is nevertheless individual or singular. For the act creates any two related determinate things together, one act for both. Although it need not be the case that any two determinate things are related directly to one another, each is related to some other, and there are no things that are completely unrelated to other things in the universe. We cannot even suggest that there are two or more radically discontinuous universes, because both would share the features of being determinate and different from one another: difference itself presupposes the ontological togetherness of mutually different essential features. Although things are created at different points in time, that difference makes sense only if time, which is also created, is one thing; therefore things in different times are created ontologically together in the same divine act even if they are created cosmologically one before the other.

In a quite proper sense, then, the divine creative act is eternal. Eternity simply means a reality that is not temporal. Temporal things are all created, and time itself is part of their determinate character.[4] From the temporal standpoint of a particular thing, it seems that its creation takes place at the dates of its existence, and that is true. But that creation is connected with the creation of the earlier and later things with which it is related, and is part of the inclusive individual act. Because temporal things are dynamic and changing, eternity is not static. Nor is it a kind of inclusive temporal event, like a day that includes twenty-four hours. It is rather the eternal creation of things with changing temporal relations. The divine life then is not dynamic in the human sense, played out one day after another. It is rather dynamic in an eternal sense, with its effects being temporally changing.

This abstract point about eternity is crucial for many Christian doctrines. It is a condition for allowing the world as temporal to have closure over against God. At the same time it is crucial for acknowledging that the identity of a temporal thing is not exhausted in its moments but rather in being its part of the individual eternal divine life. Whatever Christians believe about life after death, because of the eternity of God as ever present creator, people have a part in the eternal life of God, and the ontological quality of their life is eternal as the cosmological is temporal. Indeed, the points about the individuality and eternity of the divine creative act are what allow Christians to say that God is living. The divine life is not temporal in our sense, but still is characteristic of creative activity that includes the novelty of temporal flow within it. How is divine life eternal and yet embracing of the temporal?

A person's life embraces a past and future as well as a present.[5] The past is accomplished and fixed, a "fact." The future for the person is somewhat open, dependent on decisions yet to be made by the person and by other decisive events; the future also is determinate within bounds set by the limits of the possible causal connectors between the present and future. A person's present is not only the moment of subjective immediacy, of the feeling of existing, but also of change. Actual change takes place only in present time; because of this, the present has seemed especially important for human traits such as the free exercise of responsibility and the radical transformations associated with religion (see Cobb and Griffin, 1976; and Neville, 1974).

Although it is common in twentieth-century thinking to emphasize the present over the other modes of time in a person's (or any temporal thing's) identity, it is crucial to remember that the present is inextricably linked to the past and future. The past provides the conditions, the facts, the raw material, the true potentials out of which a present moment creates its changes; without the past, the present would be wholly indeterminate, with nothing to change or to sustain. Put in technical terms, the past provides the present with conditional features in the form of data for actualization in the present. The essential features of the present include the creativity ordering the data given by the past. The future, by contrast, provides the present with a field of possibilities for realization, a field connecting the present person with all the other present things, each realizing its own present moment. The essential features of the future are sheer logical form. The conditional features of the future are the logical form made specific to what the present has to work with (data given from the past). The future conditions the present by providing possibilities for realizing the present's potentialities deriving from the past. The essential features of the present include the creative decisions that alter future possibilities (the eating of the cake precludes the possibility of still having it in the future).

Although temporal things such as persons only live moment by moment, each moment is intrinsically connected with past and future moments. Each mode of time contains conditional features from the others; the previous paragraph showed how the present cannot be itself without being conditioned by past and future. Although not temporally together with past and future, the present still must be ontologically together with them. Eternity is the divine creative act in which past, present, and future are together. The true identity of a temporal thing, then, embraces all moments of its temporal life, and that embracing must be in eternity, not in time. In time itself, the past is gone and the future has not yet come. If the present were the whole story, there would be no responsibility.

Recognizing that a person's identity embraces all moments of the individual's life, some thinkers have tried to express this with temporal language. For instance, we can think of a person's identity as if it were all past; some doctrines of last judgment are framed with this kind of imagery. Yet this would forget that at many stages in life, the person had crucial decisions to make that determined an otherwise open future. We would remember only the decisions, not the uncertainty and responsibility involved in deciding. Other thinkers, especially Augustine, one of the most influential Christian theologians, recommend thinking of a person's identity as some kind of enlarged synoptic vision of the present, a huge Now in which both past and future are contained as if still in actualization. God, in parallel, is thought of as a great eternal now. But if everything in a person's life is a now, then there is never any definite actualization with steps, no past to take account of, no future demanding resolution; real life involves a series of irreversible decisions.

We must admit, contrary to both of these suggestions, that a person's life has its dated moments and that each of these at one point is future, at another point is in the decisive present, and at another point past. The complexity of the divine life is that it embraces all of the person's moments in all three modes of time. In a quite literal sense, then, God embraces us as we face the future in every moment, as we decide and enjoy the immediacy of each moment as present, and also as we have run the course. This is the eternal life in which we exist in God, and it is as real at any time during our lifetime as it is after death.

Although there has been powerful metaphorical play in the symbol of the afterlife and natural immortality, in a literal sense it is not of much importance. No matter how long a person lives, or how many reincarnations, the eternity of the person's life consists in the fact that any part of that life, or the whole of it, exists eternally in the divine life. This last point is what has the religious power.

III. GOD AS LOGOS

As the writers of ancient Israel attempted to understand and express the sovereignty of God as creator, they had to modify the popular conceptions with which they began. Among the earliest of those conceptions was the polytheistic belief that Yahweh was one among many gods, each attached to a city or natural phenomenon: through the covenant with Abraham, Yahweh agreed to attach himself (yes, himself) to Israel. As the covenant with Moses demanded, the children of Israel were to put no other gods before Yahweh, although the existence of those other gods, and the loyalty of other peoples to them, were acknowledged as the competitive problem for the covenant. The pantheon of gods was then refashioned with Yahweh as the chief God, not just the special one for the Hebrews. Then Yahweh alone was conceived to be God and the others were angels and other mediating divine beings. As the later writers struggled to conceive Yahweh abstractly enough to be creator of all the world, even of the other heavenly beings, they were in danger of conceiving Yahweh as so distant from worldly affairs as to be religiously irrelevant. At that point the angels were crucial for the mediating function. Under the influence of Greek thinking, introduced to the area by Alexander the Great, Yahweh was conceived to have begun creating by creating a determinate version of the otherwise transcendently indeterminate divine nature. In the Wisdom literature this was known as Sophia, and in the New Testament gospel of John, as the Logos or Word. As John (1:1–4) put it, the Logos is that in and through which everything created is made.

The Greek word *logos* means speech or discourse, especially of the sort involved in deliberation in a court by means of which a determinate judgment is arrived at. The word *sophia* also means a kind of speech that arrives at a determinate particularity, although *sophia* is the sung speech of the bard. Christian theology can take both to mean the expression of the kinds of considerations that are involved in being determinate. That is, the Logos comprises the features of determinateness as such. Because the world consists of all the things that are determinate, the Logos then is that in and by which the world is created as determinate. In this sense, the Logos is a general epiphany or revelation of the divine, whatever more specific revelations the world might contain.

Although some theologians have identified the Logos with form, more than that is involved in being determinate. There are, in fact, four elements that must be talked about in grasping something as determinate: form, components to be formed, their actual mixture, and value as the cause of their mixture. Hence there are four elements to the Logos.[6] Form, pattern, or order is one element, but inseparable from the components of the determinate thing that are formed together. A thing is thus a harmony of form and the components formed. Each component is also a thing, and thus analyzable in terms of form and components. In addition to form and components, a thing is to be understood as the *actual* mixture of its form and components: it exists as a concrete thing, according to whatever nature its form and components give. The fourth element is harder to state, given the assumptions of our secular culture. It is the *value* of having that form in those components in this existential position. Every actual harmony of form and components achieves some value, even if it is misplaced or destructive, as for instance the value of life in a tuberculosis bacterium. Part of the value of anything consists in its place among the other things, and the justifying reason for its existence has to do with how well it contributes to the harmony of the large group. The Logos is thus the character of God expressed in each determinate thing by virtue of its determinateness, and it consists in the implications of form, components, actuality, and value. To say that Jesus was the incarnation of the Logos is thus to say that he epitomized or realized these four in some perfect way. Not only will the Christology to be developed below depend on showing that Jesus incarnates the four-fold elements of the Logos, but they will be the interpretive themes of the discussions of the human condition, its ideals, its failures, and its remedies. The radical character of this conception of the Logos can be drawn out by a general consideration of its implications for the understanding of religions as such.

IV. SKY GOD, EARTH MOTHER, GROUND, GOAL

The elements of the Logos are crucial for understanding the placement and connections of the many symbols for divinity, divine action, and divine things. In the history of religions, each has been taken to be a type of manifestation of the divine.

The element of form or order has been expressed in the history of religions, as well as in the Judeo-Christian tradition, in the guise of the Sky God who imposes order on chaos. Yahweh as described in Genesis 1 makes things by imposing order on chaotic elements; God introduces distinctions. In this vein, God also imposes a moral order and demands obedience. God appears as the righteous judge. Those aspects of religion having to do with the divine origins of morality, with commandment and with human obedience, all stem from the themes of order or form in creation.

Of course, in the Christian tradition God is the creator of the stuff or chaos ordered as well as of the order. Therefore, there is a divinity in the power and careers of the components of any given order. This is associated with the religious impulses of Mother Nature, the Earth Mother (Ruether, 1983; Pamela Berger, 1985). The cult of Yahweh set itself resolutely against the feminine in religion, attempting to exclude the worship of Astarte and the Baals. Yet the counter-Yahwist cults continued to reappear, and in the later writings of the Hebrew Bible some of the feminine themes of fertility and the powers of nature that care little for moral order were attributed to Yahweh. Jesus could be seen as the righteous judge; but he also pointed out that God sends the rain on the just and the unjust, and that we should attend to holiness before righteousness because the poor we have always with us. Of course the components of nature are not really pure chaos; they only look that way from the rather insecure vantage point of the masculine concern for moral and social order. Nor are the amoral forces of nature evil, though they seem to be heedless of the needs for moral order. From the standpoint of nature, the strictures of moral and social order seem confining, a kind of bondage; but that is only when the overall frames of human life are ignored in favor of their components.

That creation is actual or existential, and not to be understood only in terms of the forms and components of determinate things, is an ancient theme. Yahweh told Moses (Exodus 3:14) that the divine name is I Am That I Am. Thomas Aquinas interpreted this to mean that God is being itself. From the human standpoint, the definiteness of our actuality, including the actual limitations on our future, are the sharpest reminders of our contingency on divine creation. Existentialism has made this a major theme in the twentieth century. But the entire emphasis on guilt and on the need for redemption illustrates a sense for the once-for-allness of actuality and its religious significance. Our actuality is correlated with God's singularity in the creative act.

That creatures are created with value means that each is related to the creator in a normative way. Most natural things simply are what they are, and glorify God's handiwork in being themselves. Human beings are changeable and responsible for those changes. Indeed, we are created to be inclusive of the activities of freedom, and thus we can be worse than we ought to be. We have a moral identity that comes from how we fulfill our responsibilities to be as good as we can be in each circumstance. And we have a religious identity in terms of how we relate our moral identity to the creator. According to Christianity, our moral mistakes are also destructive breaks in the covenant with God, and our religious identity is thus that of sinners. But we are redeemed sinners, according to Christianity. In general, the element of value in creation means that human beings have a religious path, a path of personal and social perfection.

The elements of the Logos—form, components, actuality, and value—are themselves part of the determinate creation. They are special in being transcendentals, however, characteristics that apply to each determinate thing. Moreover, they cannot be understood without one another, just as the source, product, and act in the Trinitarian conception require one another. There is no such thing as pure and separate form, or components, or actuality, or value. Rather these are characteristics begotten in the very creating of determinate things.

Just as the abstract Trinitarian conception provides a rough rubric for understanding divine creation, irrespective of how Christianity or any other religion specifies the creation, the four elements of the Logos are abstract with reference to the applications of specific symbols. Most religions symbolize the divine respecting structural and moral order, respecting the powerful natural components of the world, respecting existence itself, and respecting the senses in which the values of things determine religious paths for individuals and societies. Christianity is no exception. Therefore, the elements of the Logos are a crucial part of the overall conception of God, helpful for understanding the relative truths in the various symbols that make up the Christian tradition and that form its worship and life. They also point the way to crucial conditions for Christology, expressing something of that of which Jesus is the consummate incarnation.

A final point can be suggested here, although its real value lies in concrete applications. It is said that God is love, and that the ultimate character of creation is to love. What can this mean? At the abstract level we can begin to see that it means creating things with form, with ongoing components connecting the things with other things, with actual existential status, and with value. Perhaps the last is most important, although the first three are conditions for it: things are created for their loveliness. Even the most wretched of us is lovely to God, in our sin and suffering. Loveliness is not merely a moral quality. Indeed, it can even be positively immoral, as in a murderer or a fatal virus. Yet in its way it is lovely—ultimately, absolutely, and ontologically lovely—because it is the result of God creating. For all the differences between the world's great religions, they surprisingly agree that the rock-bottom character of reality is that the ultimate is loving, and that this transcends morality and the very importance of what we do. Furthermore, it indicates that the closure of the world is everywhere broken in upon by the creator's love. Nothing is closed to divine creativity. Nothing exists except by its loving power.

The argument that divine matters are to be understood in terms of the doctrine of the Trinity (at least that is the Christian way of putting it) is peculiarly uneven. On one level are the specific needs of the Christian community to come to an understanding of the relation of Jesus and the Holy Spirit to God. On another level is the metaphysical argument that divine matters are best understood in terms of creation *ex nihilo* and that the creation doctrine has a naturally Trinitarian form, as well as an implication that accords with the doctrine of the Logos. How can these levels be brought together?

The clue lies not in trying to squeeze metaphysics out of the puzzles about Jesus but in noting a crucial implication of the idea of creation *ex nihilo*. If all characters of God, including the divinity that might be shared with Jesus, depend on the determinate character of the world created, we must look to the world for specifications of divinity. Hence, the uneven and rough sketches of the divine in this and chapter 3 can only be completed and filled in by a consideration of the world, especially of the human condition. The analysis of the human condition will lead back to the problem of salvation with which this chapter began. Only in addressing the problem of salvation will it be possible to articulate the significance of Jesus, in humanity and in divinity. The salvific nature of Jesus itself can only be understood in terms of the actual difference it makes—that is, in history and the Church. Therefore, the full doctrine of the Trinity waits upon Christology, which in turn waits upon ecclesiology, the study of the Church in spirit and deed. The argument turns next to the human condition.

Readings in Key Texts:

1. Aquinas, *SCG*, Book 1, chaps. 26–54.
2. Aquinas, *ST*, I-I, ques. 27–33.
3. Augustine, *Conf.*, Book 11.
4. Barth, *Credo*, chap. 2.
5. Calvin, *Inst.*, Book 1, chap. 13.
6. Cobb and Griffin, *PT*, chap. 3.
7. Ferm, no reading.
8. Hildegard, *Sci.*, Book 2, Visions 1–2; Book 3, Vision 7.
9. Luther, no reading.
10. Rahner, *Found.*, chap. 2, sections 4–5.
11. Ruether, no reading.
12. Schleiermacher, *CF*, pp. 194–232, 723–751.
13. Tillich, *Sys.* Vol. 1, pt. 2, section 2; Vol. 3, pt. 4, section 4.

The Human Condition: Covenant

I. THE RELIGIOUSLY PARTICULAR ANALYSIS OF THE HUMAN CONDITION

From a logical point of view, the religious project of salvation is in response to a human problem. For salvation to be significant, we need to be saved from something. Theology thus must ask, What is the human condition such that salvation is meaningful and desirable?

Implicit, if not explicit, in all theologies is a kind of existential religious problem-response form. Paul Tillich (1951: part 1) made it explicit, that the existential human condition raises problems to which religion is asked to supply the answer, and that answer has the form of being revelation for the human condition. Part of the force of Tillich's point is that the problems in the human condition are recognized and articulated by a variety of nonreligious as well as religious critics, and thus religion needs to be able to translate its responses into terms understood across a wide spectrum of secular as well as religious cultures. In fact, if religion cannot address the secular mind with its response to the secularly perceived problem, religion not only fails to preach its gospel but it also most likely is caught within too narrow an understanding of the religious problem itself. Because of its very need to be faithful to liturgical and other symbolic forms, religion can become wedded to those forms rather to the realities they expressed when first they were vital. Tillich coupled his theory of revelation with a theory of symbols that makes this plain.

Nevertheless, there is no temporal or existential priority of "understanding of problem" to "understanding of religious response."

Rather, the religious response contains an interpretation of the problem within it, and that interpretation is as crucial as the response itself. Or put the other way, a religiously vital understanding of the problems of the human condition contains an internal, if not fully expressed, reference to the revelatory response. Either way, the religious revelation reveals the nature of the problem as well as the salvific response. Even a purely secular critique of the human condition trades on revelatory religious themes. Marxism, for instance, derives its moral force from a warmed-over old fashioned covenant theology.

There are many Christian approaches to understanding the human condition, for which salvation in Jesus Christ is the Christian response. Or if not many separate approaches, there are many different families of metaphors and historical references that need to be coordinated, such as the themes of death, immorality, suffering, disobedience, pride, and self-triviality or dependence.[1]

For systematic purposes, the central interpretive metaphor, to which the others can be related, is that of covenant. The human condition is that we are created in an ideal and normative covenant relation with one another, with nature, and with God, and that this covenant is broken; salvation is the repair of the covenant. The theme of covenant unites both the Hebrew Bible and the New Testament, and it covers both an interpretation of the religious problem and an interpretation of the salvific significance of Jesus and the life of the Christian community.

The writer of Hebrews 8 and 9 insisted that the significance of God's action in Jesus was the establishment of a new covenant, replacing the old covenant given to Moses that had been flawed because people disobeyed. The Mosaic covenant, on its side, was part of a larger development of the covenant theme. God covenanted with David to provide for his house forever. Before Moses, God had covenanted with Abraham to provide a homeland for him and his multitude of descendents, for which Abraham and his followers would bind themselves to Yahweh, with circumcision as a sign. Before Abraham, God had covenanted with Noah, representative of the entire human race, not to destroy the earth, or not to let loose the powers of chaos symbolized by the waters held up by the roof of heaven. Even at the beginning, God had covenanted with Adam and Eve to provide the Garden of Eden on the condition of obedience concerning the prohibition to eat the fruit of the tree of knowledge of good and evil.

II. CONDITIONS OF COVENANT: GENESIS 2 AND 3

Although there have been many interpretations of the idea of covenant, the theme itself has been something to which every element of the ancient Hebrew and Christian traditions has had to respond. The interpretation developed here of course is a reconstruction, looking backward from the need to articulate a contemporary theology. Yet its elements have parallels in nearly all the interpretations.

The first element of the covenant theme is that the covenant provides the most fundamental identity for the people. Through the Mosaic covenant, Israel becomes the special people of God, a nation of priests of Yahweh. The Adam/Eve covenant of Genesis 2 and 3 is even more basic: the establishment of Adam and Eve in the garden is the capstone of the creation of humankind. Human beings are created in covenant as originally good. In the original setup, prior to or apart from the fall, Adam and Eve are complete and fulfilled, in right relation with their environment and God. This covenantal element underlies the doctrine often called "the people of God."

The covenant theme of original goodness is an alternative emphasis to the theme in Genesis 1:26–27, of the creation of human beings in the divine image. The *imago dei* has often been cited as evidence of the original goodness of humankind, and indeed it is when interpreted in terms of the covenant. That is, when we understand how being in covenant is the image of God, we can see in what the original goodness consists. The *imago dei* theme, however, has often been taken by itself, and has given rise to an inappropriate individualism. It has been taken to mean that what in human beings images God is rationality, or will, or love, or some other trait that individuals have, so that it is each person individually who images God. On the covenant interpretation, it is each person in covenant with others that images God.

The second element of covenant is that the human condition involves a combination of the natural and the conventional. Before Eve was created, Adam named the animals, giving them conventional names—"whatever the man called every living creature, that was its name" (Genesis 2:19). This marks the fact that part of what is essential to human living is what is conventional or humanmade. The most important convention, of course, was the divine commandment not to eat of the tree of the knowledge of good and evil. The creation of the human race was not complete until Adam had been divided, Eve had been made, and both brought to union with each other. Both the naming of the animals and the commandment constituting the ground rules for garden life had taken place before that, when Adam was still not complete because of his lack of an associate. Development of this element of the covenant gives rise to the doctrine of the Church, the explicit organization within society that deals with the relation to God intrinsic to being a creature.

The third element of the covenant is that it stipulates how people are to relate to each other and to the natural environment. In the Adam/Eve story, the people are given specific work to do together and are given explicit freedom to use the items in the garden (save for the tree of the knowledge of good and evil) so long as they tend everything as gardeners. The Mosaic covenant focuses on rules for behavior among humans and on observances that rehearse and cement the relation of God's people with God; perhaps this shift in emphasis comes from the fact that the Mosaic covenant is guarded against the effects of the fall. This element of the covenant is the doctrine of righteousness.

The fourth covenantal element is that people, in their relations to the environment and one another, are bound also to God. Obedience regarding the forbidden fruit seems the main content of this in the Adam/Eve covenant, but it symbolizes the human acknowledgment that God is creator of the whole creation, of the special human garden, and of the people themselves. This element is the foundation of worship.

The fifth element is that God is the initiator of the covenant. Unlike an ordinary contract, where both parties have something to gain by entering into agreement, in the covenant God sets the terms and the people accept and affirm them. God also provides the means for carrying out the human side of the covenant. This element of the covenant is the doctrine of grace.

The original covenant is not the whole of the Christian understanding of the human condition, because there is, of course, the fall. Adam and Eve disobeyed God and were expelled from the garden. There have been many accounts offered for why they disobeyed: out of pride, or jealousy, or sheer disobedience. All accounts that suppose that they disobeyed out of some motive fail to make sense, however, because we can always ask how they got that bad motive if they were created good. If they were created with a bad motive, then the fault lies with the creator. The "motive accounts" presuppose a kind of technical means-ends rationality that is misplaced in the context. Rather, Adam and Eve disobeyed simply because that was the way they were.

Specifically, they forgot that the divine convention was part of their nature. The snake told only the truth so far as it went, that the fruit of the tree was tasty, good looking, not poison, and productive of very powerful knowledge. Mortality came not from any poisonous character of the fruit but because Adam and Eve disobeyed the command not to eat. That is, they took their condition to be only the natural part, not the conventional convenantal part.

The effect of the fall is that the current human condition involves both punishment and an internal corruption. The current conditions for human life are not like a garden but involve hard work and suffering. The Earth is not entirely kind, some animals are dangerous, and people are prone to be in conflict. Furthermore, despite the original goodness of human beings, and despite the continued attempt to repair and live faithfully within the covenant, human beings are filled with unnecessary weaknesses, self-deceptions, and bad motives. The original goodness of people is corrupted to original sin by repeated, free, sinful acts and omissions. The goodness is not removed; we can appeal to it, and sometimes it conquers the worst of evils. But it is corrupted to a greater or lesser degree in everyone. Though few people are so wicked as to choose to be evil, all do make evil choices, or fail their duties, or otherwise do things that lead to evil consequences in others, in themselves, or in the social and natural environment. Although the Biblical story of Adam and Eve has been taken to be an historical event by some theologians, and the presence of sin in all people interpreted to derive from some kind of genetic inheritance in the blood, the question, Why sin?, is misplaced. There is no rational reason for sin, where "rational" would mean that people sin because of a prior motive. In sinning, we give ourselves the motives of pride, greed, dependency, selfishness, slavish lust, and the rest. The human condition simply is such that people behave sinfully. Matters of blame arise because of the sinning, which is enough, not because of the human condition as such.

Recurring to the story of Adam and Eve for our theological themes, it becomes necessary to recall that the story is a myth that has been used for many purposes other than the ones intended here. Like any myth or parable, it can be interpreted in many ways, and those must be justified on the basis of independent argument, not by appeal to the myth itself. The episode concerning the expulsion from the garden, for instance, has long been used to justify the subordination of wives to their husbands, and more generally, of women to men (Genesis 3:16). This is not the interpretation intended here, and it by no means follows from the story. Indeed, the more obvious moral is that wives' subordination is the result of sin, not something mandated as ideal in the original or in a restored covenant. The story itself, of course, is a product in its final redacted form of an extremely patriarchal culture, and this must be filtered out as we attempt to build a theology that recognizes gender equality.

The limits of the story must also be recognized in its historicizing of an interpretation of the human condition. It is not uncommon to acknowledge that the story was not intended to be an historical account and that it has rather a truth appropriate to myth. Beyond this, however, we must also ask about what is intended in the mythic historic structure. Does the story require us to believe that a purely perfect and ideal situation, the Garden of Eden, is possible? Is it really possible in historical time to imagine a perfect utopia? Although the goal of Christian religious life is the restoration of the original covenant, does this demand anything more than commitment to piecemeal improvements? Does it demand a commitment to the actual historical possibility of perfection?

The question is more complicated than meets the eye. It will be argued below, in consonance with themes developed by the philosopher Hegel and by the theologian Tillich, that the conditions of actual life are intrinsically ambiguous, and that we exist in a tension between the morality of finitude and the piety of divine infinity: the poignancy of the human condition is that we are in both worlds, as it were, and the true covenant involves acknowledging both. The reconciliation of the finite and infinite is not in the actual finitude of history but in the infinite eternity of divine life; the Adam and Eve story does not suggest this.

III. THE LOGOS IDEALS OF COVENANT

Because the ideas of covenant in the Hebrew Bible and New Testament are so diverse and variously developed, it is important for theology to make an attempt to understand the covenant systematically. The clue for the attempt is to seek the basic structures of the human condition in the elements of the Logos: form, components, existential finality, and value. No one of these elements by itself constitutes the covenant. In fact, a one-sided approach seriously skews our understanding, although that has happened often enough in the history of theology to be almost unexceptionable. The ideals of covenant will be discussed in terms of each of the elements of the Logos, and then discussed in their unity as binding people to one another and to God.

The covenant is first, as respects form, an ideal of righteousness, a commitment to ways of life and social institutions that administer and express justice or righteousness, both in direct dealings among people and in the indirect effects of social institutions. Righteousness is usually expressed in rules and contracts, and undergirded by institutions that oversee it and that supply routes of appeal. Thus righteousness is most often couched in the language of order and of institutions for maintaining order. Righteousness or morality is probably associated in history with the rise of civilization, that is, of cities, when increased population required public orders that could compromise together the honest and worthy competing claims of people and institutions; in civil morality people and institutions are treated not exclusively according to individual merit but according to the merit of their claims as instances of kinds. Reflecting the Logos, the order of elements in the covenant ought to be right order, and individuals and institutions ought to serve the right orders, not the other possible orders.

Righteousness is not necessarily served by the social order or set of social habits at hand. Arguments can be made that the rules and institutions ought to be changed to eliminate injustice or to promote greater good. Social orders involving slavery, or rules of commerce that benefit the rich and powerful at the expense of the poor and weak, are orders for which more just alternatives can be imagined. The critique of a social order or rule of interpersonal justice, however, is made in behalf of a more basic form of righteousness for which institutions are available. However we arrive at our conception of righteousness, and defend it against alternatives, the covenant as normative for the human condition demands that we live in righteousness with one another. Although righteousness is a matter of order, it does not equate with the defense of order as such over against chaos, but of the right order, for the attainment of which a little chaos might be helpful.

Second, regarding the components of creation, the covenant presents the ideal of piety, a commitment to respect and appreciate the powers of nature irrespective of whether they are organized to serve the human good. The earthquake and fire manifest the glory of God, even if they treat people like straw dogs.[2] The powers of nature great and small have careers and trajectories of their own. The human social order is a precarious, extremely fragile, harmony of those powers. Of course we look at creation from an anthropocentric perspective, in which the human social order is the morally organizing principle. It is right that we do so, from that moral human standpoint. The forces of nature appear violent, in need of taming, and amoral if not immoral. Those religions that relate directly to the forces of nature, cultivating rites of fertility, fecundity, death and rebirth, have been represented as immoral and anti-religious within the Judeo-Christian tradition. The Cult of the Mother has been roundly suppressed by the Cult of Yahweh. But it rises ever again, and the extreme patriarchy of ancient Israel and the Christian movement have not been able to suppress it.[3] Although we *are* human and do have a moral perspective, that is not the *only* perspective requiring respect within the covenant. Without abandoning the moral Yahweh for the nature-cult Baals and Asteroths, we should know that the moral standpoint is not the last word: from the standpoint of the powers of nature, imposition of human order seems like strangulation and witless environmental destruction.[4] In addition to righteousness, and sometimes over against it—at the very least incommensurate with righteousness—is piety, the profound respect and appreciation for the goodness in all components of creation regardless of their measure in the human moral scale of things.

The covenant is, third, from the standpoint of existential actuality, an ideal of faith to embrace the actuality of circumstances, a respect for the finality of historical existence and of one's contingent but actual position in it. Our life has a three fold temporal structure of present, past, and future, as briefly discussed in the previous chapter (see also Neville, 1989: chaps. 9–10). The past is fully actual and cannot be changed; the future has possibilities, sometimes wide open, that can be actualized in many different ways; and the present is the moment of decisive actualization. Sometimes we are tempted to think of ourselves as always cloaked in more possibilities than are being actualized, and as regards the future that is true. But we also are bound in our identity by the past: that is what our world has become and who we have been, like it or not, and it is for that reason that we have moral identity for better or worse. The present cannot be faced squarely if we do not view our temporal lives as identified by the singularity of actuality as well as by the diversity of possibilities. Part of the covenant, as Adam and Eve discovered, is to come to terms with that finality. The forms of more or less just social order, and the powers of nature that they organize, are insignificant if not treated as progressing through time with actual finality.

With actuality, the covenant marks the religious difference between "what exists" and "that it exists," between the cosmological and the ontological. Much of religion is itself a response to the sheer fact of existence. Our gratitude to God is founded on appreciation of creaturely existence as such. Most of Christian mysticism consists in coming to terms with existential actuality. In our own century, the existential religious thinkers have focused explicitly, sometimes even reductively, on this dimension of the created world that reflects its being created. What the existential philosophers called "authenticity," existential theologians such as Tillich (1952, 1957a, 1963: 129–138) call "faith."

Value, the fourth element of the Logos, enters the covenant not just as a component in righteousness but as the orientation for the spiritual path for individuals and society, for fundamental hope. Each creature, each collection of creatures, has value, and to be a human creature is to be obliged by a kind of natural piety to be faithful to those values. This is not so much a matter of doing right as it is of being right, less a matter of morals and more a matter of being in the truth, of faithfully registering the values of things in ourselves and actions. Because we incorporate things and their values into our lives by representing them and guiding our actions by those representations, it is extremely difficult to acquire the appropriate representations. Much of the task of religion is to develop the images of true representation deep in the soul so that our actions are properly respectful. Although the universe is vast and has neither human nor geographic center, our task is to become centered with the spiritual powers to be faithful to all creation. That too is part of the covenant, individually as well as socially. Because finding our center in the cosmos and relative to God is a process, the covenant ideal imposed by the fact of value is hope.

The four elements of the Logos are abstractions from the concrete creation, and do not exist by themselves. Rather they are perspective ingredients of creation. By themselves, they are not consistent with one another. The powers of nature are oblivious as to morals; the values of things are inclusive of far more than actuality. Yet they are conjoined concretely in the creation. So too in the covenant we join them in our relations to the earth, to each other, and to ourselves. Those relations are governed by the ideals of righteousness, piety, faith, and hope.

The mode of being that conjoins them is love, which forgives the inconsistencies and embraces the alien differences. This of course is a Christian reading, which imposes Jesus' teachings about love on a much older covenantal tradition. His quotation of the Great Commandment, however, was covenantal: "You shall love the Lord your God with all your heart, and with all your soul, and with all your mind." (Deuteronomy 6:5) "This is the great and first commandment. And a second is like it, You shall love your neighbor as yourself." (Leviticus 19:18) "On these two commendments depend all the law and the prophets." (Matthew 22:37-40) The older sources quoted by Jesus are at least as old as the Deuteronomic tradition of the Hebrew Bible. For Christian theology, to be in creation is to be covenanted to love it in all its elements, elements that cannot be wholly embraced by morals, or awe at nature, or existential finality, or the spiritual path. Righteousness, piety, faith, and hope are not enough by themselves; they cannot even be conjoined by themselves. They rather are abstract components of love. The theological analysis of love is that it consists of righteousness, piety, faith, and hope combined; their combination in love is more than their enumeration separately.

As the Great Commandment indicates, love of creatures is very like love of God. In fact, given the analysis of love into the four elements of the Logos, and given the transcendental character of those elements as expressions of God in all creation, there is a close identity between love, in this sense, of creation, and love of the creator. This is indeed the normative essence of the covenant: love of creation precisely because it is God's creation—love of God precisely because that love is what mirrors God's creating from within the created order. To put the equivalences more directly: our loving of God in loving the creation is our way of imaging God's loving the world in creating it. Whereas God's love makes things be, with form, components, actuality, and value, our love of things for their form, components, actuality, and value consists in our respectful comportment of ourselves in faithfulness to creation.

Of course, nearly all the time we treat things in pragmatic ways as they enter the course of our life. This is as true of our treatment of other people as it is of our relations with the environment or ourselves. In so doing we easily lose track of the fact that things are creatures. Therefore, the first way to remember the covenant is with Jesus' first clause—love

God with whole heart, mind, and soul. The love of God recalls us to the divine presence in creation, and thus to the ontological status of the creation itself.

IV. DIVINE JUDGMENT

One more element of the Adam and Eve story needs to be recalled at this point, namely, that when Adam and Eve sinned, God judged them and expelled from the garden. The image of God as judge is unpopular today. Sometimes it is thought to be too male (as if women were less judgmental than men!). And it always seems to be in direct tension with the image of God as lover. The centrality of love in Jesus' message and in all subsequent Christian theology seems to suppress the importance of divine judgment. Even in the Genesis story, God was lover first and last: he created the ideal garden for people, and just before expelling the people after the fall he made them leather clothes to replace the puny fig leaves. If God is loving, forgiving, supportive, nurturing, and all accepting, how can God exercise judgment on people's performance with respect to the ideals of the covenant?

Although the point cannot be developed at length in advance of a discussion of sin and the ruination of the covenant, the obvious answer to the question is that God cannot truly love sinners who need forgiveness if there is no divine recognition of the sin. Sinners who are unjudged cannot be forgiven, nor loved for what they really are. Therefore God must be judge before being lover, if the object of love is a less than perfect creation. Subsequent discussion shall return to this point.

Theology must be particularly careful with the symbol of divine judgment. It is far too easy to anthropomorphize it and assimilate it to images of judgmental parents or rulers. The Christian tradition has done this time and again in its art and literature. The difficulty with anthropomorphizing divine judgment is that it suggests an arbitrariness in the divine will. This difficulty is not helped by the episode in the Genesis story according to which the covenant is established by the apparently arbitrary selection of the tree as off limits. Judgment, however, is not a matter of arbitrary divine will but is something built into the nature of things.

The covenantal character of the human condition is to have an actual state of affairs that is normed by ideals. We are created to be related to one another, to the rest of nature, and to the institutions connecting these, with righteousness, piety, faith, and hope. Yet, given human freedom, there is no necessity that people fulfill their roles in the covenant. Even if they should always do so, there is no necessity in that.

Therefore there is always a peculiar relation between the ideal and the actual: the ideal judges the actual. Judgment is not somebody's will but the real state of affairs between the ideal and the actual. Human conscience is the implicit recognition of the ways the ideals judge actual behavior. We can project our own judgments onto an anthropomorphized image of God, and there is much spiritual symbolic appropriateness in doing so if one can stop short of neurotic guilt.

The question concerning *God* as judge is whether the creator who creates in love, establishing a world with order, components, actuality, and value, also creates that world to be measured by the ideals of righteousness, piety, faith, and hope. If the ideals are real and are conjoined to an actual world, there is divine judgment, however we discern and articulate it. God's creative love embraces not only the elements of the Logos and the ideals of covenant in the human condition, but the normative relation between those ideals and the actual world. Paul Tillich (1957) expressed this as an ambiguity between essential (normative) nature and existential (actual) nature, and claimed rightly that it was an ambiguity built into the created world as such. Just as there are times in spiritual life when God's love can be symbolized as a matter of divine consciousness and passion, so there are times when God's judgment can be symbolized by conscious assessment. Yet the reality underlying both symbols is the creation itself, a creation that contains the normative tension between the ideals and the actuality.

Considerable importance lies in coming to the doctrine of divine judgment before the analysis of sin and redemption. If divine judgment—the same holds true of divine love—were a function of God's response to human sin, it would be almost impossible to avoid psychologizing it. That is, judgment and love would be *only* human projections, mere symbols, and the language of secular psychology would legitimately replace the language of the gospel. If, on the contrary, we recognize that the creation is under judgment simply in its nature as being created, and regardless of whether anything in creation fails its norms, the theological seriousness of divine judgment and love is preserved. Divine love and judgment are the most important elements of the human condition.

Readings in Key Texts:

1. Aquinas, *SCG*, Book 2.
2. Aquinas, *ST*, I–I, ques. 34–35, 39, 44–47, 90–102.
3. Augustine, *Conf.*, Book 13.
4. Barth, *Credo*, chap. 4.

5. Calvin, *Inst.*, Book 1, chaps. 15–17.
6. Cobb and Griffin, no reading.
7. Ferm, *TWLT*, chaps. 15 (by Mbiti), 19 (by Oduyoye), 30 (by Rayan).
8. Hildegard, *Sci.*, Book 1, Visions 2–3.
9. Luther, no reading.
10. Rahner, *Found.*, chap 1 (also read at chap. 2 above).
11. Ruether, *Sexism*, chap. 4.
12. Schleiermacher, *CF*, pp. 233–256.
13. Tillich, *Sys.*, Vol. 3, pt. 4N, section 1.

6

The Human Condition: Sin

No religion is organized and given symbolic form for the exclusive purpose of celebration. There is always a problematic dimension: calling in the spirits for the hunt, invoking the powers of fertility, calling upon the gods for leadership, guidance, and protection against enemies, propitiation of the lingering presences of the dead. Among the great religions that have produced elaborate literatures, the religious problem is somewhat internalized to the person or community. Not only is the power of divinity needed to get along, but at least some of the failure to get along, a failure needing divine remedy, stems from human fault. Moreover, the fault is generally limited to sentient beings and is not to be found directly in non-human nature. Roughly speaking the dominant metaphors for the religious fault in the religions originating in India have to do with ignorance, for which salvation is enlightenment; for the religions originating in China, the fault has to do with disattunement, disharmony, or inappropriate behavior, salvation from which is reconnecting or building proper links with the larger natural and cultural environment. For the religions arising from the Near East, the fault is conceived as guilt, salvation from which is divine mercy and grace that restores rectitude. There are mystical elements in the religions from all three sources that suggest that human beings live in a false separation from the divine, and that spiritual accomplishment consists in finding and letting flourish the divine within oneself and one's people as a tradition.

At the present stage of our comparative understanding it is not clear just how far the religions are in agreement and disagreement. All of the major religions have symbols expressing the pains of ignorance and the bliss of enlightenment; all have symbols for the confusions of disrelation and the restoration of ease of connection; all have symbols and rites

of purification and connect religion with virtue and justice. Perhaps
there are merely historical differences that account for the different emphases in the imageries of the religions. Perhaps, however, there are true
incompatibilities expressed in the differences of emphasis. The purposes
of the *Primer* do not require a final resolution of this question. The point
here is rather to develop a theological position that expresses the Christian emphases. The argument must develop the theme of the covenant.

As the four elements of the Logos are the clue to the normative
covenant, they also are the clue to the elements of sin. For, sin is the
perversion of the covenant in any or all of the four modes.

I. UNRIGHTEOUSNESS

Christians are accustomed to equating sin with immorality or
breaking the moral order. There is a profound truth to this. Immorality
does two bad things at once. It causes the evil or unrighteousness in
which the immorality consists. And it turns the sinner into contradiction
with the covenant that constitutes the person's identity.

To do wrong to people, to the institutions that mediate their existence, and, in an extended sense of the term, to the natural environment, is intrinsically bad. It consists in diminishing the values things
would have were it not for one's actions. Although that diminishment is
sometimes trivial, it often is serious, such as when people are given undue
burdens in their own lives because of one's actions, or are rendered less
competent than otherwise to live their lives, or are corrupted to be unjust
or otherwise sinful themselves. Similarly, institutions and systems of
nature can be diminished in value and even brought to do harm or be
self-destructive through immoral action.

The content of righteousness is sometimes ambiguous and always
contextualized to historical circumstances of life.[1] But basic elements of
righteousness are common to all human communities: honoring persons,
protecting their life save in extenuating conditions, acknowledging people's rights to the essentials of their life such as certain kinds of property
and human relations, respecting the integrity of their past and future, including rendering fair judgment on the quality of their life, and communal care for funeral rites and provision for dependents of the de-
ceased. Definitions of the margins of these, of "extenuating
conditions," vary from culture to culture, and vary again over time. But
we can usually see *why* different situations change the margins and agree
about righteousness in situations quite different from one another and
from our own.

The definition of righteousness in the case of nature is far more
controversial in our culture, particularly because it seems so often to con-

flict with righteousness toward people, as when we rue to exploit the land to produce inexpensive food for poor people or insist that poor nations not pollute the atmosphere even though that is the only apparent way they can develop an industrial economy. The content of morality is most confusing with regard to institutions and social practices that mediate individuals with each other and determine the effects of human life on the environment. The difficulty lies in the fact that a single course of action or policy or institution has good effects in one direction and bad effects in another. Sometimes the kinds of things affected are so different that alterations of their value are incommensurable. The pain of living with such ambiguity, however, is part of the moral situation. And it does not entail that in the vast majority of affairs of life, a fairly clear account can be given of what is moral and what not.[2]

The other side of immorality or unrighteousness is not the objective wrongdoing but the destruction of the moral order as expressing God's creative love. For the sinner, this is the rejection of the morally formal part of the covenant, and hence a contradiction to the person's own identity as defined by the covenant. The normative covenant is the capstone of human identity; the covenant's content is the particulars of the person's own situation plus the ideals for that situation, all understood as elements of the person's being a creature of God. To break the covenant, therefore, is to contradict the sinner's own nature at the most basic ontological level. Our own unrighteousness, by rejecting the obligatoriness of God's good, rejects God and our own nature at once. Thus we sinners live in contradiction with ourselves. As Paul put it, "I do not understand my own actions. For I do not do the thing I want, but I do the very thing I hate" (Romans 7:15). To break the covenant is to treat the world as if its form, components, existential elements, and value were not the Logos of God.

Guilt, as Christians understand it, is not only fault for doing what is objectively immoral, or shame at being identified as the one at fault. It is both of those but also and more importantly the state of being in contradiction to one's own ontological nature as created in the covenant. Harming neighbors is at the same time rejecting God, and hence it involves contradicting oneself.

Furthermore, the objective harm done to neighbors, institutions, and nature is a matter of the cosmological definition of one's moral identity (Neville, 1987: chap. 3). It defines "what" or "who" one is in a morally negative way. That much of identity can very well be mixed with other things one does to the good, giving rise to other aspects of moral identity that are positive. The self-contradiction that consists in rejecting God and the creative covenant, however, defines one's ontological identity as corrupt. Expressed in the language of the contrast between the "that" and the "what," one's existence, "that" one is, internally is at war, is self-frustrated, resonates with less than it should, "whatever" the moral identity. This produces a deep existential unease even in the best of moral persons, for all are unrighteous in at least some respects.

The ontological contradiction also frustrates God's fullness of creation. Sin, with respect to rejection or perversion of the forms expressing righteousness, consists in a breaking of the covenant through which the sinner is created in the first place. Sin as unrighteousness is far more than the objective doing of immorality; it is corruption of the covenant, a sin against God that ruins the divine creation that is oneself.

II. IMPIETY

The second ideal of covenant, destroyed by sin, is respect for the integrity and powers of nature as expressed in creation. This element of sin can perhaps best be called impiety, although that word has often been used for the rejection of God in the other ideals of covenant. The force of the word "piety" is to acknowledge the presence of divinity in a person, thing, or finite and epiphanic god. It connotes as well an attitude of respect for the divinity as so localized, and the habits and rituals of expressing that attitude.

The appropriateness of "impiety" as a name for the second element of sin comes from that element's rejection of finite things involved in processes of nature and society as bearers of the divine. As God is creator of everything determinate, every such thing is a terminus of the divine creative act, and an expression of the divine. Therefore God is in each thing. In addition, each thing is itself an existential mixture of form and further components, and thus has a value in the larger world. Impiety is the treatment of a thing as a mere thing, perhaps useful to human life, but irrespective of the fact that the thing is a creature of God, bearing the creator's presence, and expressing a worth. Impiety is the attitude that treats things only from one's human perspective, not from the divine perspective. True piety is the approximation of the divine perspective on the world, the perspective of who created something and "saw that it was good" (Genesis 1).

The second element of sin needs to be distinguished from the first because things as components of larger patterns have a creaturely status and value in themselves, in some respects irrespective of the larger forms, and they have this precisely as creatures, co-creatures with us in the larger covenant. The distinction between impiety and unrighteousness is particularly important when the larger forms are matters of right and morality. Natural piety has a heavy aesthetic dimension. Piety feels and appreciates the perspectives of things on their own, not as components of a larger process but as processes in themselves. The rocky coast has a grandeur of its own. The sea has another grandeur. That the sea grinds the stone bluffs into a beach is yet a third grandeur. From the standpoint of each "grandeur," it stands on its own, not in any order of moral or value priority to the others, although of course there is a causal order connecting them. Piety is seeing God in each thing on its own terms.

Morally, the forms of justice place an order of value priority on things. It is entirely just that a society invest resources in fighting disease, supposing that other needs are also being given proper attention. But from the aesthetic point of view of piety, the human organism as such has a grandeur, the HIV retrovirus has a grandeur, and the destruction of the human organism by the virus in the disease process of AIDS has a grandeur. Not to reverence God creating in the AIDS virus is impiety, though that reverence is not at all required by morality. It is sometimes said that the Plains Indians combined the morality of feeding their people with noteworthy piety by reverencing the buffalo before killing it and then using all its parts efficiently. From its own moral point of view, the buffalo was surely unimpressed. But from the standpoint of the covenant, the Native Americans perhaps were both righteous and pious.

Because of their very heavy emphasis on right orders, Western religions including Christianity have given short shrift to piety in contrast to righteousness. This is closely tied to the suppression of the feminine in religion and culture. As given symbolic and ritualized life in the worship of the Mother, the feminine dimension of religion focuses on the components of things organized below the level of the human moral orders, at the level of components. Of course, the components have their own order, and the feminine is related to the order of nature untamed, or perhaps tameable. Furthermore, the feminine is associated with the nexuses and connections that make possible the explicit orders of the moral and political scale, the connections of family and domesticity. The component orders of nature, of personal ties, of the holiness of the hearth, and of clannishness, often stand opposed to the righteousness of moral order even when they are the conditions for it. Whether invoking the powers of the seasons, the hunt, and fertility, or defending the wicked child, asserting family rights over those of the legal system, or insisting on network connections where these bring immoral associations, the feminine is perceived as a threat by the righteousness of the Sky God. The feminine here points up the uniqueness of piety, and its irreducibility to matters of right moral order.[3]

Many Christians fail even to recognize the distinction, and reduce piety to righteousness. Modern secularity recognized the distinction and rejected piety altogether on moral grounds. Yet piety is an essential element in the covenant; impiety is its neglect, and neither are to be reduced to the problematic of morality.

Impiety has objective expressions as well as ontological ones. Objectively it is the abuse, or neglect, or subordination to moral concerns, of the things perceived as components of our world. Direct abuse of

things is continuous with injustice and immorality, as when people tor-
ture animals or cut down trees for sheer perverse delight, or to show their
power. Neglect and subordination, on the other hand, can be consequences of preoccupations with justice and morality. Concerned to provide jobs for people, we sacrifice environmental controls; concerned with
safety and health, we kill off species that threaten human well-being.

The ontological expression of impiety is the rejection of divine
presence in the whole of the created order. This implies as well a rejection
of our own involvement and solidarity with the natural world. The East
Asian traditions, influenced by shamanism, Taoism, Confucianism, and
Shintoism, long have emphasized the continuities of nature that include
human beings and societies as specialized niches. The Western traditions,
however, have tended to define human beings as special, not just different as all things are different from others, but as set apart from and
above nature. The devices for the Western emphasis have been inten-
sified commitments to the forms of social life that define moral weight
and perspective, especially rationality and the powers of following and
applying rules. The distinction between the natural and the social is not
an intrinsic one for distinguishing piety from righteousness, however.
Many components of processes are themselves social, and piety is to be
directed toward them as well.

The impious element of sin is a rejection of the continuities of creation that make people natural creatures. It is also a rejection of the
wholeness with which God creates the world, and thus a rejection of
creation. Obviously, impiety is another form of ontological self-
contradiction.

III. FAITHLESSNESS AND DESPAIR

The third element of sin is a refusal of the existential reality of
human life and of the world more generally. Because human existence is
temporal, faithlessness takes the form of rejecting, or accepting
degenerate versions of, one or more of the temporal dimensions of life.
Tillich (1952, 1957a, 1963) is the theologian who has most explored this
element of sin, and has argued generally that sin here is a failure of ontological courage to live in the face of the disparity between the ideal and
the actual. More particularly, he argued that existence itself forces a
disparity between the ideal and the actual, so that courage is required as
part of the covenant respecting existence. By attending to the modes of
temporality, we can appreciate how this is so.

The past is to be understood in at least two ways. In itself it is essentially the fixed achievements of the universe, all structurally ordered and
determinate with respect to one another and each embodying an actual-

ized value. For the other modes of time, the past sets the conditions to which they must conform, the present by using the past as raw material for its creative immediacy and the future by presenting possibilities relevant to the actual past.

There thus are two forms of sin regarding the past. Regarding the essence of the past as fixed fact and finished achievement, we can sin with denial, supposing contrary to fact that the past was different. Denial plays into faking our moral identity, as well as our sense of what is possible in the future. Regarding the past as a condition for the other modes of time, sin takes the form of wanting to dwell in a past now gone and impossible, the sin of choosing death. Necrophilia is almost the opposite of denial, though they reinforce one another. In both cases, sin is based on a refusal to accept what is actual as actual. It is related to being mistaken, but in the case of sin, mistaken out of refusal to accept what is created as actual. Because the dynamic nature of time adds to the past moment by moment, the content of denial and necrophilia can regularly shift.

The present is also to be understood in two ways. Essentially it is the existential moment of the act of decision. We, and all our present contemporaries, constitute the present moment by our decidings. Refusal of the present thus can take the form of avoidance of decision, pretending the past to be already decided or the future to allow of no options. Such refusal is pretence because one's very nature in the present is to be deciding, and the pretence amounts to certifying the past without taking responsibility or avoiding the future.

The second aspect of the present is how it conditions the past and future. By virtue of its decisions, a thing in the present adds to the past, affecting its value and structure, and it changes the possibilities in the future, eliminating some and opening up others. The other form of sin as refusal of the present is the reduction of past and future to their functions in the present. That is, we sin by acknowledging only that part of the past that bears upon our decisions and consciousness, and we reduce that part to our representations of the past. We sin by acknowledging only those possibilities in the future that we anticipate or admit; this allows for escape from moral responsibility by eliminating the moral obligatoriness of crucial possibilities. The dual forms of refusal of the present thus combine the wimp with the superman; they are expressed as the narcissist's waffling between flattened affect and grandiosity.

Refusal of the future similarly has two forms. One is refusal of the fact that the future is normative and lays obligations upon us regardless of what it brings. Regardless of what possibilities lie open to us as determined by the past and by our own decisions, some are better than others; hence all our present decisions, trivial as well as momentous, affect the value of the world. One way of refusing the future is a rejection of the normative quality of life in the world. The other way is a refusal to accept that choices do have to be made between contradictory possibilities. Because we often want both, because we sometimes are obligated to both, we deny their incompatibility and refuse to take responsibility for having to choose. Whereas the first refusal of the future denies its value or normativity, the second accepts that but refuses its structured definiteness that defines identities as this and not that. In both cases, we sinners refuse the future's role as norming and structuring our choices, and by doing that pervert the crucial role of the future in creation.

These simple schematic observations only identify bare components of existential sin, the refusal of the conditions of existence. In real life we combine them in intricate ways. Theologians have called this the "dialectic of sin," and with good reason: each component takes on new, and often apparently opposite, meanings when combined with other factors.

In all, sin in the existential mode is lack of faith, lack of the courage to accept the conditions of temporal existence for what they are and to make the responsible best of them. All the sins of unrighteousness and impiety can be combined and recombined in the sin of faithlessness. Christian theology has long affirmed that recovery of faith is the first step toward righteousness and true piety.

The fourth dimension of sin, corresponding to the covenant ideal of attending to one's value or spiritual path, is despair, failure of hope. The ideal is to find one's own center in the universe by registering in oneself, and thus achieving the value of, all the valuable things in creation. Or, what is the same thing, to find the orientation to the creator appropriate to one's position in creation. By human powers this is of course an impossible task. We cannot possibly register all the relevant things in our world, much less comport ourselves adequately with respect to them. Nor can we envision well how we stand in the overall creation: neither science nor science fiction has that imagination. Furthermore, we are ruined by all the other dimensions of sin, afflicted by our unrighteousness, debased by our impiety, rendered impotent or uncontrollably dangerous by our faithless cowardice. Indeed, the more faith we have to accept the conditions of existence and our responsibility therein, the more hope seems absurd; this, at least, is the message of the twentieth-century existentialists. What reasonable hope have we? Despair is the only rational response to the quest for spiritual life.

But on the contrary, we are *parts* of God's creation, entitled to our own story and not that of others. Yet we are fulfilled in others and in the rest of the cosmos. It is not exactly *we* who are fulfilled, but we as participating in the larger life of God creating. Perhaps it is better to say that God as creator is fulfilled in us and in the rest of creation.

There is nothing we can ruin that God cannot redeem. The redemption is not to make things other than they are—not to transform evil to good or suffering to pleasure. Rather, the redemption is that God is glorified in the evil and suffering, or more trivially, in our incomplete and fragmented lives. This is a wholly unacceptable doctrine to those who believe God is to be understood exclusively on a moral model; morally judged, God cannot be glorified in evil and suffering. But the moral order is only one among at least three others. The heart of Christian Christology, the need for reference to the Christ, lies in the redemption of an evil and suffering world. Part of the covenant is hope for the perfection of the world in divine glory.

The fourth element of sin, then, is despair as the rejection of God's part in the perfection of the world, and more locally, of our position in it. Despair is a failure to identify oneself as part of the divine creative life. In fact, it is a rejection of God's being as loving creator. Despair says God cannot save us. This is all the more poignant the more conscious we are of the cosmic dimension of properly valuing the world as God's creation.

Despair is the element of sin most characteristic of the secular world. Secular culture has many reasons for rejecting God, but the consequence of them all is that there is no hope for the fulfillment of the finite in the infinite. For secular culture, the finite dimensions of the world are the whole of its reality. In the nineteenth century there was a great secular optimism in the slogan "I am the master of my fate, the captain of my soul." With these great secular humanistic powers, progress was simply a matter of sufficient will. But Marx and Freud undermined confidence in that slogan. "I am rather the pawn of social forces, a civilized facade over a beast's blood passion." The First and Second World Wars not only gave credence to the debunking of the myth of mastery and progress, they undermined even the partial sense of accomplishment claimed for "Christian culture." Postwar despair is the inevitable outcome of the secular limitation of hope to the finite.

Yet it is simply false that we are only finite. True, as isolated individually we are limited and fragmented. As whole individuals, however, we are connected by our conditional features with the rest of the cosmos, and the whole of history. To be sure, even the cosmos as a whole is finite; it could have been otherwise. Its existence consists in being the product of the infinite and self-finitizing creativity of God. Our true reality, therefore, is a part of the infinite divine reality. The secular view is thus a distortion, an unrealistic diminishment of the full human reality. In cultural terms, we must say the secularity requires a denial of the openness to transcendence that characterizes nearly everyone and most cultures that are not principled against it. To argue this is not to suggest that religious cultures do not go through periods of despair. Part of what makes a culture religious, however, is its openness—in principle—to the transcendent, that which can fulfill the finite.

IV. SIN AND DIVINE LOVE

Just as the four ideals of covenant are abstractions from the concrete whole that constitutes our created status, the four elements of sin are abstract when considered by themselves. Both refer to the presence and rejection of the Logos. To summarize, with respect to social forms normed by righteousness, sin is unrighteousness that rejects our very status as created in covenant. With respect to the components of the world, abstracted from the larger patterns that form them to hold the lineaments of the "human" world, sin is impiety. With respect to the conditions of existence, sin is refusal or cowardice to accept the conditions, a lack of faith. With respect to the personal human path as such, sin is despair. The opposites of these elements of sin are righteousness, piety, faith, and hope. Of course, we would expect them to be bound together by love.

What is love in this context? Love is the response to our created status that combines righteousness with piety, faith, and hope. By themselves they do not fit together in any rational pattern. But they are not by themselves because they are in fact ideal elements of the covenant constituting the fulfillment of creation, according to the Christian categories. The human theological virtue of love makes no sense without an understanding of the covenant as expressing God's love. God's love creates the world with the covenant definition of its fulfillment. The Logos is God loving in each thing. In sum, then, sin is life without acceptance of God's love as reconciling the myriad components of the covenant.

Why do sinners not accept God's love? One traditional answer is pride: People are self-sufficient and can fulfill themselves without being repositioned and saved within the divine life. But why would we be so stupid? Some people (e.g. Saiving, in Christ and Plaskow, 1979) say that pride is the male's form of sin whereas self-denegration is the female's. Perhaps then sin is nonacceptance of ourselves as worthy of covenant life. That explanation makes sense for men as well as women after the fact of sin.

But why do we forget that God loves and creates us for what we are, sins and all? God's love is an erotic creation, making us for our loveliness, not bound by any antecedent principle of creating, nor of liking what's created good or not. No motive can be given for sin. It consists simply in the consequences of inattentiveness to God's love for the world as the pervasive motive of creation. Early in the evolution of humankind, of course, there was no *representation* of the world as filled with the Logos, as God's creation. With the development of elementary reflectiveness, however, the givenness of the world is apparent and needs to be forgotten, suppressed or denied if our condition is to be sinful. Salvation consists in something that recalls us to that attention. Since the sinful state precludes the attention, salvation is no mean trick.

As remarked earlier, the Christian interpretation of sin, of the religiously needful state of the human condition, does not arise from a straightforward look at life in the absence of any religious suggestion about what to do about it. On the contrary, the Christian message about salvation is itself the interpretive tool explicating the human condition from which we need to be saved. Were there no history of Christianity informing our thinking, sin would probably be confused with immorality in the West, insensitivity in East Asia, lack of community identification in Africa; and its pain would be a vague unease. Never has there been a time, however, not even in the generation of Jesus himself, when Christians lacked a religious interpretation from the past; Jesus preached out of ancient Hebrew motifs, which themselves were developments of older Mesopotamian models, which derived from even more ancient roots. Therefore, theology (and preaching) always works with older critical interpretations to speak to the sinfulness of its world and present the salvific word. The question is not whether theology discovers new revelations to respond to a new situation discovered here and now, for even new situations are grasped with ancient symbols. Nor is the question whether theology can repeat the ancient revelatory interpretation exactly, for the situation now is somewhat different from that in which the ancient word had concrete meaning. Rather, the question for theology is how to take the old diagnostic categories, apply them to the new situation, amend them in the process, and correlate the new plea of the world for salvation with an appropriate restatement of the founding revelation, possibly vastly amended. The above is a plainly Christian interpretation of the human condition and its sinful needs.

Readings in Key Texts:

1. Aquinas, *SCG*, Book 3, pt. 1, chaps. 1–62.
2. Aquinas, *ST*, I–II, ques. 18–21, 49–73.
3. Augustine, *Conf.*, Books 2–3.
4. Barth, no reading.
5. Calvin, *Inst.*, Book 1, chap. 18.
6. Cobb and Griffin, *PT*, chap. 5.

7. Ferm, no reading.
8. Hildegard, *Sci.*, Book 3, Vision 1.
9. Luther, no reading.
10. Rahner, *Found.*, chap 3, sections 1, 3.
11. Ruether, no reading.
12. Schleiermacher, *CF*, pp. 259–314.
13. Tillich, *Sys.*, Vol. 2, pt. N5, section 1: A–C.

Salvation, Freedom, and Bondage

I. THE PROBLEM OF SALVATION

In one sense salvation is but one of many fundamental human problems, including those of economic life, the raising and education of children, the organization of society and establishment of political structures, the cultivation of beauty and the arts, and the continued acquisition of basic human pleasures, satisfaction, and understanding. Those who make salvation the sole human endeavor are unfairly reductive in their understanding of the complexities of life.[1]

In another sense, however, salvation is the most basic problem, the problem presupposed in all the others. All the other problems of life are functions of establishing the right connections and fulfillments within the world. Salvation is the problem of restoring the covenant within which the whole world is to be understood. Therefore every other field of endeavor is problematic both with regard to its own purpose and with regard to how it bears on salvation. Each field contributes in its own way to the problem of salvation, so that, for instance, there are economic and educational dimensions to salvation. And the problem of salvation underlies the problematic elements of endeavors in all the other fields. Stated in somewhat technical language, all the other fields are cosmological problems, whereas salvation is an ontological problem. Salvation is the problematic ontological dimension of every cosmological endeavor.

Expressed in the Christian symbols, salvation is the restoration of the broken covenant, which is at the same time the recompletion of the creation of the human sphere and its neighborhood. Salvation thus takes place on many levels, including the individual and the social. Furthermore, its many nuances are correlative to the nuances of sin: at least the nuances of unrighteousness, impiety, faithlessness, and despair, summed up as perverted love. Therefore a theological account must detail an extremely complex and often paradoxical story of salvation.

Since the time of St. Paul, salvation in the Christian sense has been considered to consist of two "parts." The first is justification, which Paul insisted was God's act that people receive by faith. The second is sanctification which, though dependent on God's grace in the Holy Spirit, is the slow process of perfecting individuals' life in society. People have a special responsibility in sanctification that they do not have in justification, though both depend on divine grace and both require human freedom.[2]

By employing the category of "covenant" to interpret the human condition, Christianity is committed to an approach to religious understanding and life that is both personal and social. In fact, the explication of the idea of covenant defines for Christianity the nature of both the personal and social as they bear upon the ontological fact of creatureliness. This chapter and the next three approach the interdependence of personal and social sin, relative to personal and social dimensions of salvation, from opposite poles. Here the topic is the heart's sin and bondage relative to freedom. The next chapter treats the dynamics of justification and grace. Chapter 9 considers these issues from the standpoint of social structures, and chapter 10 develops the unity of personal and social matters in sanctification. The distinction between the personal and social is somewhat artificial: both persons and their society, as well as their natural context, need justification, and both need sanctification. The division of salvation into justification and sanctification is itself somewhat artificial, as shall be made clear in chapter 8. The rough principle in the distinction is that God has primary responsibility for justification whereas people have primary responsibility for sanctification; nevertheless, human freedom is respected in both, as is the necessity of divine grace.

The great paradox of Christianity (with important parallels in every other great religion) is how sin is possible if people are essentially good. This is not a problem for most secular cultures which assume that human beings are simply incomplete as yet, lacking perfections that will come with further progress. It is also not a problem for the secular culture of late European modernity, which assumes that human nature is forever flawed and incomplete, essentially and without recourse; the Freudian conception of human nature as bestial with a veneer of civilization has no problem with the possibility of sin. Sin is a problem only when goodness and wickedness are asserted to be compatible.

The great religious cultures assert on the one hand that human beings are essentially free and responsible, except in extenuating circumstances such as immaturity, senility, or specific pathology. Therefore, people not only have the peculiar excellences of freedom and responsibility but also the goods achieved by their exercise. If people are free and responsible, then they create a moral identity for themselves through the course of life. Trees and dogs have excellences, even excellences of sensibility in the latter case; but they do not have moral identity, the excellence of being susceptible to moral praise or blame. The doctrine of the original covenant is one Christian way of stating the excellence peculiar to human beings.

On the other hand, the great religions also say that we have departed from the Tao, sunk into ontologically debilitating ignorance, fallen into the bondage of sin. This is not only bad, but a corruption of the specific human excellences having to do with freedom and responsibility. Furthermore, having corrupted the capacities for freedom and responsibility, people are peculiarly weakened with regard to improvement; trees and dogs cannot sin.

The paradox lies in the question of how something essentially good can do wrong. If there is a motive for sin, is that motive a part of human nature? If so, then people cannot be responsible for their natural motives, and freedom and responsibility are but illusions. If there is no motive for sin, then why do people choose to sin? In order to sort through these problems that lie at the heart of theology, it is necessary to examine first the natural condition of freedom and then the empirical nature of sin at its worst: depravity of the heart, mind, and will.

II. NATURAL FREEDOM

The basic distinction to make regarding freedom is between its cosmological and ontological dimensions. The ontological dimension has to do with how one relates to the world as God's creation, to one's own status as creature, and to God. The cosmological dimensions, of which there are many, have to do with how freedom is attained and exercised in the world, what it consists in, and thus what it is created to be. Both Augustine and Calvin, the pivotal figures for the problem of freedom and grace in Western Christianity, neglected to distinguish these two clearly, with the result that they both held to doctrines of predestination that seem in the end to deny human freedom, and hence human responsibility.

The cosmological dimensions of freedom can be divided into the personal and the social, and together they comprise the natural freedom of humankind. By "natural" is meant those dimensions of freedom that people have from the simple structures of human society and personality, including those that ordinarily ought to develop in the course of maturation and those that are ideal for moral society. These are worth detailing here, not for the sake of developing a full philosophy of freedom, but to show that full human freedom in the cosmological senses is compatible with the creaturely status of human beings in which they have ontological freedom while being created in every respect by God.[3] Each of these dimensions of freedom has been touted by some school or other as the exclusive or at least central freedom. Yet each requires the others for freedom in the full sense, and they must be supplemented by ontological or spiritual freedom. Furthermore, as abstract dimensions of freedom, these listed below do not indicate the personal or historical process by which they are achieved, exercised, perfected, and failed; there is a cumulative biographical sense, or sense of social history, in which a person or group is more or less free by virtue of how it adopts or relates to these dimensions of freedom.

There are at least four dimensions of personal freedom. The first, and politically most elementary, is external liberty. This is the negative freedom of not being bound, not being in jail, not being coerced. External liberties are all relative to what people would want to do and be capable of doing if there were no external constraint. The freedom of external liberties is closely allied with the freedom of intentional action. Freedom consists in part in being able to do what one wants or intends to do. This presupposes external liberty on the one hand and on the other hand it presupposes that people are capable of intending things, of organizing their behavior to achieve their purposes, and of relating to the natural and social environment in causal ways so as to be able to act. Freedom of intentional action is something that is native to human beings in an undeveloped state and thus requires development. One must learn to organize one's many impulses around goals, to act effectively with efficiency and grace, and to build up patterns of connection with the environment so that one is causally connected. Causation is very important for these first two senses of personal freedom: causation needs to be organized and tightened so that the will is effective in the world, not impeded or internally self-defeating.

The third dimension of personal freedom is free choice, and causation has a different function here. In free choice, the antecedent causal conditions allow of more than one possible outcome, and any actual outcome depends on the choice of the personal agent; the agent is the relevant cause for determining the outcome. The antecedent conditions do not have a deterministic causal control over the process of human choice and action, in cases of free choice, although they present the causal materials that the person mixes in decisive ways. From the human standpoint regarding causation, the causal influences entering the situation of choice need a kind of looseness in order for choice to be free, whereas the causal consequences flowing away from choice should be as tight at possible so as to allow for free action that extends into the environment.

The theories of causation in the modern period of European philosophy have not been helpful for understanding the combination of intentional action and free choice in responsible behavior. The deterministic theories have given a good account of how agents control action, and hence are favored by thinkers such as Calvin, Spinoza, and Jonathan Edwards. But determinism cannot stop responsibility with the agent; the antecedents are just as responsible as the person, and hence there is no real responsibility. When this is the causal theory behind predestination, it always turns out that God and God alone is responsible for everything because the divine creation is the only truly initiating cause.

Indeterminist theories, by contrast, allow enough play for agents to intervene and put their stamp on the flow of causal processes. But then the agent's choices, arising out of indeterminism, are arbitrary; for the choices to be truly responsible, they ought to arise out of the real character of the agent, as Spinoza insisted. Furthermore, if the causal processes of nature are sufficiently indeterminate as to allow a wide range of free options, then a person's actions also will be compromised by random interventions. The determinism-indeterminism controversies in modern philosophy are simply not helpful for understanding either ordinary human responsibility or the relation of human causation to divine causation.

Process philosophy in the twentieth century has provided the solution to this problem by reconstructing the entire conception of causation (Whitehead, 1929; Cobb, 1965; Neville, 1989). Whereas the older modern conception had assumed, following Aristotle, that the actualized past, the set of antecedent conditions, contains the power for actualizing possibilities in the present, process philosophy reverses the locus of power. Instead, the present moment contains the creative power that actualizes possibilities. The past consists of actualized things that enter the present as potentialities for integration into the emergent new actuality; the past thus provides the raw material, as it were, for creative integration in the present. The future consists of the logical structures or possibilities for integration. Regarding scientific regularity, the antecedent conditions in the past might allow for many ways of being resolved in the present, or only one way; if many, then some might be importantly different from others, some not importantly different. To the extent the range of options is restricted to one or to several that are extremely similar, scientific law obtains as modern philosophy has thought. To the extent that the range is broad, the causal processes will appear to be irregular, and will depend on the significant choices made among options during present moments of creativity.

For the case of human freedom, one needs not only options but significant ones. The human nervous system sorts incoming data into the pragmatically relevant classes; cultures and language systems constitute even more precise ordering systems. The result is that the potentials to which human choice has most often to respond are those that are shot through with biological, cultural, linguistic, and purposively ordered significance.[4] On the output side, human action has to achieve control over causal processes, constraining the irregularities in the environment so as to accomplish purposes. Because most of our actions relate to other people, we act with language, signs, and "significant" actions so that people will be constrained to react to what we mean, not randomly. Of course, we want people's reactions to be responsible on their part, so our constraint of their interpretations ought not be complete. Rather, our constraint aims to be specific regarding clarity of the signs, but open regarding the freedom of the interpreters to make something of our communications.

By virtue of the theory of causation arising from process philosophy, we can think of human beings as center points in vast arrays of causal processes, who can elevate certain lines of causation into significance and use them to determine far-reaching intended results, especially communicative results. It is always an empirical issue to establish just how wide a person's range of options really is, and just how much control the person has on the consequences of choice. Sometimes we deceive ourselves about both sides. Any regularity that science discovers to be empirically true should be acknowledged, and this might be a limitation on certain choices. On the other hand, one must never assume as a pseudo-scientific postulate that all behavior is absolutely regular and thus ascribe a phenomenon to regularity when that is not empirically the case. Common sense and the press of our moral problems indicate that human beings are free and responsible in nearly all aspects of life. The more technological control we develop, the more our environment is itself the result of our influence. We are responsible for the entire range of things over which our free choice has potential influence. Human beings are never the total originators of responsible action; there are always antecedents, and nature is far vaster than what we can control. Nevertheless, in the things that are of consequence for the human scale of life—for our moral character, dwellings, society, personal relations, and institutions of cultural life—people are indeed the relevant initiators that decide how things come out.

The fourth dimension of personal freedom has already been allud-
ed to in the above discussion, namely, the capacity to choose on the basis
of standards, to evaluate the standards, and to discern what is truly
valuable in order to set standards. Freedom regarding standards supposes that there are real values, or objective rights and wrongs, and that
people can have access to them, perhaps not fully or infallibly but with
some significant degree of realism. This dimension of freedom also supposes that the standards for which we take responsibility can be applied
in the process of moral deliberation and choice.

The mention of values or standards opens the door to another kind
of false determinism. Sometimes it is thought that our values determine
us in a mechanical way. This argument, deriving from certain kinds of
social science, is often used to depersonalize and delegitimate certain
classes of people by suggesting that their behavior is determined by the
values of their class or position. To say that someone is from an
"uneducated minority" or is a "dominant white male elite" is sometimes
thought to explain away the person's reasons for acting, eliminating the
need to evaluate them. People are sometimes said to be "determined" by
their "interests." This line of argument is based on a bad theory of
causation.

Rather, within the limits established by their potentials, individuals
choose the values their chosen options have, and thus give themselves the
character of being the ones with those values and interests. Suppose you
are in a position of choice, with many motives defining different options.
Option A will make you richest, option B will best satisfy your lusts, C
will bring you greatest regard, and D best expresses your image of
yourself. All the options, perhaps, affect your wealth, lust, reputation,
and self-image, but in different balances of degrees. In the act of choice,
you adopt one of the options, and by doing that adopt the motivations
and other values lying within that option as your actual motives and
values, in that mix and balance. Before the choice, any one of the options
could be the sufficient motive, although only as potential. After the
choice one option is the actual motive for your choice, but even then the
other options could have been chosen. Thus we say that you are responsible for your choice. You could have chosen otherwise. The moral
character you have is the one you adopted in choosing the option you did.
Having chosen, you have elevated the motives and values in your selected
option to be the ones that constitute your moral character. Those
motives are "why" you chose. But you did not have to choose that way
before the fact. Choosing is giving yourself the "why" of choice, and
therefore you are responsible (Neville, 1974: 163–173).

All these considerations of dimensions of personal freedom are
highly relevant to the debates about freedom and determinism in
Western theology. But they presuppose parallel dimensions of social

freedom. the first of these is freedom of opportunity, in which there is a public obligation to provide social or cultural opportunities for the exercise of personal freedom. At least three freedoms of opportunity deserve brief mention: freedom to participate in culture, freedom to participate in organized society, and freedom to participate in historically significant affairs. In all of these, opportunity requires (1) access to institutions and means of communication; (2) the education to be able to take advantage of the access; and (3) proximity to the crucial nodes of culture, social organization, and historically significant events. In a society lacking freedom of opportunity, the personal freedom of individuals is greatly frustrated in significance.

The second dimension of social freedom is social pluralism. A pluralistic society balances a complicated dialectic of ways of life based on different heritages, different weightings of social values, different cultural aspirations, and different sensibilities, over against the needs of the society for interaction that not only tolerates differences but supports them. In times of economic hardship or political distress, the needs for unity often outweigh the value of differences, but with the consequence that different cultural styles are ranked in hierarchical fashion. The historical determinants of a social order also contribute to ranking. A society is free in this second sense to the degree that it can allow a plurality of styles to fluorish.

The plurality of styles is closely related to the third dimension of social freedom, namely, the social provision for integration of social style. Human life is not a grab bag of values; they require integration for nuance and for personal and spiritual depth. Integrity of life is thus also a requirement of freedom, one that is particularly important in times of unusually great social change.

These three dimensions of social freedom call forth a fourth, namely, political freedom in which people have the opportunities to influence the conditions under which decisions are made that affect their way of life. Western modernity is no longer so naive as to believe there is any panacea for free political organization. But some form of participatory democracy seems to be required.

All of the dimensions of social freedom are cultural achievements. None is built into the state of humanity as such, although each is an ideal for human life. At the minimum, we can say that the dimensions of social freedom are ideals for righteousness within the covenant.

Natural freedom consists in the collection of dimensions of personal and social freedom. These are the elements whose characters are part of the created world. The world could have been different, perhaps, but this is the way our world is, at least as one philosopher sees it. Ontological freedom is how people employ all the elements of natural freedom to relate to God as creator, to the world as created, and to themselves as creatures. That is, an added element to all the above is not just the attainment of the dimensions of freedom but also the free response to the fact that we are created to be free. There is nothing mysterious to the dynamics of ontological freedom: it employs external liberties, intentional action, free choice, choice according to standards, social opportunities, pluralistic ways, integration of life, and political action. But these are turned to the behaviors and institutions that relate to the covenant as such. On the personal side, ontological freedom requires some considerable cultivation of will, mind, and heart; this is discussed in more detail in chapter 10, section 2. On the social side it is a function of ecclesial life for Christians, with parallel religious institutions in other traditions; this is discussed in chapter 13. Thus with regard to ontological freedom, as well as cosmological or natural freedom, human beings are significant initiators, and hence responsible where the empirical circumstances indicate, because the same dimensions of freedom are used.

III. DIVINE AND HUMAN AGENCIES

The question of divine agency relative to human agency can now be reformulated. The Christian tradition acknowledges God as creator of everything, and in response to the modern principle of closure, it has been argued in the *Primer* that this means God creates everything determinate. As human beings are determinate, they are created. What this means for the unfolding of human life within time is the following.

In every present moment, a person is creatively mixing the potentials given by the past into a new actual thing. The spontaneity in this creativity is divine action, and it can be said that this is the Holy Spirit (see Neville, 1982: chap. 3). The raw material for creating in the present is provided by past things actualized; each of those consists of its series of present moments, with divine spontaneity in each. Furthermore, God creates the determinateness of logical form in which the future consists, relative to each present moment of decision; God therefore creates the possibilities, although they are relative to what has been actualized and what is in process of decision. Therefore, for any present moment of creative decision, God has previously created the past data that come to it, as well as the future possibilities. God is not at the present moment creating the past and future, but they, like the present, are created within the eternity of the divine created act in which each moment is contained in its future, present, and past modes. There is nothing in a person that does not come from God.

Where then is human freedom? It lies precisely in what is created. If God creates a world with external liberties, freedom of intentional action, free choice, and the rest, then human beings are free. They are personally free if they initiate significant actions in such a way as to give themselves a moral identity, and they are socially free to the extent they have opportunities, and so forth. People are ontologically or religiously free if they can turn these freedoms around to address the conditions of the covenant as such. As the Christian tradition has said, God creates us to be free and, in that, also to be able to respond to God and the creation.

But then is God not responsible for our freedom in the sense that what appears to be our free choice—to take that crucial dimension of freedom—is really God's creating in the spontaneity of the moment of decision? Yes, in the sense that God creates everything and is responsible for everything. That does not in the least diminish the sense in which the individual also is free and responsible, because the individual's freedom consists precisely in what God is creating there at that moment; or if the person is not really free, God is creating that alternate condition instead. It is the person, not the environment, not the force of the tempting motive, not the genes or bad upbringing, that makes the relevant choice, and the person is thereby responsible. Or, perhaps it is in fact the environment, the motive, the genes or the upbringing, in which case what is created is not an instance of freedom. The fact that God creates all the determinate elements in free human life does not make the life less free; freedom obtains when the right created conditions are there.

The fact, however, does mean that there are two authors of every significant free human action. One is the free human agent, and that person is just as free as the situation allows. The other is God who is the ontological cause of the deciding person, of the conditions with which and about which the decision is made, and of everything else connected with the context. We ascribe moral identity to the human agent because the agent gives itself the value of adopting the worth of the options chosen as the motives for action. Do we also ascribe moral identity to God? It cannot be in the same sense for each action. God has the moral identity of creating the world with the value it has, and this cannot be measured from any finite human standpoint for which the values of most things are distorted to means and ends relative to human life. God's identity is not exhausted in moral order; God is the source of the components of the world, the ground of existence, and the orientation point for how people ought to relate to creation. Judged from a moral standpoint alone, God is responsible for hardening Pharaoh's heart as well as for Moses' inspired speech. But as responsible creator, God's moral identity is but an abstraction. Because we live by that abstraction, it seems sometimes that God is more to be feared for being beyond morality than congratulated for moral goodness.

Regarding human freedom, God is closer to us than we are to ourselves, as Augustine and others have observed. But the question of whether we are free, in what respects and to what degree, is not answered one way or another by observing that God creates us; God's creation is trivially true of everything. The question rather is the empirical one of whether we really possess or have exercised the relevant cosmological dimensions of freedom. In the ontological sense, God is the author of everything. In the cosmological domain in which people are free or not, the individual is the free and responsible author if and only if some other conditions or persons are not the authors instead. God is not another author within the cosmos. The famous controversy over free will and divine coercion comes from distinguishing those acts in a person that are of the person's own initiative, and those to which the person is forced by external circumstance. Divine grace is then likened to an external circumstance, so that an act caused by grace is one to which the person is forced, and an act in which the person is free is one in which divine grace can at most be an influence or allure. But God is not another external cause, contrary to what many process theologians say. God is an interior cause, at the heart of human freedom itself.

IV. DEPRAVITY AND BONDAGE OF THE WILL: ORIGINAL SIN

Having discussed human freedom and divine agency at length, the argument can now return to the problem of salvation with which this chapter began. Human beings are sinners in at least the senses discussed in chapter 6, namely in their unrighteousness, impiety, faithlessness, and despair, adding up to a corruption of love.

We can now say that the sinful state is freely chosen, albeit with continued naiveté about the consequences. There was no special motive, in the Genesis myth, for Adam and Eve to sin. Rather, they simply adopted the motive suggested by the snake, to eat a beautiful, tasty fruit that would make them wise. They were created by God with the capacities to do that. Similarly, each of us is faced with many motives for good and evil, for different kinds of goods and different kinds of evils, for different mixes of good and evil, and we seem inevitably to adopt at least some of the evil motives and make them ours. Then we have fallen into sin.

The consequences of sin are of two sorts. First is the evil done. This is to be understood as a cosmological matter, specific to the created world. The second is that we have broken the covenant, disrupting our ontological relation to God and the created world. The cosmological evil can itself lead to a corruption of character and of our institutions, as for instance is the result of escapism through drugs. But the ontological evil leads to a severe corruption that Christianity has called depravity. The consequence of depravity is a bondage to the sinful state from which only the special grace of God can release people. Depravity is the corruption of the heart, mind, and will with regard to their powers that stem from being at ease in the covenant.[5]

The heart is the collection of faculties having to do with desire or love. In ordinary development, one must learn to love the right things and to love in appropriate ways and degrees. But in the condition of depravity, one's love is turned to a kind of bondage. Like being caught up in sexual lust (St. Paul's favorite image) in which one can hardly feel other things and one's desire becomes blinded to its harmonious disposition regarding diverse objects of love, depravity of the heart consists in fixations and obsessions. A depraved heart may still be capable of loving, even organizing a love life. But it is susceptible always to fixation and obsession.

The mind is the collection of rational faculties that imagine, understand, theoretically appreciate, analyze, classify, and integrate things, and that evaluate things critically and dialectically. Depraved, the mind can still do those things, but with an irrational skew that tends to regard things very much according to the ways they relate to our depraved fixations and obsessions. The mind is not entirely blind, but is always susceptible to falling into distortions.

The will is the set of psychic faculties that have to do with integrating one's activity for free and responsible behavior. Under ordinary circumstances it might be weak or immature. Under the circumstance of depravity, however, it falls into bondage to the objects of obsession, and is deceived by the distortions of the depraved mind. The result is, as Paul described (Romans 7:15-20), a will that does what it wants not to do and fails to do what it wants.

To say that a person is depraved is not to deny that it can do good things. In the secular or cosmological sense, individuals are a mixture of good and bad. While perhaps everyone is unjust, impious, faithless, and given to despair sometimes, nearly everyone also has some positive moral accomplishments, is not totally blind to the grandeur of things, has a modicum of courage in the crunch, and may be open to pursuing a special meaning in life. Moreover, we often and without much controversy make distinctions between people on the basis of how much virtue they have, and how much vice. There are very good people, rather good people, thoroughly mixed people, rather bad people, and downright villains. We also note how people change in this regard. Therefore it is empirically silly to say that no one has *any* worth on the human level. That cannot be what the doctrine of depravity legitimately means, though perhaps some people have meant that.

The doctrine of depravity says rather that, despite the good that can be done by great effort and good fortune, the heart, mind, and will cannot return to the covenant, to the right relations in which they should live to God, to the created world as created, and to the person as creature. There is a debt of guilt that comes from the ontological contradictions of denying the covenant in oneself. This debt causes people to deny God's love of them, and secretly, or not so secretly, to hate themselves. Obsession of heart, narcissistic distortion of mind, and internal destructiveness of will are functions of self-condemnation. Because sinners are indeed guilty of breaking the covenant, they cannot just agree to forgive themselves. Rather, the originator of the covenant must forgive them, and they must accept that they are accepted in love as sinners. Salvation means being freed from bondage, from the will's bondage in confusion, the mind's in distortion, and the heart's in obsession. However great an individual's powers of virtue are, depravity cannot be overcome by the individual's ordinary powers. Rather, because the offense is against the covenant and its creator, the creator must overcome depravity, and people are dependent radically on God.

The Christian doctrine of depravity, especially as developed by Calvinists, has not fared well in the modern era. It stands directly opposed to humanism. The doctrine is that human beings, because of their sin, are utterly without power of their own to help themselves in the matter of salvation. For salvation they are utterly dependent on God (and if there is no God, they are utterly without hope of salvation, as existentialists and other disappointed Calvinists have declared). Furthermore, even if God "offers" salvation, human beings are incapable of accepting or appropriating it except insofar as God moves them to do so. At this humanism takes offense.

Christianity simply stands opposed to modern humanism at this point, and the dispute is an empirical one: Do we experience ourselves and others as sinful in the Christian sense? The events of the twentieth century give profound support to the Christian analysis.

It should be understood that there is no necessity in creation that people sin. Rather, the fact of sin is simply empirical. Look around, and you see that the world is sinful. Look within and you see the same thing. On the covenant analysis of creation, however, there is a necessity that the breaking of the covenant is not something that can be repaired like something broken *within* the covenant. Our standing in the covenant, whole or broken, is the condition for relating to the creation as such.

The adjacent doctrine of original sin complicates the picture by affirming that no one is sinless, that merely being born into the human community is enough to guarantee that one is sinful. Does a person ever have a time before the fall into sin? That question is like asking whether there is ever a first responsible choice, or a first appreciation of the beauty of something. All human responses are learned in their vocabulary. Although elders do not literally make choices for babies and children, they do decide the things that the youngsters will later decide for themselves; they model decisionmaking; and they provide the initial terms that structure growing responsibility. We grow up learning that the normal world is the sinful one of our parents. That we follow it is our responsibility after a while, not theirs. There is no metaphysical necessity that our choices or responses are sinful, but there is a practical inevitability that comes from becoming individuated through membership in a human community. From this we conclude, with abundant empirical evidence, that individuals, either on their own mature recognizance or as "innocent" children, will corrupt any good thing, in small if not large ways.

In this sense sin is "original": all-pervasive and inevitable. Sin is not inherited like a genetic disease, as some have thought. Nor is it the fault of any historical Adam and Eve. It is rather part of the continuity of a community in broken covenant. Institutions themselves are sinful in a derivative sense when they exhibit the injustice, impiety, faithlessness, and despair of the broken covenant. Salvation from sin thus requires not only the repair of the covenant for each individual, but also for the community at large. For this, Christians look to the grace of God.

Readings in Key Texts:

1. Aquinas, *SCG*, Book 3, Pt. I, chaps. 63–78; Pt. II, chaps. 88–100; pt. 4, chaps. 50–52.
2. Aquinas, *ST*, I–II, ques. 78–89.
3. Augustine, *Conf.*, Books 4–6.
4. Barth, *Credo*, chap. 12.
5. Calvin, *Inst.*, Book 2, chaps. 1–8.
6. Cobb and Griffin, *PT*, chap. 4.
7. Ferm, no reading.
8. Hildegard, *Sci.*, Book 1, Vision 4.
9. Luther, no reading.
10. Rahner, *Found.*, chap 3, sections 2, 4.
11. Ruether, no reading.
12. Schleiermacher, *CF*, pp. 315–354. 536–560.
13. Tillich, *Sys.*, Vol. 2, pt. 3, section 1: D–E.

Justification, Grace, and Love

I. THE QUEST FOR GRACE

If sinners are indeed depraved, then even the intent not to be sinful must come from God. How is this so? The Christian answer to this question is the center of the doctrine of grace. In its most general sense, grace is divine provision for the welfare of the world, especially that which is more than might be naturally expected. The word has been used with a very wide compass, however, so that some people speak of the creation of the world as itself a matter of grace. Perhaps the best usage is to say that grace is the divine provision for all aspects of human life having to do with the ontological dimension, with relating to the creation as created by God, with a proper orientation to the covenant as binding God and creation. Thus grace has to do with original right relation with God and with salvation. How do we find God's grace manifest in this sense?

The argument so far has spun out the metaphors of covenant, a symbol so potent in the Judeo-Christian tradition as to seem self-justifying. We must now make a more critical appraisal of the notion. The critical question is not whether the idea of covenant can be demythologized into the thought-forms and favorite categories of our own time. The question rather is whether it can be particularly illuminating of our cultural forms and issues. Let us set aside as a promissory note the problematics of community, society, organization, nationality, and related issues so vexing to our world; the following chapters will address some of these from the standpoint of covenant. Let us focus here on the topic of the individual's relation to others, to nature, and to God, how the individual's heart bends to these, and how the situation might be illumined by the notion of divine creation through establishment of the covenant.

Regarding the secular or humanistic dimensions of sin, the cosmological dimensions, it is not difficult to imagine how individuals might come to regard their errors as faults in need of remedy. But how might individuals come to interpret this as ontologically significant, as having to do with their very being, and with the being of the cosmos? The answer given in the Judeo-Christian tradition is that people are created in the image of God and that, although this is distorted or tarnished by sin, the image of God is not entirely lost. Therefore even in the worst of persons there is a spark of divinity or a divine image that serves as a reminder of our true ontological origins, and of the normative ideal of living as God's creatures in covenant. Before exploring this, we can quickly survey the universality of this mode of thought.

In the traditions arising in the Indian subcontinent—Hinduism in its many forms, Buddhism, and Jainism—the human condition is interpreted as a kind of ignorance of the true reality of individual life.[1] The true reality is an identity of what is most authentic in people with the absolute, usually interpreted as an Absolute Mind whose thoughts are creative of worlds (Kung, 1986). Even in the depths of ignorance, prior to any enlightenment, the reality of the authentic identity exerts a call, elicits an unease about ignorant life, and often incites a panic to do something about the swarming concerns of life. What is most real about individuals is the Unconditioned or divinity within them. Often the Unconditioned is not personalized at all, nor interpreted as an agent with substantial actions. Nevertheless, when the Unconditioned is finally realized, it is seen to have been there all along.

The traditions of China—Taoism and Confucianism—and the maverick religion of Chinese (and Korean and Japanese) Buddhism, similarly believe that the human condition at its worst is but a deviation from the reality that funds it (Kung and Ching, 1989; Park, 1983).[2] We can depart from the Tao, but only by employing the powers of the Tao itself; and the result of departure from the Tao is not getting somewhere else but simply self-destruction. In Confucianism, the human condition can fail to fulfill the mandate of Heaven and Earth to manifest their conjunction with self-reflective clarity. But it can do so only by clouding over or not fully realizing the antecedent input of Heaven and Earth. As Confucius said, "humanity" is always close at hand (Chan, 1963; chap. 2). The principle of Heaven, as the Neo-Confucianists developed the notion, is the creative principle, identical with love, that nudges civilization and individual spiritual life along. And it is always available as a resource for those whom it moves to grasp it (Tu, 1985).

The Judeo-Christian notion of the image of God requiring covenant is thus a version of a vague but universal sense that the religious ideal is implicit even in its denial, and that the power to achieve it is presented even when it is rejected. The Christian tradition, in fact, has given even greater weight to the notion of image of God, found in the first creation story in Genesis 1, than to the covenant notion in Genesis 2. There has been much debate concerning in what the image consists: Reason? Will? Creativity? Consciousness? Capacity for moral judgment? Love? All of the above? The disadvantage of the strong emphasis on the image of God in human beings is that it fosters an unwonted individualism. It suggests that each person, individually and without intrinsic connections with other parts of creation, images God. The better strategy is to give priority to the covenant relation between God and the entirety of creation, and then interpret the image of God in terms of covenant.

Within the context of the fundamental metaphor of the covenant, the image of God means the affectionate and supportive regard for the well-being and mutual support of all things in the created order, as God creates them so. Alienated though we are from this image, which is nevertheless ineffaceable within us, it returns as the Great Commandment: "You shall love the Lord your God with all your heart, and with all your soul, and with all your mind. . . . You shall love your neighbor as yourself" (Matthew 22: 37–39). For us within the broken covenant, acting in expression of the image of God is no longer second nature. But it is the first nature underneath. The Confucians make a similar point with great power. Mencius, a third-century B.C.E. writer, noted that no one, no matter how depraved, lazy, angry, or selfish, could help but feel a start of sympathetic panic at the sight of a small child about to fall into a well; we might cover up quickly, blaming the parents for not keeping better watch, but even the worst of persons skips a heartbeat (Chan, 1963: 65). This immediate compassion is the source of all fine moral intuitions when developed and, even when stunted or demolished, it remains minimally operative and tries to reassert itself. Mencius likened the original goodness of human nature to a mountain that is completely logged over but whose tree stumps in the morning send up new shoots. Later Confucianists developed this theme in connection with the metaphor of "being one body with the world." Wang Yang-ming (Chan, 1963: chap. 35), a contemporary of Martin Luther, admitted that we might have fellow feeling with babies because they are so like ourselves that the feeling is merely extended selfishness. But we are also pained at the death of a bird, or the felling of a tree, even at the breaking of a tile or the crushing of a rock. So Christians believe that the covenantal image of God can be enslaved by the bonds of sin but still struggles to be free. In every Scrooge there is a good soul ready to be awakened, and in fact fighting against the forces of depravity. Even Hitler loved his mistress and Stalin his family.

On one level, prevenient grace is the image of God in every person. Although different symbologies are used to express it, that image is analogous in all peoples and cultures. But not every individual is roused to recognize and hate the sinful state, and will to do something about that. Scrooge gave himself over to charity, but Hitler and Stalin were villains to the end, and many other people are just as bad, if less powerfully placed. The universal prevenient grace of being a creature is obviously not enough. What more is needed?

A second level of prevenient grace is necessary. St. Paul (Romans 1, 2) discussed two kinds of grace, religious and natural. For some people, historical contingency or providence brings them an explicit religious reminder or goad to recovery of the true covenantal image, for instance the giving of the Torah to the Jews. For Paul, the Torah of the Jews was entirely valid as far as it goes, which is not far enough.[3] Presumably he would say the same for the serious religious heritage of the Hindus, Buddhists, and others, had he come to know them intimately in their depth. Failing a serious religious cult that spurs one to covenantal life, other people are reminded by nature and history, as Paul regarded the Gentiles of the Empire to have been. This is enough to have made many Gentiles naturally moral and even God fearing, though still it is not sufficient for salvation. Nevertheless, if not sufficient for salvation, religious culture and the contingencies of nature and history are often enough to jolt people into wanting salvation, and that is our issue here. The question is why the sinners come to see the sin as bad and want salvation at all.

A third level of prevenient grace is also necessary, the movement of repentance itself. Repentance is not just the resolve to treat people better. Rather, it has to do with the ontological covenant, with recognizing that the covenant is broken and that one is thus in existential contradiction to one's created status, alienated from the creator; and it is a resolve to have all that repaired. Or if the Christian language is foreign, then it is a recognition of whatever functions as the symbolic analogue, and a resolve to have it repaired. Repentance is impossible without being confronted with both the broken covenant and one's own sinful deviance from it. This requires a confrontation with the gospel itself, or its analogue, and an acceptance of the gospel as a mirror that shows one one's own sinful state. More grace. And then, from the confrontation and self-revelation, one repents. Even more grace. Because the level of grace involved in repentance comes from the gospel itself, repentance is inseparable from justification.

II. JUSTIFICATION: OBJECTIVE AND SUBJECTIVE

Justification is the Christian doctrinal name for what God is understood to have done in Jesus Christ about people's salvation. Justification is traditionally thought to have two sides, an objective one, concerning what God did in Jesus Christ, and a subjective one, whereby individuals' lives are transformed by a faithful appreciation of God's action.

The objective side, which will be explored at length in the Christological chapters 11 and 12 below, has received many interpretations, none of them especially convincing or significant as we approach the Third Milennium. One such interpretation is that Jesus was a temple sacrifice, substituting for the lamb that would not have been sufficiently valuable to restore the covenant broken by our sins. The sacrific interpretation, whereby we are "cleansed by the blood of the lamb," supposes a basic interpretation of the covenant as governed by the retribution and substitution mechanisms of the Torah and temple law. Small wrongs or defilings could be rectified by sacrificing a pidgeon, larger ones by a lamb or bull. But nothing could work to rectify a complete breaking of the whole covenant, except the sacrifice of Jesus, Son of God. Even if the logic of the substitution interpretation could be developed fully, it would not be an effective symbol for cultures such as flourish now in which temple sacrifice plays no part.

Another interpretation, varying the first, is that the magnitude of human sins requires the sacrifice of the human race itself; in this pass, Jesus, Son of God, comes to substitute for the human race, not for inadequate lambs. This interpretation too presupposes an impotent symbolism of temple sacrifice. Both of these interpretations of the objective work of justification or redemption assume a kind of magical relation to God, a manipulation of divine action by doing or failing to do the right ritual act.

A third line of interpretation sees the story of salvation as a fight between God and Satan. Since human beings have broken the covenant and accepted the sinful temptations Satan offers, we belong to the devil, not to God. Jesus wins us back for God by substituting for us in Satan's kingdom; because Jesus is the Son of God, Satan thinks he has the better bargain. But Jesus fools him and rises from death to triumphant life. Although there are many situations in life that seem like a contest between God and the devil where we are both the operative players and the ultimate prize, the metaphors are rather too fanciful in the personification of good and evil to serve as root tools for understanding justification.

Furthermore, all these ways to interpret the objective side of justification, including those that have Jesus acting in such a way as to change God's mind from just anger to mercy toward us, function on a kind of supernatural plane oddly unrelated to real history. This was part of the natural cosmology during the Hellenistic period, and Paul accepted it quite without pushing it to the extremes of gnosticism (Jonas, 1958; Pagels, 1979). The double history, one of Earth, the other of "Heaven," is too far from our own cosmology to be religiously helpful; it surely ignores the sense of closure that marks the modern cosmological sensibility. Moreover, it obfuscates the historical character of the Christian view of salvation, transforming it into a matter of heavenly "types" by which to understand historical reality. The Christian witness is that God acted directly in human history to save the human race, and that the life of Jesus was the central and dateable divine action that made the difference.

A minimal interpretation of the objective side of justification, then, is precisely that the life of Jesus, as communicated to people by direct confrontation, by the witness of the first-generation disciples, then by the scriptures, by the rites of the Church, and by other witnesses, makes a decisive historical difference so as to effect subjective justification, the transformation of lives so that they are back in unbroken covenant as far as possible. The life of Jesus by itself does not do this. Only as interpreted and responded to in ways that constitute the subjective side of justification is Jesus the agent of salvation.

The Christian tradition, emphasizing grace, has said that people receive Jesus as justifier only through the action of the Holy Spirit. The Holy Spirit acting contemporaneously in us moves us to be transformed by the life of Jesus which is represented to us in the Bible, through preaching, or in some other way that by itself is not efficacious. The technical theological principle at work here is that the action of any one Person of the Trinity is at once the action of the other Persons. The objective side of justification can be understood to be whatever is graceful in history to effect the historical or subjective side of justification.

"Subjective," as a characterization of justification, does not mean what goes on interior to the mind or consciousness, but what happens in the subject undergoing justification. The objective side is what God does; the subjective side is what is done in the human subjects of justification. There are at least four "moments" of justification (all of which are preparatory to sanctification): (1) repentance of one's sins, and the sins of one's world; (2) acceptance of God's love of us despite the sin, as manifest in Jesus; (3) the exercise of faith so as to bind up our lives into a new form, a "new creation;" and (4) commitment to membership in the renewed covenant, the Kingdom of Heaven, as disciples of Jesus Christ. The next two sections shall spell this out.

III. DYNAMICS OF FAITH AND REPENTANCE

Because Paul so closely associated justification with faith, we may begin with faith despite the fact that it presupposes both repentance and acceptance of divine love as preconditions in an ordered process of justification. In the seventh chapter of Romans, Paul described the sinful state as one of bondage to obsessions, the paradigm of which is lust. Sinners are broken apart by their obsessions, made to do what they know good and well is wrong and harmful, and set in a state of swarming confused consciousness which he said, in Romans 1, leads to perversion of natural sexual impulses, "wickedness, evil, covetousness, malice. Full of envy, murder, strife, deceit, craftiness, they are gossips, slanderers, Godhaters, insolent, haughty, boastful, inventors of evil, rebellious toward parents, foolish, faithless, heartless, ruthless" (Romans 1:29–31).

All the while, the sinful people know these things are wrong. Yet the sinful obsessions are in control. In fact, the person of the sinner dissolves: "For I do not do the good I want, but the evil I do not want is what I do. Now if I do what I do not want, it is no longer I that do it, but sin that dwells within me" (Romans 7:19–20). As if this demonic sin-possession were not bad enough, when sinners do manage to do something right, it is not themselves but God acting within them. Sinners have neither identity on their own, nor identity within God, but are a mere field in which the obsessions of sin and the meritorious acts of God jerk the person around like a marionette.

Faith is the discipline of will or spirit that binds up the fragmented parts of the sinner and makes them whole. It is not that the objects of desire about which the sinner previously obsessed are rejected. Though Paul sometimes spoke ill of sex, he did not claim that erotic love itself is bad. Rather, those desires are reconstituted in faith so as not to put people in bondage; they are integrated into a whole and harmonious life, at least potentially. In faith, a person can take possession of the passions that othewise would possess the person. Furthermore, the good a person does, in faith, is no less to be attributed to God; but it is also to be attributed to the faithful person who is now a free agent within God's creation. As remarked in earlier chapters, faith is the peculiar virtue of that part of the covenant having to do with mixing the components of life in actual existential ways. Faith is the courage to live singlemindedly in a world filled with ambiguities and incompletions. Where does this faith come from? It is, of course, God creating in the sinner's soul to make a faithful, renewed person. But how? How is faith both a gift and a free human act?

Revert to the prior question of repentance. To repent is itself a complex process. In logical order, one first must come to recognize one's sinful life for what it is. Such recognition involves the objective and public aspect of one's injustice, impiety, faithlessness, and despair about ultimate things. It also involves the ontological implications of these such that one's founding covenant lies in self-contradiction and that one's life is refusing its own created self. Moreover, the recognition of sin extends beyond personal actions to the social and natural structures within which one lives.

Having recognized all this, repentance requires a self-reflexive moment of acknowledging the sinful state as one's own, as definitive of one's identity, or broken identity, or dispersed identity. Human beings differ from other creatures by having an identity that includes reacting to representations of one's identity, a kind of doubling back on identity. The sinful part of identity is perhaps the most important element to be represented in repentance. And then repentance moves beyond acknowledgment to taking responsibility for the sinful state, for having established it and for continuing it. Involved in taking responsibility is the admission of depravity, that sin has indeed enfeebled one ontologically so that one is powerless to change it. Anything short of this is a denial that sin has reached to the ontological constitution of oneself as a creature in covenant.

Then, and finally, having identified one's life as sinful, both cosmologically and ontologically, having recognized that it constitutes one's true identity, having taking responsibility for this, and admitting that one is powerless to turn it around, then and only then the repentant sinner *desires to be saved more than any other desire.* Then and only then the sinner wills purely the one thing sinners cannot will, that their will be blown away and replaced by God's desire. We abandon the last bit of hope in self-correction, push despair to the limit, and cry to God for help. I capitulate to the final judgment of my own depravity, relinquish any merited claim on mercy, and cry that God be glorified without me, I am so sorry.

Without reaching the point of willing my own damnation in agreement with divine judgment, I short-circuit confession and repentance and am not open to the enormity of God's love. Without willing that God's good be done over our own, we continue to choose the broken rather than whole covenant. The sinner must repent of the whole sin, including the obsession with salvation. Only when one puts the entirety of the religious problem in God's hands has one repented of one's attempt to live out of the covenant in which one is created.

Although people can strive for greater virtue, with success, and work together to build a more just society, they cannot will their depravi-

ty away. Indeed, the attempt to overcome depravity by their own effort
only marks the obsession in which depravity consists. Religious obsession is the paradigmatic example of deravity, a great lie about the world,
the greatest bondage of the will. Although this emptiness is most often
associated with Buddhism (Panikkar, 1989), it is at the heart of the
Christian rejection of the instrumental use of righteousness or Torah for
salvation, and the gospel of divine grace.

IV. DIVINE LOVE: CONVICTION AND COMMITMENT

But how in the world can the sinner repent? If sin is a bondage of
commitments, how, with no real power of our own, can we abandon
those commitments? The Christian answer is that God's grace provides
the power to make a free choice in the matter. How is that? For this, we
should look at the second moment in justification, acceptance of God's
continued and infinite love.

Sinners cannot truly repent until they are "convicted" of God's
love. This is not to say only that we don't have courage to loosen our
own striving until we know there is a divine safety net below, although
knowledge of that net might help. Rather, encountering God's love
shames us into repentance. God's love overwhelms our rationalizing talk
and makes us pour forth our sins and helplessness to make sure God
loves us despite even that too. In the face of God's love we can will our
own damnation confident that, if such is required as part of that divine
love, the divine love is infinitely better than our "salvation" would have
been anyway. Our true salvation is in the glory of God's creative love,
not in some good things happening for us bad people. This is what an encounter with God's love would show us.

All this talk ,about encountering God's love sounds very
premodern. The metaphor comes from human relations, encountering
some person who loves you. God the creator is not a person in this sense,
although God is sometimes symbolized this way. Rather, the point is that
the fundamental constitution of the universe is loving in the healing way
required here. Understood from the cosmic perspective of creation, to be
at all is to be an object of creative love. This might not at all result in
good things for us considered in terms of our personal interests in our
neighborhood of the cosmos. But, understanding the scale of creation
allows us to see that, sometimes, what looks bad for us, for instance our
depraved life, is in fact something redeemed and fulfilled in the larger life
of the creator. Our very existence is an expression of creative cosmic
divine love, and depraved sinful existence is just as much an expression
of this as is the polis of virtue. There is no a priori reason to think that
the universe at bottom is loving. It is, however, the testimony of all the

great religions, each in its own way, and for each love is not just morality but piety, grounding, and orienting. According to Christianity, the culture of the Near East had forgotten that love is more basic than all the other epiphanies and secularities. To counter this, Jesus Christ came to recreate the presence of divine love in history. Here is the central symbol of the Christian religion, the reason why Christians follow the cult of Jesus.

The encounter with Jesus Christ is precisely the point at which we meet and can accept God's love. People in other religions might have alternatives; but for Christians it is in Christ. Jesus Christ was an historical figure. Therefore our encounter with God's love is historically based. Without the historical Jesus we would have to have some other full and extraordinary demonstration of divine love, or would get along with none. Jesus is important not just because he was an interesting man, or a great teacher, or the central or perfect illustration of a general divine love. Jesus' historical life was and is the very actual way by which God loved and loves those who could be Christians (others might have alternate actual modes of divine love, or none).

Jesus is not complete, however, as the actualization of God's love unless sinners, including us, actually take him to be God's actual love. That is, unless God's love has effect in us, so that we are loved, the actuality of God's love has not gotten to us. So the completion of God's love in Jesus Christ, according to Christians, is the continuing activity of the Holy Spirit. Jesus is not the Christ of God, the Love-Bearer, without the continuing creativity of the Holy Spirit.

The Holy Spirit is extraordinarily economical. Moved to see and accept God's love in Christ, in that same act we repent with absolute tears. Regardless of how we interpret Christ intellectually, the point is the acceptance of God's love in what we find there. And in that very same act also we have faith once again, or for the first time, becoming our own selves, at once dying in repentance and accepting new life free from the bondage of sin.

The "moments" of justification are logical distinctions, not necessarily temporal ones. Our conscious realization of the moments, and of their own internal differentiations, may come in just about any order. But the existential act of faith (1) receives Christ as the down payment on God's love, (2) repents of the sinful life, and (3) commences the new life in faith. That act reconstitutes us as free creatures in the ontological sense, so that we are at once the recipients of God's historically based creative love and responding acceptors of it. Christ, as we receive him through the inflowing of the Holy Spirit, is the beginning and center of it all. Before Christ, and apart from Christ, salvation at best is different. For Christians, the meaning of salvation is indeed justification in Jesus Christ.

The fourth moment of justification, commitment to life in the Kingdom as disciples of Christ is simply the existential content of the other moments. As the author of Colossians put it, we have already died with Christ and risen with him. So get on with the business of life, of personal self-improvement and the establishment of a more just society. Though we still are unjust, impious, backsliding in faith, and nervous about our hopes, we are no longer in bondage to the weaknesses of sin, and we should get on with eliminating those weaknesses as quickly and thoroughly as possible.

Thus life in the Kingdom is the process of sanctification. The special point of the Kingdom, however, is that we behave as disciples of Christ. We have the mind of Christ through many avenues of testimony; life in the Kingdom is the institutionalization of that mind in personal habits and social structures. Some people, perhaps those whom William James called the "once born," are already living in the Kingdom before they recognize that their life is because of the love of God in Christ, before they realize they are in a sudden state of repentance, or that they are girded about by faith. The order of realization is not important. Nor is the duration of the act of receiving God's love in faith and repentance. The important point is the reality of divine grace making us free as Christian disciples.

Readings in Key Texts:

1. Aquinas, *SCG*, Book 3, pt. II, chaps. 111–119, 147–163.
2. Aquinas, *ST*, I–II, ques. 109–114.
3. Augustine, *Conf.*, Books 7–9.
4. Barth, *Credo*, chap. 15.
5. Calvin, *Inst.*, Book 1, chaps. 1–3, 11–15, 21–24.
6. Cobb and Griffin, no reading.
7. Ferm, *TWLT*, chap. 13 (by Libanio).
8. Hildegard, *Sci.*, Book 3, Vision 2.
9. Luther, *TT*, "A Treatise on Christian Liberty."
10. Rahner, *Found.*, chap 4.
11. Ruether, *Sexism*, chap. 7.
12. Schleiermacher, *CF*, pp. 355–373, 476–505.
13. Tillich, *Sys.*, Vol. 2, pt. 3, section 1: A–B, E.

Sin and Society

I. A SOCIAL METAPHYSICS OF THE COVENANT

Perhaps the most important contribution of the Wesleyan heritage to world Christianity is its insistence that holiness is a public and social matter as much as a private and personal path. Wesley observed that the social conditions of his time for most people in England were oppressive and degrading. Poverty and economic exploitation are bad in themselves and are disastrous in their consequences for character and spiritual life. A converted heart, therefore, must turn as much to the alleviation of the social conditions of the environment as to improving its personal holiness. Put another way, personal holiness includes what we now call "social action" as much as it does prayer and meditation. On the other hand, Wesley recognized that humanitarian social action itself can be hollow and self-seeking, even if reasonably effective. Social action therefore ought not be uncoupled from the life of prayer and meditation: social action ought to be undertaken as a form of holiness. The transformation of the heart by an encounter with the love and holiness of God is the center that needs to develop in both personal holiness and social sanctification.

Wesley, of course, was not entirely original in the insistence on the integration of personal piety and social action in the playing out of salvation. The English Puritans of the late sixteenth and early seventeenth centuries believed the same thing, calling for spiritual renewal and social reform at once (Haller, 1938; Neville, 1987). Because of the cataclysmic political upheavals of England in the seventeenth century, however, that early Puritan movement in its progressive side was transformed into classical liberalism. John Locke was the son of the Puritan movement, yet was the chief instrument in the invention of the liberal sense of autonomy that denies the social connections essential to seeing personal piety and social action as intrinsic to one another (Leites, 1986). Liberalism in the classical sense has become the ideological rallying point for those who want to make religion and spiritual concerns entirely private, to be protected by the laws of privacy, in contrast to public matters that deal with social conditions and are obligatory only on those who hold public office. Wesleyanism was an eighteenth-century alternative to classical liberalism. Of course, the story of the Wesleyan movement is by no means unambiguous (Semmel, 1973; H. R. Niebuhr, 1929). The Puritan-Wesleyan heritage now, however, is an important resource for asserting the integral character of the social and personal sides of spiritual life.

That personal piety and endeavors to make the world more in keeping with the covenant imply each other derives from human nature itself. Or rather, it derives from even more basic metaphysical characteristics defining what it is to be a thing. Chapter 3, section 3, provided an analysis of determinateness that argued that identity consists in being a harmony of essential and conditional features. This can now be made specific with regard to human beings.

Human beings are combinations or harmonies of both essential features and conditional ones.[1] The essential features are those unique to each person, and have mainly to do with how each person orders connections with other things so as to have a unique perspective and identity. The conditional features are those a person has by virtue of relating to other things, the "conditions" of life. Among the conditional features are those that are functions of systems in nature and society. People play roles in food chains and metabolic systems, for instance, and they occupy ecological niches, social offices, and cultural functions. The roles people play in the systematic conditions of existence affect the systems on the one hand, and also provide characteristics for the people. The conditional features, including most of the natural and social systems in which people participate, are just as necessary for an individual's identity as essential features. A person is no more the essential features than the conditional or relational ones: a person necessarily is a harmony of both.

The above sketches a metaphysical theory underlying the idea of covenant. Things are created to be in relation with one another, a relatedness or "conditionedness" that is just as necessary and important to identity as their essential uniqueness. For people, it is often assumed that other people are the most important things to which they are related within the world. Even relations with other people, however, are mediated by systems whose elements are themselves conditions. For instance sheer biological responses are mediated by systems of sexual attraction and repulsion, aggression and flight, empathy and cooperation.

Social organization systematizes food production and distribution, economic development, use of space, provision of shelter and clothing, and perhaps most of all child rearing, cultural transmission, and education. Therefore, even if relations with other people were the only important conditions of human existence, instrumental to that are relations with many conditioning systems that provide the necessary context for human relations. There is, however, no reason to believe that human relations are the only ones important for their own sake. People are related in essentially transformative ways to the mountains, the sea, the fruitful earth, and the starry sky. They are in equally important relations with social institutions or systems such as government, the judiciary, the arts, and learning, among others.

The covenant of creation is that each determinate thing is created with its own excellence, which consists in part in its conditional connections with other things. The great *shalom* of the covenant is that each thing be allowed to flourish according to its excellence. True, many of the relations are instrumental ones from the standpoint of certain things: little fish are food for big ones, acorns have a divided destiny as oak trees and squirrel food, and when in the Peaceable Kingdom lions lie down with lambs, as the old joke says the lambs don't get much sleep. Nevertheless, even if a thing's excellence is only to support something else, which is unlikely, the ideals of the covenant call for that excellence itself to be supported.

A Christian covenantal analysis of a complex of social systems such as the contemporary world exhibits therefore has to attend to how the interweaving of conditions provides for or detracts from the excellence of the people, of nature, and of the systems themselves. This point is extremely important in the contemporary situation, for it is truly revolutionary. Most social analysis through the first third of the twentieth century was based on liberal notions of progress toward perfection, usually with the classical liberal understanding of the autonomy of the agent of change. Since that time, especially during the last two decades, most Christian social thought has taken the form of liberation theology, much of which is based on Marxist assumptions about social analysis. Those assumptions are that people are principally defined by how they stand in relation to the means of production, ownership of land, and other economic entities; more particularly, the most important thing to know about people is the economic class to which they belong, where class is defined by relation to the economic system. Early in his career, Marx was a humanist, in the sense that he took the purpose of the economic system to be to enhance the community of human beings in all its complexity. He later came to see, as Hegel had before him, that the implication of the class analysis is that individuals are important only with regard to their

membership in the class, and that the descriptions of other aspects of individuals' lives, such as religion, art, family structure, character development, and so forth, are really ideological covers or distortions that express the interests of class membership. From humanism, Marx turned to
a kind of mechanism he called "scientific materialism."

Christian liberation theologians have all the resources of the gospel
for the preservation of a focus on human beings in community, not
reducible to class membership. Yet any analysis based on social class will
tend inevitably to suppress the nuance of individuals in community in
favor of the ways people function as tokens in their economic class, with
their class's interests. Further, because the class analysis sets the interests
of classes in opposition, it compels an adversarial mode of understanding: we understand ourselves in terms of who we are against. The opposition then becomes more important than the need to make specific
changes, and social analysis tends to blur all opponents into a Wicked
Other in which individuals are not distinguished from the institutions
causing suffering. At this point ideological jargon takes the place of
serious social analysis.[2] This, of course, is directly contradictory to the
Christian ethic of love, especially that of loving enemies: you cannot love
enemies if you cannot find the individuals because they have been folded
into the Wicked Other of the system.

These reservations about the Marxist base of much liberation
theology by no means constitute a direct critique of that movement. In
the first place, liberation theology usually is an indigenous form of
reflection, rising from below out of the experience of a specific group of
people who have not been in close touch with the elite intellectual tradition; therefore, for them the Marxist categories are foreign imports performing perhaps temporary functions for the organization of the community. The Christian vitality of base communities in Latin America is
far more important than the political meaning and viability of the
economic class categories in which much of their thought is expressed.
Second, liberation theology is a young movement whose thought is only
now maturing. What categories will survive into mature theology and
which ones will be dropped or transformed beyond recognition remains
an open matter. Because liberation theologies arise indigenously from
local areas, the first phase of theological maturation is the comparison of
one region's analysis with another's. The universal language of economic
class analysis provides an initial set of categories for conversation; but it
is unlikely that they will end up meaning the same thing for Afro-
American liberation, the liberation of peasants in Central America, and
the liberation of workers in the Republic of Korea. The systems within
which liberation is sought—American welfare state capitalism, Hispanic
feudalism, and industrialized Confucianism—are vastly different. The

position of Christian *systematic* theology is not one from which liberation theology as a system can be seriously addressed at this point. Liberationist arguments, of course, must be taken very seriously.

The attempt here to circumscribe the social class analysis in liberation theology should not be taken as a rejection of the contributions of Marxist analysis. Precisely because relations to systems and institutions constitute class definition and membership, Marxists have often been the most acute theoreticians regarding how systems and institutions work. Furthermore, because of their theory of ideology—the self-deceptive description of society as distorted by one's class interest—Marxists have often analyzed social entities with a "hermeneutics of suspicion," not taking systems at face value. In addition, perhaps because of its vast oversimplifications of the good oppressed versus the wicked oppressors with their systems, Marxist social theory has been effective in mobilizing people to undertake social change at some potential cost to themselves. Cornel West (1982) has analyzed the implications of Marxist analysis for a revolutionary Christianity with uncommon subtlety, and shown its great power. The point of the *Primer* is to call attention to the range of interactions of people with institutions that go far beyond the economic dimension, and yet are determined by the broken covenant and in need of repair. A Christian social analysis must deal with a vast range of institutions and various relations individuals might have to them (Neville, 1988).

Human beings, perhaps all rational beings, are what they are in part because they relate themselves to an idea of themselves that represents, with more or less accuracy, who and what they are in their situation. To have a moral identity, with responsibility, blameworthiness and praiseworthiness, a person must act in reference to a conception of the person's identity over time in relation to the things involved in the situation. Even to have speech is to represent to oneself what is appropriate for anyone to say in the situation, so as to be understood by one's particular audience. Similarly, people are what they are in part by representing the various systems in which they participate, to the extent they know them, and controlling their actions more or less well to act in the systems according to their ideas of what is appropriate.

The heart of covenant theology is that people necessarily represent themselves and their world as created by God, as loved by God, and as meriting their diverse excellences because of that divine creative love. These representations might be directly in the cultural terms of the Judeo-Christian tradition of covenant, or they might be in analogous terms; how far the analogy can be stretched is a matter of debate. The systems of religion arise from the ways by which people relate to the representation of themselves and the world as created. The *broken* covenant involves a misrepresentation of the created status of things, or a failure to represent it at all. Sin consists in activities that involve misrepresentation or denial of created status and its normative elements. A *renewed* covenant requires a re-representation of the created status of things, a symbolization of the world as God's Kingdom, and a reordering of activities so as to reconstitute the *shālōm* or peace in which each thing is supported in its excellence.

II. SOCIAL SANCTIFICATION

Sanctification, therefore, cannot be conceived merely as a personal matter, a function of developing an individual character. It must also, because the harmony of essential and conditional features is a necessary one, involve a rectification of the social and natural systems with which one is connected so they conform to the ideals of covenant. The systems must be understood by means of representations of how they jointly contribute or should contribute to the *shālōm* of the Peaceable Kingdom. Although Jesus assiduously avoided involvement in moral causes as a political matter, he was clear that the proclamation of the Kingdom is a call to righteousness, piety, faith, and hope, and that this has social consequences. The Christian tradition long has been developing what is now known as the social gospel, or the social justice movement. The point of social justice for Christians is not merely the justice, though that is worth an absolute commitment in itself. The point is that justice is a necessary expression of discipleship in the Kingdom.

In order not to fall into an overemphasis on individualized sanctification, it is necessary to call attention to certain aspects of social structures. In the first place, they have a nature of their own within which people play roles defined by the system. Sometimes whether an individual plays a particular role is voluntary, other times not. Some systems present roles that can be played without much alteration to the player; others require radical alteration. In nearly all instances, social systems do have consequences for the lives and characters of the individuals they embrace. Systems also have consequences on the other systems and things in the natural and social environment within which they operate. A theory adequate for social analysis needs to be able to trace out the causal consequences of systems on one another, on the natural environment, and on the individuals who play various roles within them. By the very nature of systematic movement, the causal features of systems are recursive, that is, they influence themselves, which in turn influences themselves once again, and so on. Systems do not exactly repeat themselves. The idea of systematic equilibrium is a fictional ideal case. Rather, because of their recursive function, systems are constantly changing in their structure and consequences. Indeed, systems are affected sometimes by the individuals who play roles within them, and hence are responsive to the nonsystematic influences of human freedom. Social analysis needs to be able to identify the nodal points at which systems are changeable and do change in their consequences.

In the second place, those consequences all have some value or other, affecting the people and things touched by the system for better or worse. Therefore, the systems have a moral character, though perhaps a complex one: good effects here, bad effects there, the good effects depending on the bad effects and vice versa. Indeed, systems may have effects that can be called righteous or unrighteous, pious or impious, faithful or faith destroying, hopeful or hope destroying.

When Biblical authors wrote darkly of "the powers of this world," they knew that certain social structures have bad consequences and have also an integrity that maintains those structures against the simple will of good people to change them. The seventeenth-century political theorists such as Thomas Hobbes, Nicolo Machiavelli, and John Locke, and the eighteenth- and nineteenth-century economists such as Adam Smith and Karl Marx, developed theories of social structures that attempt to give causal explanations for morally freighted social consequences. But they are so far much too simple. Marxism is attractive to many Christians in our time because it cites the distributive principle of giving to people in accord with their needs and requiring from people in accord with their abilities. The Marxist theory of social structure, however, attempts to reduce all social systems to the economic one, and from the basic definitions of the economic system, for instance of ownership and wage labor, to derive a theory of social class that is supposed to be more important than and explanatory of any other classification. By suppressing all the systems that affect motivation (for instance, age characteristics, gender, ethnicity, political and religious persuasion), into the bare rational economic motive, Marxism prescribes an economic polity that seems to actually reduce wealth rather than increase it as Marx hoped. Furthermore, by deligitimating all the systems, such as those mentioned, that affect the distribution of wealth, Marxism requires as a polity a class-based tyranny of economic experts that broadly suppresses freedom, and hence suppresses even more areas of motivation. The recent repudiations of Marxism by Eastern European countries marks its inadequacy, especially its totalitarian defects.

The lesson to be learned from the sad experience of Marxism in this century is that *the objects over which the social gospel should advocate control are the systems themselves, not the classes of people as defined by a particular system.* Informal Marxism picks up the power differential between the wealthy and the poor, and then sets the poor in anger against the wealthy. The apparent simplicity of this ideology for raising consciousness and effective organized opposition has made Marxism attractive. But by feeding class warfare it violates the covenantal ideal of the Kingdom, and vastly oversimplifies the real complexity of interacting systems, each of which has consequences for justice. Liberation theology often uses Marxist analyses to provide a perspective on the Christian commitment to social change on the part of those who are in disadvantaged positions. But, as mentioned above, the degree to which liberation theology employs a genuine Marxism remains to be shown. Perhaps only where it feeds anger rather than organized action for deliberate change of institutions is liberation theology genuinely Marxist.[3] Much work needs to be done to identify the actual causal structures of social systems and to assess how they interplay and affect one another and the individuals within them.

From the standpoint of theological analysis, it is clear that social systems as well as individuals can be sinful, though in different senses. Individuals break the covenant by causing harm to people and other things within the covenant, but they also do so with personal responsibility and in a way that violates the representation of the Logos, the created status of the covenanted creation. Social systems do not behave as persons; they are causal agents of good and bad consequences, but not morally culpable ones. That a system can be identified as in need of serious changes need not require that individuals can be identified as morally culpable for the system's bad effects: few if any people "will" an economic system to be exploitative, only to make themselves wealthier. On the other hand, *if* a system is to be changed, individuals do have to be identified as having the responsibility to move the pieces that make the changes. Although it has become common in theology to speak of social systems themselves as being "sinful," sometimes it seems as if it would be better to speak of them as "evil," reserving "sin" for individual agency. Nevertheless, in a broken covenant, everything is broken, social and natural systems as well as the human heart. In that added sense, systems can be sinful.

III. OPPRESSION AND BLASPHEMY

In earlier chapters, "righteousness" was associated with the moral element of the covenant, in contrast with those elements corresponding to the ideals of piety, faith, and hope. The purpose of that contrast was to draw limits to the role of moral righteousness in Christianity, especially in light of the overuse of that notion in contemporary theology. "Justice" carries a deeper connotation than righteousness or morality, however, namely that of being rightly related to things so as to affect them in ways that are their due. In this sense it applies not so much to individuals, although this is part of the meaning of personal justice, as to institutions and social systems. Those systems are just insofar as they support the covenant; and they are unjust or sinful insofar as they express the brokeness of the covenant and lead other systems, individuals, or nature to sin or disrepair. Therefore, we can examine the sinful nature of institutions not merely in terms of their moral quality, but in terms also of their effects on those elements of the covenant whose ideals are piety, faith, and hope.

The key here is the Logos: that by which the covenanted world is created includes order that should be moral, components with intrinsic value that should be respected, actuality that should be embraced as given, and a value centering the whole on its creaturely status. Injustice thus has four parts, which will be discussed under the following labels. Injustice of social order is *oppression*; of relation to the components of the world, *blasphemy*; of relation to the givenness of actuality, *alienation*; and of relation to transcendent centering value, *secularism*.

The moral dimensions of the sin of systems or institutions can be called "oppression" because of the power of systems to make things conform to them. We should be wary not to thematize power and oppression too much in the mode of modern European thought, which has used those themes to replace classical notions of worth and acting within appropriate limits. Still, systems or institutions primarily are destructive of the covenant by the effects they have on individuals, parts of nature, or other systems insofar as those other things must conform to the system's roles. It is systems and institutions that are oppressive. Rarely would an individual have such personal control over a system as to be the system's author and therefore an oppressor.

A sinful or oppressive system exerts a power of conformation that can be ruinous to a thing's excellence. Individuals can be made into brute laborers by an economic system, rewarded according to the system's resources rather than by the individual's deserts, or by the bounty of nature, or by the mutual care of an ideal community. People can be forced by the draft to participate in a wrong war, or by taxes to support a wrong war, or by an educational system that makes them think a wrong war is good, to support a wrong war. People can be diminished into demeaning domestic roles by a system of gender discrimination; the same system can inflate their hypocrisy, falsify their true potentials, and distort the participation of people in nearly every other system of life.

Mountains can be grossly logged over in conformity with a government program for subsidizing the pulp industry. Lakes can be polluted by cities' sewage. Near-space can be cluttered with artificial satellites. Political systems can ruin judicial systems; judicial systems can ruin an economy; economies can ruin a society's support for the arts. In our day we have seen how a national sense of identity can oppress minorities, how an economic system can oppress its poor people, and how gender role definitions can oppress women and gay people. Although we have tended to radicalize the Christian sense of injustice in simplistic ways, blocking out good and evil people in clear stereotypes, now it is becoming apparent that the victim in one system can be the oppressor in another, and that any action to cause a social change will bring evil as well as good. None of this is to say that disciples of Christ are excused from attempting to rectify their society just because action is complex and multivalued. It is, however, to indicate the complexity and multivalued consequences of social action.

The above has not attempted to provide an analysis of how systems and institutions can be oppressive, or to provide a history of how they are. Rather, it has attempted to illustrate certain classes of oppression to make the point that systems and institutions have causal powers to bring suffering to people, to harm nature, and to make themselves worse. These all illustrate the broken covenant, and the systems call for removal, replacement, or reconstruction so as better to approximate the situation of the covenant.

Blasphemy is the injustice of social systems regarding piety toward the components of things. Social systems that demean or deny respect for the grandeur of the processes of nature and of society are blasphemous. "Blasphemy" is not a popular notion in secular culture because it suggests that there is some public good or evil in what people take to be holy, and that therefore public sanctions might be warranted to preserve it.[4] Yet the total rejection of blasphemy as a form of injustice entails either the belief that nothing is holy and that all claims to holiness are idolatrous, or that social systems and institutions cannot embody beliefs in holiness without destructive consequences.

Blasphemy is intended as the characteristic of broken social systems and institutions that is parallel to impiety in individuals. Impiety is an attitude that neglects the intrinsic worths of the components of things and treats them only insofar as they add up to something of interest on the human scale. Impiety rejects the presence of God as creator in the whole of creation. Blasphemy is the characteristic of institutions that does the same thing. An economic system, for instance, necessarily uses elements of nature to accomplish the ends built into the system; but it need not treat those elements as if they had no other value, a value intrinsic to them and from the perspective of which the system's uses are abstract. The economic system is blasphemous when it suborns reverence for the natural systems in which it lies. It can also be blasphemous when it regards the persons who play roles in it only according to those roles; the system needs to acknowledge, if only by openness, the plethora of other connections and essential values its players have.

Blasphemy is not a moral fault of utilitarianism, although a system may have related utilitarian faults. The reasons to protect the natural environment, for instance, include utilitarian ones (so that we will not run out of fuel, for example) and also pious or reverential ones (the forests should be revered as parts of the creation). Morally, we should see the AIDS virus as greatly destructive to human life, and should mobilize the medical and social institutions to eliminate it and discover means to reverse its effects. As a matter of piety, however, we should honor the virus as a particularly clever part of creation. And the medical and social systems would be blasphemous if, in attempting to eradicate the virus, they cause us not to ponder its wonders.

If the ancient Christian belief that everything in God's creation is good in its way, and as such is an expression of divine creativity, is true, then everything is holy in context. And thus everything is subject to blasphemous destruction. Most of modern secularity, particularly the Marxist and capitalist economic elements that construe everything primarily in an instrumental relation to economic development, is blasphemous. Christians tolerate that only because the social price of condemning blasphemy is so high, namely, the restriction of people's freedom and the imposition of the Christian valuation of things on non-Christian people. But the acceptance of what is indeed socially blasphemous has come round to haunt European and North American culture already with regard to environmental issues, and will soon manifest its way of breaking the covenant in social relations and in the treatment of individuals.

IV. ALIENATION AND SECULARISM

Alienation is not the right word, being insufficiently inclusive, to indicate the ways in which social structures undermine faith and integrity. As a metaphor, however, recaptured from Marxism by the existentialist literature that has called attention recently to the problems of existence and faith, alienation might indicate the effects sinful social systems can have in putting people in bondage to their passions. Alienated consumerism is the obsessive culture that exercises a twofold dialectic. First, it represents the values of things to be only the values they have for individuals, groups, or institutions with which people identify. Then, it defines the value of those individuals, groups, and institutions solely in terms of their possessing the value of the things. Alienated consumerism can lead to an oppression of people and a blasphemous treatment of the social and physical environment; but its intrinsic injustice is that it causes people to define themselves in terms of possessing, and thereby being possessed by, other things.

Social systems and institutions are alienating insofar as they lead people to ontological hyprocrisy. Ordinary hypocrisy is when people behave in ways that dissimulate what they truly believe and feel in order to deceive others. Ordinary hypocrisy is for the sake of sustaining a public image that is different from one's reality. Ontological hypocrisy is when the dissimulation aims to deceive oneself. Of course it is logically impossible to lie to oneself. But human beings have many repressive mechanisms to let them believe on one level what they know to be false on another. Institutions are alienating when they force people to live a lie to themselves.

The consequence of alienation is that people cannot live in faith. They cannot embrace the historical particularity of their situation and make themselves at home in it. They insist on being strangers to their situation and to their own possible actions. Economic institutions force bad faith when the impoverished have to pretend that a miracle might enrich them the next day, when the rich believe they deserve their wealth because they work harder than the working poor, or when they convince rich and poor that the system is the only way the system can be. Family institutions are alienating when they make people believe that their true identity is exhausted in the family role, or that the family role justifies them. Religious institutions are alienating when they lead people to accept unacceptable conditions here because there will be better ones by and by, or when they persuade people that conformation to a religious culture is sufficient for salvation, or when they teach idolatry. Social institutions are alienating when they prevent people from embracing the creation as it is actualized in their neighborhood and in their own person.

Secularity, of course, is the teaching, the tradition, of systems and institutions that require players to assume that the system or institution is self-contained and all there is. Secularity is the mode of spirit to which some systems and institutions force people to conform that says, not that things within the created order should be supported in their excellence, but that things are good insofar as they are fulfilled on their own terms. Secularity suppresses excellence for the sake of fulfillment, and defines fulfillment in worldly terms that ignore the essentially finite and fragmentary character of existence.

Christians believe that they are fulfilled in the infinite life of God, and seek a path to acknowledge that, a path that also leads to as great an excellence as is possible for their finite position. The secularity forced upon us by so many social structures waffles between idolatry and despair. Sometimes it promises that we can in fact be fulfilled in terms of finite systems. Other times it tells us there is simply no fulfillment. The spiritual center of Christianity aims to recognize the integrity of the world in itself, but also to reveal the infinite divine creative ground in which things achieve their true fulfillment, actually, a divine fulfillment.

In the face of all these forms of injustice—oppression, blasphemy, alienation, and secularity—Christian discipleship requires subtle critique and social action. To live in the renewed Kingdom of God is to work to perfect the whole covenanted creation. If we were to think that the obligation to sanctification is meant only for ourselves, or for persons, we would have succumbed to the individualism that is a chief manifestation of the break in the covenant. Even individuals cannot be perfected without perfecting the social structures and nature that constitute their environment and their conditional features. An exclusive focus on personal perfection and piety usually reflects an unmentioned affirmation of the unjust social structures characterizing the broken covenant in one's neighborhood. The "social gospel," therefore, is an intrinsic and necessary part of sanctification.

Readings in Key Texts:

1. Aquinas, *SCG*, no reading
2. Aquinas, *ST*, I-II, ques. 90-100, 106-108.
3. Augustine, no reading.
4. Barth, no reading.
5. Calvin, *Inst.*, Book 3, chaps. 18-19; Book 4, chap. 20.
6. Cobb and Griffin, no reading.
7. Ferm, *TWLT*, chaps. 3-5 (by Gutierrez), 29 (by Mar Osthathios), 33 (by Kim Yong-Bok).
8. Hildegard, *Sci.*, Book 3, Visions 4-6, 12-12.
9. Luther, *TT*, "An Open Letter to the Christian Nobility of the German Nation Concerning the Reform of the Christian Estate."
10. Rahner, *Found.*, chap 5.
11. Ruether, *Sexism*, chap. 9.
12. Schleiermacher, *CF*, pp. 517-524.
13. Tillich, *Sys.*, Vol. 3, pt. 4, section 3: B-D; pt. 5, section 1.

Sanctification

I. SANCTIFICATION AND JUSTIFICATION

The point stressed in chapter 9, that sanctification requires commitment to the perfection of society insofar as that is possible, has been the hallmark of liberal Christianity in Europe and North America since the latter days of the nineteenth century, and in much of the rest of the world more recently. That point needs to be balanced over against the hallmark of conservative Christianity, namely, the importance of personal sanctification. In truth sanctification does not have two types, social and personal. Sanctification is rather one thing, the restoration of the covenant in oneself, in one's relations, in the institutions of society, and in the natural world with which people interact. Personal sanctification is necessary to the pursuit of social justice in the large sense, and the pursuit of justice is necessary for the life of prayer and discipline.

The necessity to recover and integrate both dimensions of sanctification arises from the fact that their unity is no longer an obvious truth. It has been argued, for instance, that in deeply entrenched patriarchal cultures such as the European, North American, Latin American, East Asian, Indian, Oceanic, and African, women cannot seriously approach personal sanctification without first transforming the patriarchal culture. For, the very definitions of holiness express oppressive male views rather than the potential excellences of women (Daly, 1973, 1984). Therefore, political change must take place before serious religion is possible. Similarly, it has been argued that one should not expect personal piety of the poor, for instance the rejection of class anger, until after the conditions of their poverty have been alleviated. These arguments have great persuasiveness if solidarity with that point of view, or a privileging of the epistemological perspective of the victims, is made a precondition for reflection and conversation.

Yet the prior Christian principle is that people are created in covenant *not* to be reduced to the environing systems that condition them. In the broken covenant, those systems might attempt a dehumanizing reduction. But that is precisely the problem. An essential part of a renewed covenant is that people take back their integrity from the systems that would wholly define them, and take responsibility for their own holiness. Much should be understood and forgiven in people who bear a far greater burden than others. The forgiveness is especially obligated when the potential forgivers are beneficiaries of systems that oppress, blaspheme, captivate to lust, or break the hopes of others. None of us is in a position to condemn what others see as necessary for the Kingdom, though we might not agree and have to oppose them. What can be more understandable than the anger of people at the institutions that oppress them and the people who benefit from and maintain those institutions?

The love of God in Christ, however, sets people free from the bondage of sin, including the bondage of anger. Precisely in conditions of social injustice, the gospel of Christ frees people to seek their own holiness and, with that, the justice of their context.

The unity of personal and social sanctification can be seen in the connection of sanctification with justification. Justification is the action of God as Trinity by which individuals become convinced of God's love, a conviction that actually sets them free from depravity and bondage to the lost state of sinfulness. With justification alone, individuals do not change personal ways or habits; nor does justification change institutions. The process of sanctification is the work required to make those changes. But justification as an actual fact sets the individuals free to begin that work. The dialectic of faith and repentance, conviction and commitment sketched in the last chapter shows something of the underlying structure of the changes in the subject of salvation wrought by justification. Chapters 11 and 12 shall detail this further with reference to Jesus Christ, whose identity on the one hand stems from embodying the creator's Logos and on the other hand requires the continued action of the Holy Spirit through history. Jesus is *not* the savior unless people are saved actually, not in principle or in some divine mind but actually.

Justification is something that happens in the heart, and thus is ineluctably individual. When groups of people suddenly break out of their bondage to sin, that is because enough individuals in the group do so that the rest are carried along. The personal interiority of justification, however, cannot be mistaken for an individualism of sanctification, for the individual is both essential features and conditional features. By its conditional features, an individual is part of a family, of social groups, of political units, of economic and religious institutions, and a host of other systematic connections. Perhaps deepest of all, an individual is part of a system of signs including language and all the meaningful signallings of daily life, and that system has no reality save in its being exercised by the situations of meaning. Therefore, if justification is to lead to sanctification, it must do so in all the connections by which people are conditionally connected to one another, to institutions, and to nature. Saying a prayer in private and marching with a crowd in a demonstration might be extremes of behavior susceptible of sanctification; but they themselves are abstractions. There is no such thing as praying by itself: it is the prayer of the one who marched or did not march, the prayer of one whose symbols come from the Christian tradition, or some other, the prayer of one of a certain age, with certain experiences, and occupying certain roles, probably changing, in various communities. Marching is also merely a part of a richer life. The change of heart in justification needs to manifest itself in sanctification throughout the whole of people's lives, and those lives are defined not individually but in terms of their connections in the covenant.

Salvation, which embraces justification and sanctification, thus also embraces the whole of the created covenant. Salvation is enacted first in a change of heart in individuals, and then in changes in all the things affected by the heart, including personal character and all parts of the created world over which human causality might exercise some influence. Without the justifying change of heart, both the improvement of character and the achievement of social justice are possible to some degree, and this is not to be scoffed at. Yet without the change of heart, the other changes are religiously hollow, good in themselves perhaps, but having nothing to do with salvation. For, salvation is not merely cosmological changes in people and societies, but also an ontological repair. Salvation has to do with how behavior within the created world reflects on the creator, either denying the world's created status or acknowledging it and imaging the divine creative love as much as possible. For this reason, salvation requires the explicit acceptance of divine love in the creating of oneself, originally and in the point of repair. This means acknowledging the Logos as the presence of God in creation, as the source of order, of the components, of the actual existence, and of our ways of relating to the creation. Having broken the covenant and lost the power of righteous, pious, faithful, and hopeful living, justification restores that power. Having been "reborn" with the power, to use Jesus' image, we still have the hard work of exercising the power together to effect repairs in the covenant.

Sanctification is the process of exercising the power of the renewed covenant with God to effect a reconstruction of the covenant in the actual world, insofar as that is possible in our neighborhood. With this understanding of the unity of sanctification, we may now turn to its personal and social modes.

II. PERSONAL SANCTIFICATION: SPIRIT, MIND, AND HEART

What then are the steps to personal sanctification? There are of course many spiritual routes, appropriate for different kinds of people. In a profound sense, each person seeks an individual and unique route, for it should lead to a personal centeredness in the context of the entire creation. Certain general elements can be identified, however.[1]

First, sanctification for Christians means taking on the mind of Christ so that it informs one's life. To do this requires study about what that mind is. For many this begins with the presentation of Jesus in the Christian community. But for the serious it means also a personal study of the Bible, the tradition, and the meaning of the Church and larger Christian community.

Second, sanctification requires an understanding of the life that is to be sanctified, one's own and the determinants of that life in context. Intelligent self-knowledge, as well as critical appreciation and appraisal, are required for deliberate sanctification.

Third, continual reflection and prayer are needed to join the mind of Christ to one's own situation. The joining will not be by clever intellectual connections but by the Holy Spirit working within the soul to give power and sensitivity to the mind of Christ.

Fourth, support of the Christian community, in its liturgies that join one to the Church across space and time, in its preachments, and in the personal encouragement of the saints, is a crucial tool in sanctification. There are, of course, examples of hermits and others who have foresworn the Church as wicked or corrupt, or simply unnecessary, and have themselves gone far toward perfection. Such isolation, however, runs counter to the recovery of the covenant community about which the discipleship of renewal is in the first place. At best it can be a temporary expedient.

Fifth, and most of all, the process of sanctification needs to be made a personal, deliberate, and habitual project. It moves so slowly, and with so many apparent backslidings, that the pursuit of holiness needs an internal momentum relatively free from the vicissitudes of external circumstances. Furthermore, even within the Church, the project of sanctification is easily misperceived and made lonely. The continuing renewing strength of God must become the sustaining and encouraging force for personal life.

If these and like things are elements of spiritual life, in what does personal perfection consist? The answer to this question depends on one's model of the self, and there is no one Christian answer. The following is an ancient model, however, that has been influential in European-based Christian communities. The various potentialities of the self can be divided into those having to do with the development of psychic integrity, which Plato called the "spirited" part of the soul, those having to do with learning, reason, wisdom, and guidance, which Plato called "reason," and those having to do with desire, appetite, love, and the organized activity productive of satisfaction, which Plato called "eros" and Christians better call the heart (Neville, 1978). Although each of these families of elements in the self is related to the others, each of the families undergoes a spiritual development or dialectic of its own. Together they correspond to the three forms of depravity discussed in chapter 7, section 4.

The perfection of one's psychic integrity or *will* begins with the attainment of an image of oneself as loved by God and thus worthy. There are, of course, many levels of this, and one returns to a renewed and deepened self-image many times. Before his Aldersgate experience in which he felt himself personally loved by God, John Wesley's despair of the Christian life was utter frustration to his spiritual development; that experience gave him the start for a lifelong project. He rarely referred to it later, because it was only a beginning; yet it was an essential beginning.

The second level of psychic integrity is the attainment of competence as a self in acting. From physical activities to intellectual, from inner actions to abilities and skills in community, psychic integrity requires skill at action. Christianity has not often paid sufficient attention to the cultivation of skills of action. The military virtues of the medieval knights are perhaps not the best model. Nor is the focus on "enabling," the current fashion in some Christian circles, for it suggests a passivity of the person, depending on someone else or some institution to make the person able. The same fault lies in the language of "empowerment," and it has the added deficit of employing the metaphors of dehumanized objectification, of power and matter in motion. Rather, the focus should be on the person's acquiring competence.

The third level is a cultivation of consciousness so as not to be hounded by obsessive passions or defined by the inner dialogue that reinforces needs to be justified by things other than God's love. This is not so much mind control as mind purification. The arts of meditation and prayer are most relevant here; this is the focus of hatha yoga.

The fourth level is a perfection of devotion, so that in living diversely through all the relations of the many contexts of life, one is devoted to manifesting and promoting the covenant of God. At the beginning, devotion is rather like taking an external vow, coupled with emotional enthusiasm for the project; as one progresses in spiritual depth, the devotion becomes a defining habit of the heart. Devotion is the opposite of dependence, because it must begin with the development of autonomy in self-image, action, and the rest. But it shares with dependence a giving over of oneself to God. Unlike mere dependence, devotion is the free and responsible offering of oneself, and therefore a relation to God like friendship rather than like the dependence of childhood.

Sanctification of the mind or reason is perhaps the best understood element of holiness in Western society, and is equally the burden of the chief traditions in India and East Asia. One begins by coming to know oneself. Obviously correlated with obtaining a proper self-image, self-knowledge means knowledge of inner motives, talents, and weaknesses, as well as an understanding of one's situation.

Beyond self-knowledge, holiness of mind requires understanding the world, not just in its basic causal connections but with regard to what is important for what, and how. Worldly wisdom is required for the recognition of the covenant, and criticism of its fissures.

Beyond the level of worldly wisdom is its internalization, indeed a personal "becoming true," so that one lives in such a way as to accurately represent in one's life the real values of things in the world around. Becoming true is the subjective way of living in *shālōm*, allowing and supporting other things to be in their excellence. None of this is to suggest that the world can be made compatible within oneself, only that one is true to the extent one does make it compatible. Fulfillment of becoming true is possible only insofar as one's life is viewed as a part of the divine life embracing all creation.

Enlightenment is the capstone of cognitive sanctification, the ability to understand in a bifocal way: with the close lens we see the world and ourselves from the perspective of our own finite position, and behave in ways that actualize the covenant proximately; with the far lens we get a distant view of the creation from God's perspective, in which the creator is equally close to all things and in which all things, as harmonies of their essential and conditional qualities, are uniquely valuable. Christians do not go so far as the religions of India in suggesting that we actually attain to God's view of the world; we are created as normatively finite. Yet we can come to appreciate God's glory as such, even though we are but a small part of it.

Sanctification of the heart begins with the building of good desires, those that enhance the covenant. This means pruning away bad desires, and becoming detached from those that captivate. But more it means the creation of worthy desires. The great fault of sinful life in a broken covenant is the general impoverishment of the desires. Sinners desire too little, not too much. Just as erotic, sexual desires are paradigmatic of the bonds of sin, so free erotic and sexual desires are paradigmatic of joyful life itself.

Beyond desire, disciples need to cultivate the capacity to love. Further, not just many loves with permanence and devotion, but a comprehensive love such that one's many loves are integrated in a unified love of God in the world. This recurs to the Great Commandment associating love of God with love of neighbor.

Although will concerns disciplined organization, and mind concerns direction, the passions of the heart concern power. The perfection of power is based on the folding in of desires and loves on one another, each reinforcing the other, each connecting us with some part of the world, each taking in the world's powers. Power in this sense is not the mechanical power of physics but the personal power we often call "charisma." In some traditions, it is alleged to be able to perform magic or miracles. In all traditions it is a mark of advanced spiritual development. Power, of course, is as dangerous as it is useful: Satan was the most powerful of the angels, most glorious in heaven for the integration and focus of his heart (according to John Milton if not the Bible).

Finally, the sanctification of the heart leads to communion with the divine, and with the rest of creation as bound together in the covenant. Communion can be experienced at just about any stage of spiritual development, though at first it is fragmentary and "amazing." As communion develops, aided and paralleled by developments of spirit and mind, it becomes more and more frightening, less like conversation than like an overwhelming sexual experience. It is, after all, a meeting with God who loves us into being, a meeting enabled by modest gains in our own capacity to love and respond to love, a meeting that is not relational as if to another finite being but that is our own creation, our completed birth, a completion that climaxes our own loving. Certain feminists (e.g. Harrison and Heyward in Brown and Bohn, 1989) believe that this interpretation of the culmination of divine communion is simply a function of patriarchal civilization. Erotic imagery for divine love, they suggest, is male imagery which serves to reinforce feelings of powerlessness and dependency in women, and it reflects a homosexual undercurrent in male spirituality, sadomasochistic in both cases, according to the feminist critique. Neither in the classical spiritual literature nor in contemporary experience, however, is it clear that the divine lover is experienced as male rather than female, only creative; nor is it clear that the human response in divine communion transfers dependency on God to dependency on other things within the world rather than energizing the beloved for more courageous life. Because mature communion depends on mature enlightenment and mature devotion, being consumed by and with the Creator is a free acceptance and giving.

Because spiritual development or personal sanctification is so complicated, with so many faculties related by different projects, filled with backslidings and cross-fertilizations, the following summary chart may be a helpful map.

Will	Mind	Heart
Purify Self-image	Know Thyself	Perfect Desires
Purify Action	Understand World	Perfect Love
Purify Consciousness	Become True	Perfect Power
Purify Devotion	Enlightenment	Perfect Communion

The paths of sanctifying the spirit, mind, and heart are obviously intertwined. Other cultures sort the components of self differently, and thus represent its perfection according to a different analysis. Furthermore, the sanctification of the personal self cannot be separated except abstractly from personal and cooperative activity to sanctify the environing society and nature. To that last topic we now turn.

III. SANCTIFICATION AS SOCIAL JUSTICE

Because human beings are harmonies of conditional as well as essential features, thereby intrinsically related to other people, to nature, and to systems of interaction connecting all these, the process of personal sanctification cannot be limited to one's own character save by denial of one's involvements with the rest of creation. Indeed, if the doctrine of repentance was correctly analyzed in chapter 8, to the effect that one must go so far as to abandon hope in one's own salvation and agree with the divine perspective that one is worth no more than the rest of the fallen creation, then one has no more reason to be concerned with one's own sanctification than with that of anything else.

The grounds for the focus on one's own personal sanctification are purely pragmatic: one's own character is the thing most constantly affected by what one does, and therefore deserves the lion's share of one's attention. Furthermore, no one else has any special responsibility for one's character, and part of being responsible at all is taking responsibility for oneself. The practice of holiness is self-reflexive. The path of becoming holy is part of being holy. One cannot be holy for someone else. Nor can one make someone else holy except in the derivative sense of providing a favorable environment and support.

From this follows a negative generalization or principle concerning sanctification as social justice, namely, to respect the personal responsibility of others. We can no more sanctify others than we can make others moral. Sanctification, like morality, is a matter of the exercise of each individual's responsibility. Nevertheless, just as we can steer people toward or away from opportunities for moral behavior, so we can steer people toward or away from the supports for sanctification. We can present them with various witnesses to the love of God in Christ, though we cannot cause the Holy Spirit to graft it into their heart. We can surround people with others who are also disciples, struggling with sanctification, but we cannot guarantee that the saints will not be a blatant turn off. We can bring people into our own projects of social justice, incorporating them into our Christian community. According to the James/Lange theory of emotion, acting in a charitable way is likely to lead to intentions of true charity; but that cannot be guaranteed because there are so many other motivations having to do with attempts at self-salvation or personal fulfillment that propel people to charitable work. We can pray for people, regularly and intensely; but God is not moved by prayer as if by magic. In the long run as well as short we must respect the responsibility of others. Not to do so is to sin the way so tempting to Christians: the imposition of a totalitarian Christian regime on other people.

Nevertheless, amendment of the social systems in one's environment so as to heal their broken nature and cause them to affect people, nature, and each other for the good, is entirely compatible with respect for the responsibility of others. Because the systems have a character of their own, that character can be understood in terms of its effects on other things and, insofar as subject to human control, amended so as to produce effects conformable to the renewed covenant. The principle of sanctification here is that we should affect all of the systems in which we play or can play roles, subject to respecting the responsibility of others, so as to conform them as nearly as possible to the ideals of the covenant. Social systems and institutions are the mediating links by which people relate to one another and to nature; further, they have excellences of their own. In both roles (the former are their conditional features, the latter their essential ones), social systems should fulfill the great *shālōm* of God's creation, and thereby be holy expressions of the creator.

We have come to realize in our time that there is no univocal outcome for justice in the larger sense in any state of a social system. What has liberating effects for some is oppressive for others; what turns some people to piety is blasphemous for others; what satisfies healthy desires in some enslaves others; the very source of some people's hope fixes despair in others. No story has only one meaning: the Christianization of Europe meant the corruption and ultimate destruction of the Druid Cult of the Divine; Elijah's vindication of Yahweh on Mount Carmel was a holocaust of 450 priests of the Goddess (I Kings 18). Yet for all the ambiguity of *shālōm*, it is still possible to distinguish in the large between good and bad systems, and to discern improvements in the ones at hand. Ambiguity is no excuse for abandoning the world with which our lives are necessarily tied.

Social justice in our own time has come to be associated with negative causes, for instance the elimination of racism, sexism, military weapons that do more harm than possible good, the bellicose political mentality, and structures of poverty that breed generations of the underclass. Important as these movements are, they are large and crude. They do not attend to subtle causal structures in the systems involved but tend to generalize to the persons, making broad classifications of oppressors and victims on the basis of perceived benefits and harms that come from the systems. There is a truth to this, of course. Those who benefit from a system that victimizes others, and those in position to control the system (often the same people), are highly likely to resist changing the system to alleviate the victims if they themselves lose benefits or power. Generally, however, the enjoyment of benefits from the system, and exercise of control over its effects, are the very things to be desired in the *shālōm* covenant, though not with the victimization of others. The obligation of holiness is to change the system to benefit all, allowing each a proper exercise of responsibility in affecting the system; the obligation is not to make the current beneficiaries into enemies for destruction.

As argued so eloquently by Martin Luther King, Jr., and by Gandhi before him, social action requiring resistance must be taken in love, not hate or anger. The danger with large-scale negative causes is that they foster, indeed depend upon, hate and anger. Part of the problem is with some of the newly developed technologies of mass movements: overstatement, use of language to develop political consensus rather than to express truths that can be ambiguous, use of ideological theater instead of analysis and persuasion, symbolic (and not so symbolic) acts of terror, and the like. These technologies of mass mobilization seemed cheerfully right-minded in the early stages of the American civil rights movement, but became murky when the black power movement broke the initial consensus; pouring blood on draft files seemed to many a legitimate way to symbolize resistance to the American war in Vietnam; but then both sides in the abortion controversy in America learned the technologies of creating a movement, and suddenly each side perceives the technologies as morally dangerous, and remembers the Nazi movement.

The positive side of social justice must be determined contextually according to the criteria of the Spirit: does the social system produce love, joy, peace, patience, kindness, generosity, faithfulness, gentleness, and self-control (Galatians 5:22) in the community? The social forms that do are just, those that do not, or that do so preferentially, are not.

Most definitions of justice in the modern world turn on what we have, or fail to have, or how we distribute what various people can have. The language of possession and consumption seems second nature. But it is not. The covenant is an ontological state, and what matters is what we are, not what we have. Possessions, of course, determine a great deal about what we are, but in various ways and in different contexts. So too the various polities for distributing possessions have equivocal consequences. The pragmatic test of justice in every situation is whether the social form at hand or envisioned produces good *being* in people, that is, love, joy, peace, patience, kindness, generosity, faithfulness, gentleness, and self-control.

IV. SANCTIFICATION IN LOVE

The principle of social ethics for Christians can never be an identification with an initially plausible "right side" in a "struggle" against the "evil side." It must rather be a continual witness to loving each participant, to supporting all the excellences of the systems involved, and to discerning the subtleties and ambiguities of the truth. Care for truth always weakens a movement that otherwise could appeal to diverse motives, elevated and base, and energize them with hate for a common enemy. Christians must choose that kind of weakness. If they do not, the goal is not sanctification of the world in terms of the Kingdom, but rather the victory of one's faction's vision of justice.

It might seem to some that the ambiguities involved in sanctification as social justice are not to be found in the more personal side of sanctification. Perfecting the spirit, mind, and heart seems so much more straightforward, albeit difficult. Lack of ambiguity there, however, is also an illusion, sometimes a tempting one. First, there is no such thing as sanctification of spirit, mind, and heart that does not also involve participation in the sanctification of the world, both individually and in cooperation with others. Second, the finiteness of an individual's life, like that of history, means that its fragments can be made excellent but that there is no pattern for the whole with univocal value. As our society is fulfilled in God, not in itself, so our souls are potentially holy only as parts of the divine holiness. The world, including ourselves, can be holy as expressions of the divine. But the reference to the divine is crucial. In a complete sense, only God as creator is holy.

On a covenant analysis of social justice, love is not just one motive among others but the summary motive that combines righteousness, piety, faith, and hope as applied to institutions. Because social justice is of interest to religion because its pursuit is a requirement for sanctification, love has two orientations. One is toward the rest of creation (oneself included), and that involves relating to the world by living in righteousness, piety, faith, and hope. The other is toward God whose creative love is mirrored or imaged in our own love. The purpose of sanctification is that God's creation might be more nearly complete in our neighborhood. That purpose is accomplished insofar as our love sustains and repairs the covenant as God's does.

Readings in Key Texts:

1. Aquinas, *SCG*, no reading.
2. Aquinas, *ST*, II–II, ques. 1–7.
3. Augustine, *Conf.*, Book 10.
4. Barth, *Credo*, chap. 13.
5. Calvin, *Inst.*, Book 3, chaps. 6–10, 25.
6. Cobb and Griffin, *PT*, chap. 7.
7. Ferm, *TWLT*, chap. 24 (by Koyama).
8. Hildegard, *Sci.*, Book 2, Vision 7; Book 3, Visions 3, 10, 13.
9. Luther, no reading.
10. Rahner, *Found.*, chap 8, section 1; chap. 9.
11. Ruether, *Sexism*, chap. 10.
12. Schleiermacher, *CF*, pp. 505–517.
13. Tillich, *Sys.*, Vol. 3, pt. N 4 section 1: A; pt. 5, section 3.

Christology: The Cult of Jesus Christ

Because Christianity is not merely a general cultural expression of the human religious response to the createdness of existence, but one founded in particular reference to the historical person Jesus, the unique focal point of its theology is Christology, the study of how Jesus is the Christ, and what that means. One might wonder, therefore, why the direct discussion of Christology is postponed to so late a position in the *Primer*. In the Apostles' Creed, which forms the plot line of most systematic theologies, Christology is part of the doctrine of God, focused on the second person of the Trinity, following the discussion of God as creator and preceding that of God as Holy Spirit. In the *Primer*, the Logos holds that middle position, but not in a discussion focusing on how the Logos was incarnate in the human person of Jesus of Nazareth; the incarnation is a subsequent topic.

There are several reasons for the order here, although it would surely be possible to follow the traditional one. First, the *Primer* moves from general considerations to more specific ones, aiming to identify contemporary Christians in the concluding chapter on the Church; Christian symbols have been used throughout, and they too move from the general to the specific. Second, in deference to both European modernity's emphasis on the human condition and the fact that human experience is the point of contact in the comparison of Christianity with other religions, the human condition needs to be discussed immediately after the doctrine of God in order to show what is religious about the enterprise. Religion is about salvation, and salvation refers to some flaw in the human condition; therefore the nature of the ideal covenant and sin must be discussed before the work of salvation. Flaws in the human condition are religiously interesting, of course, only because of its relation to the Creator; therefore (unlike most anthropological theologies) the *Primer* insists on treating God first, the human condition second.

Third, the specific Christology of the *Primer* argues that the identity of Jesus as the Christ depends in the main on the work of salvation in Jesus and the Holy Spirit. Therefore salvation, including both justification and sanctification, must be introduced before a direct discussion of the identity of Jesus Christ. And, fourth, the identity of Jesus Christ is intimately tied to people's responses to him, and therefore is the prelude to the analysis of the Christian life, or the Church. The adjacency of Christology to ecclesiology is the principal reason for the order of topics in the *Primer*, which only now can be understood.

Although Christian theology by and large has made good use of philosophical concepts, adapting them where necessary and moving beyond them when no longer useful and better conceptualities become available, Christology has been singularly trapped by bad metaphysics. Aristotle taught that the way to understand something is to know what kind it is, or to what kinds it belongs. Falling in with this, Christology has assumed that it has to classify Jesus Christ as a peculiar kind of entity that has two natures, divine and human. There is good reason indeed for calling Jesus both human and divine, but not necessarily because of his "kinds." Rather, a thing can be known by what it does. This is especially true of an historical being such as a person. Christology should be "functional," not "sortal."

The way to formulate the Christological question, then, is to ask whether what Jesus did is human on the one hand and divine on the other. Because we are not inclined in our day, as was the case in the first century, to believe that Jesus was an angel who only looked like a human being, there is not much problem regarding the human nature of his actions. The relevant issues regarding Christ's humanity have to do with whether he can be imitated or his ministry extended by others. Regarding the claims to divinity, the Christological question is whether the specifics of his life and its extension in the Church play a part in the ontology of divine creation. Does Jesus complete the creation in some sense, or recreate the covenant? This and the next chapter will explore these issues.

Some theologians have exaggerated Christology to the point of Christocentrism. Christocentrism is a lopsided distortion of the Trinity, something of the opposite sort of heresy from Arianism.[1] Rather, Jesus is the Christ because of the Creator and the Holy Spirit; God is Creator in the Christian way because of Jesus Christ and the Holy Spirit; the Holy Spirit may have many forms but is the Christian Holy Spirit because of the creator and Jesus Christ. The Trinitarian balance requires to be maintained.

Christology needs to be approached from two problematics between which a continuum should be constructed. One problematic emphasizes the divinity of Christ, representing him, according to Paul and John, for instance, as having come from the Father, done God's work, and returned to Heaven. The other problematic has emphasized the historical Jesus, the teachings of Jesus, and his humanity, and thus has focused more on the synoptic gospels. Both sides are true, and a viable contemporary Christology must be able to give new life to the symbols that have been important in both approaches. More than that, the two problematics express the different sides of the problem of the two natures of Christ, as defined by the Council at Chalcedon.[2] The present chapter shall develop the problematic of the historical, human nature of Jesus Christ; chapter 12 will develop a theory of the divine nature. The unity of the two natures, according to the Christology presented here, consists in the historical actuality of Jesus' life and influence which re-empowers the covenant community so as to recreate in finite forms the work of the Logos in the elementary covenant-creation. The approach to the historical, human side of Jesus Christ, must thus begin with the Church.

I. THE CULTIC COMMUNITY OF JESUS

Since the beginning of contemporary historiography in the early nineteenth century in Europe, scholars have been deeply concerned with the "quest for the historical Jesus." What can be known of the historical character of Jesus? How are the gospels and other reports of him to be evaluated? After an initial period of increasing skepticism about the historical usefulness of the Biblical accounts and corroborating ancient writings, scholars have now amassed an extraordinary amount of relevant material that paints a detailed picture. Furthermore, the extensive use of various techniques for reconstructing the social context of the first century has given rise to many new questions to ask of the biblical material. Particularly, the cooperation between Jewish and Christian scholars, and the recent flourishing of scholarship concerning other Hellenistic religions, has been very important. These findings are summarized in any number of up-to-date introductions to the New Testament (for instance Kee, 1980, 1983; Koester, 1982; or Perrin and Duling, 1982).

Historical understanding of the life of Jesus and early Christianity is not sufficient for contemporary Christians' interest in Jesus Christ, however, although it is necessary for that interest. Contemporary Christians aim to be disciples of Jesus, to "have the mind of Christ" (I Corinthians 2:16), and to understand how that relates to the mind that should inform their own situation in culture. The Christians' question is how the covenant might be renewed in the context of their own society and life. Thus there are a number of factors that need to be taken into account by any Christian in his or her situation, including the following:

1. How do the gospel and the tradition of Christianity illuminate one's own situation, proximately and more broadly?

2. What does the Christian understanding of one's own situation add to what the tradition has understood before?

3. What is there in the historical life of Jesus, especially his teachings, that can be applied to one's situation? What is irrelevant? What in Jesus' teachings is a misplaced emphasis, or misleading, when applied to one's situation? What arguments justify the answers to any of these questions?

4. How do the Christian traditions come from Jesus to one's own situation? Through the European churches, or Indian, or African, Chinese, Oceanic, etc.? Through underground currents in these?

5. How have these connecting traditions been affected by missionaries from different cultures? By encounters with religions other than Christianity? Has the Christian gospel grown normatively in these interactions? How or how not?

6. By what means is the appropriation of the mind of Christ for one's own situation to be understood as part of the Great Cloud of Witnesses (Hebrews 12:1) in other parts of the world and other periods in history?

7. In light of answers to the above, how is one to organize one's own spiritual path of prayer in the search for holiness? To what voices of the Spirit ought one be specially attentive? How is Jesus to be imaged in one's own soul, given its particularities, its history of repentance, and needs for renewal?

8. Where ought one wait upon the Lord, and how is the Lord to be recognized, in one's daily life, attempting to renew the covenant in all the social and natural systems in which one participates? What is the critical edge of the gospel, built from Jesus to one's own situation? What is the cultural achievement that the gospel has brought to one's situation? In particular, how is one to be a Christian in the secular world of modern development?

The answers to any one of these questions obviously suppose answers to the others. The actual process of historical thought, as well as the Christian community's actual practice of worship, prayer, and mission, encompasses a subtle dialectic interweaving all these topics, correcting approaches to one by results in another. None can be left out. None has any normative priority over the others, save the line of covenantal faithfulness connecting one's Christian life to Jesus Christ. Christianity is a cultic community, deliberately cultivating personal and social characters reflective of Jesus. There are, of course, other religions with other cults, whose religious achievements may be more or less profound than Christianity's but at least different. When persons grasping the grace of God in Jesus Christ find that the line connecting them with Jesus is irrevocably broken, not merely corrupted and itself in need of critical renewal, but genuinely broken, where the answers to all the above questions are negative for the cult of Jesus Christ, or null, then they are no longer Christians and should seek some other cult.

II. THE TEACHINGS OF JESUS

There are four general teachings or activities of Jesus that figure largely in the image of him as normative for our own personal and communal sanctification. These correspond to the elements of the Logos and the ideals of the covenant.

The first, in continuity with John the Baptist, the Essenes, and the Pharisees, was the teaching of righteousness; the Kingdom of God is the reign of righteousness, and God shall judge the righteous and unrighteous. Jesus preaching of the Kingdom was in continuity with the tradition of the Messiah. yet as noted above he minimized the royal ruler of the Kingdom in favor of the creative Father who judges according to standards divinely established.

The second theme has positive and negative aspects. Postively, Jesus taught trust in God's presence in nature, in the powers of creation a bit irrespective of moral righteousness. Negatively, he pointed out (Matthew 5:43-48) that the rain falls on the unjust as well as the just and that, without diminishing the obligatoriness of morality, there is a respect for God in the larger creation that puts a limit on the applicability of moral law. The piety of Mary and Mary Magdeleine is somehow more basic than the moral service of Martha (Luke 10:38-42) or the disciples who thought expensive ritual materials would be better used for the poor (John 12:1-8). When Jesus answered that "the poor you have always with you," he put a strict circumscription on the claims of morality.

The third theme of Jesus' teachings was the honest facing of one's existential position in the world; this was presented in his critiques of hypocrisy (Matthew 6:1–18) and his parables, such as that of the Good Samaritan (Luke 10:25–37) or the discussion with the rich young ruler (Luke 18:18–27), that forced people to face up to who they are and what their real commitments are.

His fourth theme was the worship of God and the role of that in one's own spiritual life. He shifted the focus from the adoration of a warrior king to devotion to a creative and loving Father, and taught his disciples to pray in this regard (Matthew 6:7–14).

Clearly, in our own time, the preaching of righteousness, and the Christology emphasizing Jesus' role as liberator, has taken great precedence over the other teachings, and there is a need to recover piety, faith, and hope in the light of the limitations of morality. Yet the current emphasis on righteousness itself arose from a perception that Christianity had lost its moral cutting edge, and had become, in many areas of the world, a mere political ideology for preservation of an unjust status quo. Because situations differ, the balance of these teachings that preserves the integrity of the gospel differs from case to case, and that balance is found only through a complex dialectic integrating many concerns. This is as true for understanding the proper image of Jesus in one's own meditational life as in presenting Jesus as a model for social reform.

There are four particular situations in which the teachings of Jesus are specialized and controversial from the standpoint of representations of the tradition of the whole Church (representations that should be distrusted, for few if any are in a position to represent "the tradition"). They are the situations of widespread extreme poverty, of political bondage, of most women generally, and of cultures to which Christianity initially comes as an alien culture and needs to be made indigenous.

One of the reasons Christianity has been successful historically as a religion of world scope is that it addresses all conditions of society, rich and poor, young and old, weak and powerful. But it has a special appeal for the poor whose lives seem to show very little benefit from the love of God. Jesus gave priority to the poor over the rich, both in beatitude and in position, perhaps mainly because the poor are relatively free of hypocrisy. At the same time, he laid obligation on the rich to share with the poor. Although Jesus did not mention social structures, it is but a small and obvious application of his teaching to say that the rich and powerful ought to cooperate in alleviating the conditions that make people poor, and that the obligation to love the poor as neighbors cannot be qualified by their lack of readiness in dress or manners to sit at sumptuous tables. There have been several times in which Christianity has been called to take on special forms to address the needs and culture of the poor. The medieval period in Southern Europe, culminating in the Franciscan movement, was such a time, as is our own, both in underdeveloped countries and in developed ones.

Christianity has also been called upon to take special forms for the liberation of those in political and economic bondage, conditions in which the gospel is addressed particularly to the power structure of a society. This particularization of the teachings of Jesus is by no means obvious, because Jesus himself repeatedly declined to take up a revolutionary posture and Paul was explicit about not doing so. The theological justification for the careful extension of the gospel to support for those caused to suffer unnecessarily by unjust power structures comes again from the general obligation to love and the particular concern Jesus evinced for those abused by power. Jesus preached what is now fashionably called "solidarity" with all people as creatures in the Kingdom, children of God. His point is illegitimately extended when taken to mean solidarity with the poor in contrast to solidarity with others, based on resentment of the powerful and rich. But the opposite point is also true: it is illegitimate to interpret Jesus' call to universal family ties to apply only to those who benefit from and have reason to be supportive of a particular social arrangement.

The most powerful particularization of the teachings of Jesus in our time is its reinterpretation in terms of the experience of women. The reason for its great power is the extent and depth of its scope. The religious soil within which Christianity originally grew had been biased for at least a thousand years against allowing the expression of femininity in the terms represented by the Earth Mother and fertility goddesses, and which have been expressed here in terms of the transcendent power of the forces of nature in creation, and the covenantal ideal of piety before created things irrespective of their roles in patterns oriented to human society. The books of history in the Hebrew Bible tell repeatedly of the warfare between the masculine cult of Yahweh and the cults of the Baals and other fertility deities (even reference to Baal obscures the fact the religion centered on Astarte). When Jesus personalized God, the only obvious parental referent was Father. As if the male-oriented development of Judaism, Christianity, and Islam were not biased enough, the cultures of India, East Asia, and much of Africa have been even more extreme. With the feminist movement, all this has suddenly come to consciousness (Elisabeth Schussler Fiorenza, 1985; see also the Bibliography of Feminist Theology, appendix B). Dimension after dimension of experience has been uncovered and criticized for male bias, and the gospel has to be rethought in each instance. Despite the male-oriented language, and despite the composition of the Biblical canon by subsequent generations of Church leaders who represented an anti-female hierarchy, Jesus' own treatment of women offers many clues for the development of his teachings in ways directly redressing much of the traditions' neglect of women's experience (Fiorenza, 1984, 1985).

Care is needed, of course, to avoid the assumptions that all women are alike, or that generalized stereotypical traits such as the "feminine" and the "masculine" apply directly and exclusively to individuals. Much of the particularization of the teachings of Jesus to the situation of women also applies to the situation of gay people, who not only have had the special characters of their experience neglected but have been persecuted and, in many conditions, forced to hide their gender identity.

From the beginning, Christianity has extended Jesus' teachings from one culture to another. St. Paul's letters are textbooks about the difficulties of extending Christianity from the Jews to the Gentiles. But they curiously are lacking much discussion of the ways Jesus' own teachings are transformed when taken from Jesus' culture. The New Testament Gospels are themselves documents representing Jesus' teachings as already filtered through to the Gentile community, and only with great painstaking have scholars been able to reconstruct their Palestinian meaning. In our own day, the spread of Christianity through the Western imperial movements of the modern period has given rise to new contexts for making the gospel relevant to cultures to which it is new. The issue is complicated because of the mixture of Christianity itself with the political and economic forces of the imperial powers.

Theologians are now attending with considerable sensitivity to the special applications of Jesus' teachings to situations significantly different from that of Western Europe which has defined the North American theological situation. The multicultural embodiment of Christianity is by no means new, however. Within a century after Jesus' life there were Christian communities in Africa, India, and probably China, as well as the Near East and Europe. In each of those traditions Christianity has had a history with many turns. The ecumenical movement in the World Council of Churches and the special attention given to non-European churches in worldwide denominations such as the Roman Catholic and Methodist churches have brought the dialogue among religious cultures to the center of Christian theology. Each situation presents a challenge for interpreting the teachings of Jesus; each presents special opportunities for the development of spiritual life as disciples of Jesus Christ.

III. JESUS CHRIST THE REDEEMER: RESURRECTION AND THE KINGDOM

The Christology focusing on the teachings of Jesus and the specifics of discipleship needs to be supplemented by an interpretation of the person of Jesus Christ as redeemer of the world. The need comes from the point stressed earlier that Jesus is taken by Christians to be, with the Holy spirit, the actualization of God's love restoring the covenant. Jesus is not only the teacher and model for imitation; in those roles he is like many other religious founders such as Gautama Buddha, Confucius, and Muhammed. The Christian claim in addition is that Jesus himself was God acting in history to make a salvific difference. In a crucial way, different from other religious founders, Jesus is taken to be divine himself. The New Testament epistles and the Gospel of John are the main sources for the identification of Jesus with God, although it was only in the later theological speculations that the precise doctrine of the Trinity was elaborated. This section shall focus on the historical presence of God in the world, in the person of Jesus Christ. The next chapter shall deal with the Trinitarian conception of Jesus and the Godhead.

The argument was made in chapter 8 that Jesus, in his own life and through the witness to him made in the early generations, actually transformed the religious situation so that people accepting his gospel are saved in a sense other people are not. As sin entered the world with "Adam," it is overcome by Jesus, the "second man Adam," according to Paul (Romans 5:12–21; I Corinthians 15:21–49). Christians date their era by the distinction brought by Jesus' historical work of redemption. The question for Christology, of course, is the precise nature of the salvation Jesus worked.

Salvation in the New Testament meant several things on the superficial level (Fredriksen, 1988). For John, salvation had to do principally with joining God, being in the presence of the Father. For Mark, on the other hand, salvation is being gathered with the elect by Jesus at the end of the age (Mark 13:26–27). Mark's Jesus presented a new model of salvation: the righteous one who was defeated and suffered, but triumphed through the resurrection, showing that loving humility is stronger than apparent power. Mark's theme was how Jesus was consistently misunderstood by friends and enemies alike, who looked for something different in the Son of Man.

Unlike Mark who took Jesus to be alien within Israel, Matthew traced Jesus' identity back to Abraham, founder of the Jewish people, and forward to postresurrection appearances that extend the mission of Jesus through the disciples to the Gentiles (Mark began abruptly with Jesus' baptism and ended with the empty tomb). For Matthew, salvation meant being brought to the elect by obeying Jesus' specific commandments, and Jesus was presented as judge of Jews, Gentiles, and Christians alike; Matthew's chief problem was with people who failed to appreciate or, worse, betrayed Jesus.

Luke extended Jesus' identity farther back, beyond the founding of the Jewish tradition to Adam, the founding human being; Israel was

represented, not as rejecting Jesus as it always had the prophets (the way
Matthew thought), but as awaiting him and predicting his coming; and
Luke's book, in the portion we call Acts, extends well beyond Jesus' own
life to the continued life of Jesus in the Church. Salvation for Luke is
participation in the larger body of Christ.

For Paul and his school (for instance the author of Colossians),
salvation is participation in the cosmic drama in which Jesus is the major
player; as he died, we died with him in baptism; as he was raised, we
already in this life are with Jesus at the right hand of God. Through Jesus
Christ the world was created. And in our flawed history, Paul advised:

> Let the same mind be in you that was in Christ Jesus,
> who, though he was in the form of God,
>> did not regard equality with God
>> as something to be exploited,
> but emptied himself,
>> taking the form of a slave,
>> being born in human likeness.
> And being found in human form
>> he humbled himself
>> and became obedient to the point of death—
>> even death on a cross.
> Therefore God also highly exalted him
>> and gave him the name
>> that is above every name,
> so that at the name of Jesus
>> every knee should bend,
>> in heaven and on earth and under the earth,
> and every tongue should confess
>> that Jesus Christ is Lord,
>> to the glory of God the Father.
> (Philippians 2:5-11)

The point of salvation, for Paul, is to participate in the divine life
through participating in Jesus' resurrection; John, by contrast, who
equally emphasized Jesus' participation in the Father, speaks much less
of salvation by resurrection than of salvation through the possession in
this life of the Father through the Holy Spirit.

Underneath these differences of emphasis and of the sense of the
"religious problem," there lies a complex but common conception of
salvation. It is that, by virtue of God's action in Jesus Christ, the broken
covenant can be renewed, or the Kingdom of Heaven realized, in such a

form that people participate in the character of Jesus. To understand this, we must first note carefully the things that are *not* essential to this salvation.

Although resurrection of the saved is central to Paul's expression of salvation, it is not necessarily meant in a literal sense. On the one hand, being raised from the dead is not itself eschatologically special: no one took Lazarus or the others Jesus returned to life to be saved in the religious sense. What is special in resurrection is God's power in Jesus to accomplish it, first for Jesus' "patients," then in Jesus himself, and finally in those who are "fellow heirs" (Romans 8:17; Ephesians 3:6) with Jesus.

On the other hand, resurrection is the symbol of God's power to defeat death and create us as "new beings" (II Corinthians 5:17; Galatians 6:15; Ephesians 4:24; Colossians 3:10), thus restoring the covenant. Whether this is conceived to take place in this life, as in the "realized" eschatology of John and the author of Colossians, or in some future life as in the cosmic fulfillment eschatology of Paul's letters, the point is that death, the power of the broken covenant, is overcome. The result of God's work in Christ is that now we are free of bondage to sin and are enabled to get on with the life of love of neighbor and God. And *that*, the life of freedom and love serving the restored covenant, is itself participation in the life of God. The fulfillment of individuals is in the whole divine life, irrespective of whether there is a heavenly life for the subjective individuals after death.

Although political imagery is often used to depict the reign of God, salvation is not tied necessarily to a political transformation of history. Of course, such a political transformation to establish the earthly kingdom of righteousness was the early belief, probably the belief of Jesus himself. But that did not take place in the first generation of Christians, or the second or third, or in ours. In contrast to both Jews and Gentiles who looked to an apocalyptic transformation of history, the Christians came to understand salvation as the renewal of the covenant within the life of God who transcends history. For our part, our salvation requires living in such a way as to influence things toward the renewed covenant. This means seeking personal sanctification as well as a social life of righteousness, piety, faithfulness, and hope. In our historical situation we are enjoined to go to the death for God's Kingdom, but not to abandon hope if the Kingdom fails to be manifested in ordinary affairs. Our hope is in God's infinite love. Justice cannot be abandoned for pie in the sky by and by. But neither is salvation pie here and now.

The tension between historical life being modelled on crucifixion, which is the shape of salvation here, and the sense of salvation that involves enjoying God's love, led Christians to understand providence to be a mystery. As Calvin put it, providence is "immense," by which he meant it is unmeasurable, and *shālōm* is incomprehensible when viewed at large. Perhaps the unmeasurability consists in the fact that every measure assumes some finite standpoint, for instance the welfare of the Christians, or human beings generally, whereas the scale of the created world bound in covenant is far broader than that. Only God can determine the true fulfillment of excellence in each thing relative to the others. With regard to righteousness, which wholly binds us but not wholly God, we of course are finite and therefore our perspective defines suffering and injustice.

IV. THE UNIVERSALITY AND PARTICULARITY OF SALVATION

For some Christians, there is only one salvation, that deriving from Jesus Christ; all other people are not saved but damned. They cite, for instance, John 14:6, "Jesus said to him [Thomas], 'I am the way, and the truth, and the life; no one comes to the Father, except through me,'" Damnation was interpreted in the apocalyptic passages of the New Testament in terms of a time of divine judgment at which the saved shall be separated from the damned who shall languish in punishment and separation from God. Kenneth Cracknell (1986) has shown how limited a view of the New Testament authors this is.

Although Christian salvation is presented as universal, available to all who accept Jesus as Christ, not everyone does accept Christ, and there might be other senses of salvation available to them. Some construe salvation in terms of enlightenment, which overlaps much of the Christian notion but is not its central component; Christianity rejected its gnostic strain which led in the direction of enlightenment as the fundamental metaphor. Others, for instance Taoists, construe salvation as living in conformity with nature; related to that yet others, for instance Confucians, take it to be the development of a cultural life that fulfills the potentials of both matter and creative moral form; again, there is overlap with the Christian form of salvation but not identity.

In contrast to these conceptions of salvation, Christians believe that it consists in relating to a particular historical figure and living in a particular way in a particular, if temporally and spatially extended, community. Among the historical and theistic religions, Christianity differs from Judaism by the Christian rejection of a wholly historical form of messianic fulfillment. It differs from Islam by affirming salvation as love in priority to justice. Christianity differs from all the other religions by its emphasis on the cult of Jesus: Christian salvation is the impressing of the person of Jesus on the new covenant by virtue of incorporation of his image in the lives of disciples. This is Christianity's chief particularity.

The emphasis on the particularity of different approaches to salvation is, by itself, wholly agnostic with respect to whether the approaches other than the Christian have merit. Perhaps some do and some do not. Just as the Christian tradition has often undertaken internal criticism and reformation, so the other traditions have internal divisions, and not all can be equally authentic. As to the particulars, the point is that the determinations of salvation are simply different, not competitive regarding the same sense of the religious goal. The experience of dialogue among world religions has been that deeply spiritual people in any tradition feel a camaraderie with deeply spiritual people in other traditions, a camaraderie greater than any feels with the superficial cultural hangers-on in their own tradition. Perhaps that feeling of being in the same place adumbrates a deeper sense of salvation than any particularized in the various traditions, a sense of unspoken and perhaps unspeakable agreement. As for Christians, however deep and culture-transcending their spiritual practice might be, they are cultic disciples of Jesus Christ.

Therefore, it is a plain historical fact, not a theological conjecture or dogma for belief, that Jesus did change history, for better or worse; the Christians and their works are that. Beyond this, it is a matter of Christian faith that salvation in Christ is a genuine salvation, *the* salvation from the sins of the broken covenant that are revealed in Jesus Christ. If we were to say that sin and repentance could be defined antecedently and in neutrality with respect to Jesus Christ and his reception, then it might be possible to compare various traditions regarding salvation to see which best fulfills the job. This seems most plausible in the comparative case of Christianity with Judaism, because both take the core of their salvation metaphors from the same Hebrew Bible. Yet, they clearly differ in the meanings assigned to the messiah, which is the key notion between them. And from this they differ in their interpretation of the meaning of the promises of God and of the nature of their fulfillment. From this they differ in defining the community of the faithful, and its place: for Jews, Israel is home base, whereas, for Christians, we are pilgrims passing through someone else's home. In a strict sense, Christians would agree with Jews that salvation in the Jewish sense of messianic return and the conversion of the world to righteousness has not yet occurred.

Because God is creator of all, and nothing happens that is not part of that creation, God was in Christ accomplishing the Christian salvation. God is also in the Torah, in the Muslim community, and in all the other religious traditions; but whether God is there in genuinely salvific ways, salvific in those other senses, is here a matter of conjecture. A crucial part of the theology of dialogue is the construction of common but vague categories by which the religions can be compared as different specifications of vaguely common truths (Neville, 1991).

Nevertheless, Christians, reflecting on the sweep of history, must insist that the whole of the world's cultures across time and space are included in the covenant of creation, and thus subject to renewal by the actions of Christians. Part of the gospel is loving those who are alien to ourselves, even alien to our religion. Disciples of Jesus Christ are a small saving remnant. Whether people in the other traditions pay attention to the Christian claim for the universality of the covenant-creation is another matter. They may be like the Jews who were deeply annoyed when Karl Rahner called them "anonymous Christians." The Christian sense of world mission depends on this commitment to the universality of the covenant; and its effectiveness depends on Christians making the Christian sense of salvation plausible, and with it the Christian sense of sin. Several religious traditions regarding the religious problem and its answer might be plausible together in an intellectual sense. That they can be made compatible cultically is a more difficult matter, although all known religious cultures nowadays are amalgams of diverse antecedents. In dialogue, Christians experience difference in considerable unity with people of other faiths.

Readings in Key Texts:

1. Aquinas, *SCG*, Book 4, chaps. 1–26.
2. Aquinas, *ST*, I-I, ques. 34–35, 43.
3. Augustine, no reading.
4. Barth, chaps. 5–8.
5. Calvin, *Inst.*, Book 2, chaps. 9–12.
6. Cobb and Griffin, *PT*, chap. 6.
7. Ferm, *TWLT*, chaps. 8 (by Boff), 10 (by Sobrino), 12 (by Gulilea).
8. Hildegard, *Sci.*, Book 3, Vision 8.
9. Luther, no reading.
10. Rahner, *Found.*, chap 6, sections 1–6.
11. Ruether, no reading.
12. Schleiermacher, *CF*, pp. 374–376 425–275.
13. Tillich, *Sys.*, Vol. 3, section 2: B.

Christology: The Divinity of Christ

I. A LOGOS CHRISTOLOGY

Whereas chapter 11 developed some of the main themes of the historical particularity of the person of Jesus and the elements of salvation attendant upon that, it is necessary now to attend more directly to the senses in which Jesus is to be understood as divine. Many conceptual models have been employed for this in the history of Christian theology, and the one to be developed here is usually called a "Logos Christology." Jesus Christ is the incarnation of the divine Logos, fully divine by virtue of the divinity of the Logos, fully human as the person in whom the Logos is incarnate. The biblical text for the source of the metaphors in this theory is the prologue to the Gospel of John:

> In the beginning was the Word, and the Word was with God, and the Word was God. He was in the beginning with God. All things came into being through him, and without him not one thing came into being. What has come into being in him was life, and the life was the light of all people. The light shines in the darkness, and the darkness did not overcome it.
>
> There was a man sent from God, whose name was John. He came as a witness to testify to the light, so that all might believe through him. He himself was not the light, but he came to testify to the light. The true light, which enlightens everyone, was coming into the world.
>
> He was in the world, and the world came into being through him, yet the world did not know him. He came to what was his own, and his own people did not accept him. But to all who received him, who believed in his name, he gave power to become children of God, who were born, not of blood or of the will of the flesh or of the will of man, but of God.

And the Word became flesh and lived among us, and we have seen his
glory, the glory as of a father's only son, full of grace and truth. (John
testified to him, and cried out, "This is he of whom I said, 'He who comes
after me ranks ahead of me, because he was before me.' ") From his fulness
we have all received, grace upon grace. The law indeed was given through
Moses; grace and truth came through Jesus Christ. No one has ever seen
God. It is God the only Son who is close to the Father's heart, who has
made him known.

The notion of the "Logos" came to John from many quarters of
Greek philosophy, from the Jewish tradition of wisdom or sophia (Cady,
Ronan, and Taussig, 1986), and from Roman notions of order and law.
John connected it: (1) with the Genesis 1 creation account, paraphrased
in the first statements of the prologue, (2) with Jesus' special depiction of
God as the Father who at once is expressed in the Logos and is the source
of the historical Jesus, and (3) with a special embodiment in the historical
Jesus who was pointed to by the prophets and John the Baptist and who
died after having been misunderstood. Although the Logos in a basic
sense is in everything that is created, and might be exemplified in special
ways by prophets and teachers, in John's theory the Logos is *incarnate* in
Jesus, a unique kind of embodiment. ("Incarnate" is a word with Latin
roots for "embodied" or "enfleshed.")
    The chapters above have developed a contemporary theory of the
Logos as the elements of order (including moral order), components, actuality, and value that go into any determinate thing as conditions of its
being created. To pull the earlier discussions into a proper doctrine of the
Logos, two points need to be made.
    It has become customary to associate Logos principally with form,
to the relative neglect of the elements of components, actuality, and
value. Partly this custom has arisen from the influence of Neo-Platonism
which depicts the Godhead as first Pure Oneness, then Sheer Difference
(form), and finally Soul moving to integrate unity in difference. On the
Neo-Platonic view, there is an ontological order moving from the most
real Oneness which overflows into the Dyad or Duality of formal Difference, which in turn overflows into the World Soul, which overflows
into many finite souls of various descending grades and finally into matter. Only the last material "emanations" would count for what Christians call the created world.[1] Neo-Platonic thought-forms have been
tempting to Christians because of the Trinitarian character of the
Godhead and because Christians have tended to blame the body for sin,
or at least have interpreted sin on the analogy of bodily lusts that puts us
in bondage.
    To the contrary, however, there are no forms without components
to be formed; form and components are created together, and exist only

insofar as there is actual creation with the actual value of having those actual components harmonized that actual way. The Neo-Platonic preference for form over multiplicity and materiality is an unchecked imposition of the masculine reading of righteous order. Rather, we should say that, just as nothing is made without form, nothing is made without components to be formed, without actual existence, and without the achievement of some worth.

As surprising as the need to balance form with the other elements is the need to avoid asserting that the Logos is some *one* thing. The usual image people have of the Logos is some superpattern for the cosmos, unified and capable of existing by itself or with the Father but apart from the created world. Yet what the Bible asserts is only an order of creation or dependency: The Logos is that through which the world is made, and it is eternal with the Father whereas anything in the world is temporal. Nothing identifies the Logos except references to the created world; without those references there would be nothing to say about the Logos. Because the Logos is the transcendental structure of the creative act, and the act is eternal in the sense of creating time itself as well as all temporal things, the Logos is what makes the Father the source.

The Logos is not some one thing that exists in the Godhead in abstraction from the created world; yet it is not simply the created world. The four elements of the Logos are real only in their togetherness in the creating of the actual world. Although they are specific and distinguishable from one another in abstraction from the world, in the world itself they are unified in concrete things. To speak only of their unity in things is not helpful, however, because then there is no way to describe the Logos except to say that the world embodies God's creative love. "God's creative love" is an empty notion on the ontological level if it does not follow upon an understanding of how love unifies form, components, actuality and value.

A Logos Christology is one that understands Jesus Christ to be the special and unique incarnation of the Logos. How can the Logos as described here be "incarnate," and how does incarnation differ from other expressions or exemplifications of the Logos?

II. INCARNATION AND THE TWO NATURES OF CHRIST

In one sense, the Logos is in everything created, as that through which created things are made determinate. Hence everything is an exemplification or expression of the Logos insofar as it is determinate. In a second sense, certain individuals can exemplify the Logos in special ways. This is to say, they can, in their teachings or lives, show how to put ideal form with ideal components in an ideally actual historical context with an ideal result in value. Teachers represent how to do this, heroes manifest some special version of it in their lives, and great religious founders such as Moses, Confucius, Lao-tze, Muhammed, and Gautama Buddha exemplify the Logos through both representation and manifestation. Jesus was a founder and special exemplification of the Logos in at least this sense.

But in a third sense, incarnation is more than exemplification. Incarnation is the presence of the Logos in Jesus such that the historical person of Jesus does a special work to complete the creation of the world. Specifically, as the original human condition is to be in covenant, in the ways expressed above, and that original human condition is broken or distorted by sin, God restores the covenant, thereby completing the creation made incomplete by the fall, in the historical person of Jesus. Were there no sin or fall, the creation might be complete without Jesus as redeemer. But there is sin, and the covenant is broken; the restorative work of God in Christ is thus a new creation, completing the old, according to the Christian gospel. What are the considerations that make sense of this?

First, the covenantal character of the human condition must be taken to be an ontological matter. That is, part of the very creation of human beings is for them to be in covenant, so that a breaking of the covenant is a breaking of human nature. The covenant is not made inoperative or nonobligatory by sin, only distorted and somewhat ineffectual. Restoration of the covenant is thus the recompleting of the original creation, as it were.

Second, the character of the fall and redemption must be conceived as historical in a sense. Not that humankind fell in the actions of common ancestors, as if the Adam and Eve story were to be taken literally, but that the condition of life in the broken covenant was an historical reality. Then, at a certain time in history, something historical happened (the life of Jesus) to change the conditions of the broken covenant. Precisely because of what Jesus taught and did, and because of the response of people informing the Church, God's power to redeem the covenant was loosed in the world. The historical "work" of Christ, discussed in the previous chapter, is what makes the real, historical, ontological difference. After Christ there is not just a new doctrine but a new power at work in the world, in the disciples of Jesus.

Third, the new power is meaningful only in historical terms. If there were not the tradition of the Hebrew people articulating the covenant, the messiah redeemer, and all the rest that gives significance to the "names of Jesus" (Son of God, Son of Man, Son of David, Holy One of God, High Priest, and so forth), then Jesus' actions would not have had the significance they did, even if they physically had been the same.

Lacking that significance, they would not have unleashed the redemptive power of God. Because of this, John wove the Baptist's prophetic identification of Jesus with the Messiah of Israel into the abstract discussion of the Logos. Jesus was historical in two senses, first in being a flesh and blood person, second in having an historical identity as determined by his role relative to Israel. The particular historical identity of Jesus, combining both senses, was to embody the Logos in a way so as to redeem and hence recomplete the creation.

To recapitulate the doctrine, Jesus Christ is wholly God in being the incarnation of the Logos, combining in his wholly human identity the particular synthesis of form, components, actuality, and value that restores the covenant and recompletes the creation. Put the other way around, Jesus Christ is wholly human in giving flesh and blood, historically particular, identity to the creative power of God redeeming the world.

Furthermore, it is the historical particularity of Jesus that is the unifying element combining the two natures, divine and human. There is no need to appeal to an underlying substance, or a person beyond the human and divine. Nor are the humanity and divinity funny kinds of essences that need to be combined in a substance in ways that are usually mutually exclusive. Rather, because of the historical identity of the man Jesus, and because of God's creating an historical world, whose ontological status is corrupted by historically contingent sin, Jesus is the redeemer.

At this point, it is necessary to remark on certain elements often claimed for Christology that are not rendered in this theory.

In what sense can Jesus be said to pre-exist his earthly life? As a conscious person, Jesus of course cannot be said to pre-exist his birth, because that would destroy his human nature; it simply does not make sense. On the other hand, the Logos in general is present in all temporal parts of the created world, those events that preceded Jesus as well as those contemporary and subsequent. In a deeper sense, too, the entire creation is eternal, and the historical event of Jesus Christ in that deeper sense is eternal. It is more than just the dates of Jesus' life, though the "more" is not more dates. The "more" is the total role of Jesus in the inclusive life of God in which Jesus is the redeemer of the world. Because of that role, Jesus, not merely the Logos incarnate in him, is God.

Is Jesus God for non-Christian peoples in a sense that makes his historical identity an incarnation of the Logos? That question requires analysis into parts.

One part is the question about people who do not understand the human condition in terms of the covenant, nor identify with the tradition of the Messiah. For these people, Christians can argue objectively that the covenant analysis is better than its alternatives, that it has effective analogues in some other traditions, and that where it is unknown, it would be helpful to be known. Insofar as the covenant notion can be stretched to accommodate other traditions, non-Christians can understand the completion of creation in terms of renewal of the covenant.

But could they accept that Jesus is the redeeming completer of creation without Israel's understanding of history, of the Messiah, and of the importance of historical particularity, another part of the question? That is doubtful. The issue for Christian missions, then, is whether the teachings of Israel about the historical context for making sense of Jesus Christ are compatible with the ways non-Christian cultures think about related matters, or are in competition, or simply are a new dimension that can be added on to the culture.

Does Jesus Christ effect the redemption of parts of the world and other cultures that cannot relate to the particularities mentioned above? In one sense the answer is negative, because the particular meaning of Christian salvation is renewal undertaken because of the power of resurrection in Jesus, a renewal taking the form of Christian discipleship. Christian discipleship is different in small and large ways from other kinds of discipleship, and from no discipleship. In another sense, the incarnation of God in Christ is but one element in a vast divine love that repairs the covenant in a multitude of ways. Christians as such are in no position to limit God's redeeming love and activity in other peoples, places, and times. There are no grounds for cosmic exclusivism in Christology. Yet, the particular character of Christian salvation, with its necessary reference to the history of Israel and the specific character of Christ imitated in the Church, is exclusive of all but those relating to that particular character. There are no incarnations of the Logos besides Jesus because incarnation requires the historical identity of Jesus. There may well be other salvifically effective expressions of the Logos.

III. CHRIST AND THE HOLY SPIRIT: THE *FILIOQUE*

The discussion of Christology seems to be of a whole because of the wholeness in the person of Jesus Christ. Yet it is peculiarly truncated without a discussion of the Holy Spirit.

The Holy Spirit, in general, is the divine creative act, giving rise to each thing in the world, relating them ontologically as harmonies with essential and conditional features; and, in creating the world the Holy spirit also gives God the character of being source. With regard to human beings, living in the broken covenant, that creative activity involves particular nudges toward the restoration of creation. The Holy Spirit in Jesus Christ, that which creates him in relation to the rest of creation, is the agency by which his historical identity is formed to incarnate the Logos. The special and particular work of the Holy Spirit for Christians, however, is to witness to the Christ.

Part of the historic identity of Jesus essential to redemption is that his resurrection was interpreted as displaying the power of God that can be appropriated to others, that his teachings were interpreted to be true and to have redemptive power, and that discipleship to him constitutes a path of salvation defining the Church. Without people actually following out the implications of Jesus' life, Jesus would not be the redeemer in actuality. The particularly Christian identity of the Holy Spirit is to witness to Christ in the lives of subsequent people, interpreting the Scriptures, inspiring congregations, entering into individuals' spiritual life, and actually fulfilling the course of redemption. From the appearance of the Spirit at Jesus' baptism through the Pentecost experience, Jesus was who he was because of the explicit witness of the Spirit.

In the early Church, controversies about how to understand the divinity of Christ preceded those about the status of the Spirit, and were far more vociferous. Partly this was so because the Holy Spirit seemed so obvious as the startling and self-authenticating presence of God in congregational and personal spiritual life. Partly also it was so because the question of whether the Spirit is a full-fledged Person of the Trinity comes up only when Christology forces recognition of such notions as "Persons of the Trinity." As the act of creation mediating between the creative Source and the Logos through which the world is created, the Spirit is interdefined with the other Persons of the Trinity.

A fundamental issues of pneumatology (study of the Holy Spirit) continues to divide the Church, however (the separation of the Eastern Orthodox from the Roman Catholic communions in 1054 was allegedly focused on this issue, although other historical factors may have been far more important). The creed adopted by the West asserts that the Spirit "proceeds from the Father and the Son" ("and the Son" is *filioque* in Latin), whereas the East restricted the procession of the Spirit to the Father alone. East and West agreed that the identity of Jesus Christ requires the Spirit, and that the Father is source because of both the creative Spirit and the Logos through which the creative act receives actual determinate expression in the creation. They disagreed over whether the Spirit must have the form of Jesus Christ or might take other forms as well. The details of the early debate are not all to the point here (see Grillmeier, 1965: chap. 1); but the issue arises with new urgency in this time of dialogue among world religions.

We may suppose that the Holy Spirit proceeds from the Father with creative power and from the Son with the function of creating things with the dimensions of the Logos. But does the Spirit have to have the form of the historical Jesus Christ? Many contemporary Roman Catholic thinkers, defending the classic Western position, answer affirmatively.[2] There is no manifestation of the Holy Spirit, they say, that fails to have the form of Christ. In the past ages, the inference from this was that only Christianity was valid religion, and that God acts only through Christian forms. Recently, experience has shown that many non-Christians are deeply spiritual, and the folly of attempting to limit God's powers of salvation to Christian forms has become obvious. In the face of this, theologians affirming the *filioque* have developed the notion of the Cosmic Christ, a Christ not of historical particularity but of mystical cosmic identity. Consequently, when persons or institutions of other living faiths show the apparent marks of the Spirit, it can be said that the Cosmic Christ is manifest there in ways foreign to the historical Jesus. Jews, Buddhists, Muslims, and Hindus, then, can be called "anonymous Christians" even though they explicitly reject Christianity and the central Christological claims about Jesus (see the subtle discussion of this point in Rahner, 1978: 311–321).

There are two difficulties with the strategy of the Cosmic Christ. First, it is offensive to seriously religious people who define themselves explicitly to be non-Christian. Second, it dilutes the historical particularity of Jesus Christ, smoothing off the edges and turning him into a representation of general spiritual cosmic religiosity. As a result, being a Christian is not much different from being a Saivite, or Buddhist, or Taoist, or Cabbalistic Jew. Yet this is deliberately to fudge religious differences. It might turn out that all paths of spiritual perfection lead to the same perfected state. It might turn out that the particularities of the several spiritual paths are only trivially different. It might turn out that the various traditions overlap and dovetail so that each fills in lacunae or weaknesses in others. But then again, it might not. The question is an empirical one, to be decided only after years of serious dialogue, sharing, and communication at all levels of abstraction and concrete practice. To force an "in principle" agreement is unwarranted both because it restricts the forms of God's saving activity and because it imposes Christian terms as conditions for the debate.

The better strategy is to loosen up the claims about the *filioque* and say that the Holy Spirit always has the form of the Logos, but not the form of the Logos as incarnated in the historical Jesus Christ. The Holy Spirit then can be acknowledged in any expression of the Logos. For Christianity in particular, it is essential to acknowledge that the Logos is expressed in the Torah, the law defining the meaning and significance of Jesus. Expression in law is different from expression in a person who teaches the Logos in a particularly apt way, which in turn is different from its expression in a person who exemplifies it in other ways. Buddha,

Confucius, Muhammed, Lao-tze, and many other religious "founders," express the Logos in ways different from what Christians claim about incarnation. Those ways are different from one another, and none would be claimed by adherents of their respective faiths to be competitive versions of incarnation. Even the Avatars of Hinduism are not claimed to be historically defined incarnations, because Hinduism does not acknowledge historical identity of the sort supposed by the cult of Jesus Christ.

IV. CHRIST AND HISTORY

The question of the nature of history has emerged as one of the most central questions for Christianity and its doctrine of Spirit. Beginning perhaps with the rise of Enlightenment historical consciousness at the end of the eighteenth century, running through the historical investigation of scripture and the "quest for the historical Jesus," and culminating in the theory of "salvation history" in the mid-twentieth century (Cullmann, 1962), a strand of Christianity has attempted to give history the form of a single story. Emphasizing the sovereignty of God and leaning heavily on metaphors of God as an individual cosmic agent, this theological movement has represented history as the story of God's dealing with people, a story with definiteness and a univocal meaning (Altizer, 1977, 1985). For various reasons, this is hopelessly reductive. At the very least, univocal salvation history must be rejected because any historical incident plays roles in many individual stories, often with quite opposite meanings. There is no one meaning to any event (Tracy, 1987). Not even a single human being can be reduced to a story; a biography is always a highly selective representation.

Two positions about history therefore seem to be incumbent upon theologically astute Christians. One is an openness to the approaches to history, or lack of such approaches, in other religions and in secular culture. "Openness" does not mean agreement, only a willingness to investigate and take the opposing arguments seriously. One of the essential tasks of comparative religions is to show the variety of approaches to history manifest in the great spiritual traditions.

The second Christian position about history is that the history defining Jesus as the Christ should be seen as multifarious and ambiguous. Perhaps Christianity need not approve all the culturally vigorous approaches to history. Nevertheless, a wider variety than usually acknowledged needs to be lifted up to make sense of Jesus' historical identity. An illustration that has repeatedly arisen here is the recovery of the feminine in the Judeo-Christian tradition. The unique one-sidedness of Yahweh's acts of war, reducing history to the oppositional dichotomies of struggle, needs to be balanced with the cyclical and repetitive elements of the feminine piety toward nature on scales irrelevant to human affairs.

Another illustration lies in the relation of Christianity to Israel. According to the model of the unique story, Christianity must supersede the Hebrew religion, displacing rabbinic Judaism completely. Yet there seems to be little Christian ground for saying that God ceased working with the Jews according to the life of Torah simply because a non-Torah-oriented Gentile community arose as disciples of Jesus. Christian and Jewish history have paralleled one another in the Common Era with a notoriously bad fit. Although Christian history should be seen as ambiguous, polysemic, and multifarious, the limitation on that is whatever is required to understand Jesus as the redeemer through whom our life can be brought to perfection in the life of God.

Christians hold at least this much to be true, whatever other saving activity is manifest in other faiths and cultures. Christians hold this even when faced with the wretched perversions of the mind of Christ that have been established in the name of Christianity. Christians hold to this even when contemplating the scale of nature in creation extending beyond human history. Who knows what civilizations of intelligent creatures have arisen throughout the galaxies? Who knows what their "condition" is? Or what would "save" them if salvation is their problem? Christians have been extraordinarily parochial in assuming an exclusive or even very important place for the human sphere. Within the cosmic temporal and spatial span of creation, human history might be but a speck, and God's love for us but a wee quark of the totality of divine love, all of which bears the form of the Logos. Nevertheless, within that human sphere, within people who can identify with the history in which Jesus has identity as the Christ, the way of Christ is a way of salvation.

Jesus is the Christ because in actual history he is actually salvific in the sense of transforming the hearts of people and, through that, transforming other elements of creation to work toward restoration of the covenant. The actual course of this history, ambivalent and polysemic as it is, is located in the Church, the cult of Jesus Christ. Because of this locus of the actuality of Jesus as savior, the Church is called the Body of Christ.

Readings in Key Texts:

1. Aquinas, *SCG*, Book 4, chaps. 27–49.
2. Aquinas, *ST*, I-I, ques. 36–42.
3. Augustine, no reading.

4. Barth, *Credo*, chaps. 9–11.
5. Calvin, *Inst.*, Book 2, chaps. 13–17.
6. Cobb and Griffin, no reading.
7. Ferm, *TWLT*, chap. 26 (by Song).
8. Hildegard, no reading.
9. Luther, no reading.
10. Rahner, *Found.*, chap 6, sections 7–10.
11. Ruether, chap. 5.
12. Schleiermacher, *CF*, pp. 377–424.
13. Tillich, *Sys.*, Vol. 2, pt. 3, section 1: C–D.

The Holy Spirit in the Church

A great many Christians, surely those with the curiosity to read a *Primer*, regard the Church with ambivalent judgment, loving it for what it ought to be and sometimes is, hating it for its failures and wickedness. At its worst, organized Christianity has been the cause of great wickedness. In our century two world wars have been fought between Christian nations, each side blessed by at least some of its Church bodies. European Christianity's missionary efforts over the last three hundred years have been inextricably tied to imperialism with its attendant evils. The Christian Church often has been a principal agent in the suppression of the public expressions of women, homosexuals, and minorities. At its best, the Church's effective discipline has required structures of authority that hurt those who bump them the wrong way. This is as true of "free church" polities where authority lies in the discernment of Spirit as of hierarchical polities with official authoritative structures.

The temptation is to separate the normative definition of the Church from any actual organization and say something like, the Church is wherever the Holy Spirit operates in the world. Paul Tillich (1963), for instance, discussed not the Church, but the Spiritual Community which was ambiguously related to the churches, sometimes expressed there but often hidden. This strategy might in fact be the final court of appeal in the long run. In the short run, however, it fosters an ecclesiastical gnosticism, degrading the actuality of the churches. The Church must be actual or it is nothing; if the Church is not actual, then Jesus Christ is not the actual savior.

The Church is better identified as the actual churches as normed by the mind of Christ.[1] The actual churches are all those groups that iden-

tify themselves as a cult of Jesus Christ under some or other set of symbols. In some terms or other, the groups conceive of themselves as embracing disciples or followers of Jesus Christ. The churches are the
Church insofar as they are subject to the norms comprising the mind of
Christ; how they actualize those norms is another matter—it is the
Church either way. Those norms are not the same as any church's
representations of the norms; rather, the true mind of Christ is the norm
by which representations are to be judged. The polities of the churches
are not normative in themselves; rather, they ought to be as the mind of
Christ would dictate for the churches' conditions. Thus, they must take
into account varying traditions and cultures, varying social classes, varying personalities, varying ethnic groups and hosts of other varying
historical elements. The Church exists wherever people gather to
discipline themselves to continue the ministry of Jesus in their own
neighborhood.

The Church, so identified, is always to be described as under judgment, as it were. Any church situation should be understood in terms of
how well or poorly it embodies the norms of the mind of Christ for its
situation. Even the German churches supportive of the Nazis were part
of the Church, albeit a very corrupt part. The imperialist collaborations
of the European and American missionary churches are genuine parts of
the Church, albeit counterproductive to the mind of Christ. The depreca-
tions of women, homosexuals, non-Christians (especially Jews), and
various minorities are also elements that have characterized the genuine
Church, but should be recognized as failures of, indeed offenses against,
the mind of Christ. The other side of all this is that, where the churches
have in fact been the communities where the mind of Christ has entered
into the actual salvation of people and the renovation of their lives and
the institutions of society, that is the normatively positive description of
the Church.

The mind of Christ present in the world after the historical presence
of Jesus himself is the Holy Spirit in special Christian form. The Holy
Spirit is present in any created thing, of course, but present as the effective witness to Christ in the Church. There may be other gracious saving
forms of the Holy Spirit—God's grace cannot be limited. But at least the
Christian Church is defined as the community which exists by the norms
of the mind of Christ being brought to bear by the Spirit on gatherings of
self-identified disciples and those whom they touch.

The discussion here, at the *Primer* level, has four principal topics:
sacraments, church life in the community, the Church in relation to God,
and the relation of Christianity as a special cult to other religions.

I. SACRAMENTS: BAPTISM AND EUCHARIST

Protestants generally recognize two sacraments, baptism and the eucharist (or Lord's Supper or Holy Communion). Both have to do with membership in the cultic community of Christians and thus with the special means of grace associated with that community. Baptism is the rite of entrance into the community, and the eucharist is the rite of exercising membership in that community as such. A great many things about the community are special means of grace, including the fellowship, the teachings, community service, music, liturgies, and so forth. The rites claimed also to be sacraments by Christian groups other than Protestants—confirmation, marriage, confession, penance, extreme unction, burial, ordination, and sometimes others—are surely means of grace, although they do not have the meta-graceful significance of baptism and the eucharist, namely, affirmation of membership in the community of the cultic graces of Jesus Christ. Baptism and the eucharist are the special cultic graces by which people gain access to the cultic graces of Christianity.

Baptism is the rite of acquiring membership in the Christian community. Reflective of the salvific grace of God coming to us because of God's love rather than our merit, baptism is essentially something done to us. We are submerged under the water and then raised up. This symbolizes dying to our old life, to the world, to bondage to sin, dying as a participation in the death of Jesus, and then being raised up to new life by God. We are washed in the baptismal waters of repentance and forgiven our sins, as we mimic John the Baptist's prefiguration of Jesus. But Christian baptism is more than a restoration of righteousness: it is a taking on of the death and resurrection of Christ and thereby becoming a part of the Church.

Whether baptized in infancy or adulthood, the rite symbolizes God's action to draw us in to the saving cult of Jesus Christ. That is a pricey action, costing Jesus' struggle of death and rebirth, and so serious to us that it is to be understood in those extreme alpha-omega terms. Though something done to us, not by us, membership in the Christian cult is not something in which we are wholly passive. For adults, from the earliest days of the Christian community there has been a period of instruction prior to baptism during which the candidates, the "catechumens," study what Christianity means. Although the content of that study has varied widely over the centuries and elaborate "catechisms" have been developed and criticized, from the second century on the test has been to understand and affirm a version of the

Apostles' Creed. When Christians today recite that creed, it is less a statement of theological doctrine on their part than a reaffirmation of their baptism and an act that both symbolizes and in part constitutes their unity with all other members of the Christian community. For Christians baptized as infants or young children, subsequent confirmation studies are crucial for the understanding of baptism, that is, of membership, itself.

The Christian community has been described here as the *cult* of Jesus Christ. The word "cult" is not used in the sociological sense to signify a sect rather than a highly institutionalized denomination (H. R. Niebuhr, 1929). Rather it is used to suggest the cultivation of character. Specifically, the Christian community is aimed to draw people together to take upon themselves the mind of Christ, and to do in the world together what is implied by Christ's character to renew the covenant. Therefore, everything that happens in the Church—its worship, preaching, teachings, fellowship, place, architecture, art, and myriad of actions in the world—are all to be designed to cultivate the Christian character in the members and the social consequences of that character. The cult of Christ is the community of those cultivating in themselves the mind of Christ. In this, it is to be understood as differentiated from those cults organized to cultivate the life formed by Torah, the law of the Koran, the Buddha-mind, or the sagehood of Confucius. The cult of Jesus Christ is a cultivation of his image, not that of other religious founders or centers, although there may be overlap of character.

The Lord's Supper or eucharist, therefore, is the sacramental rite that focuses membership in the cult of Jesus Christ. At once it does two things. First, it celebrates God's grace to save us and the rest of the world. Second, it rehearses the work of sanctification according to the cult of Jesus Christ. The unique center of the Christian cult, of course, is the death and resurrection of Jesus. The death is symbolized in the bread for broken body, the wine for spilt blood. The resurrection is the availability of the elements for the communicants so that they consume and, being what they eat, are the risen Christ. The death-conquering life of Jesus is made the power of our lives as communicants. In a suggestive, if inexact, formula, Jesus, who was raised from the dead and ascended into Heaven, is still alive in the Church on Earth insofar as the Holy Spirit instills his character in the members of the Church, individually and collectively. The symbol of the Church as the Body of Christ is a different metaphoric route to the same point.

The eucharistic rite is specific to the community of Christ in several ways. Its symbols, the bread and wine, come from a particular incident in Jesus' life, the Last Supper, which is also celebrated with a particular place in the liturgical calendar for Passion Week. In this way, the Christian emphasis on historical particularity is reinforced. Jesus' death, symbolized in the elements, was of course not an accident. Through it we understand the course of Jesus' ministry and the place of his execution in its drama. We understand also something of the persecution of the teacher of righteousness, something of the betrayal by disciples, and something of what to expect for ourselves because of the commitments of discipleship. At the same time, the elements in their repetition symbolize not only the resurrection but the continued life of God quickening the Church.

Participation in the eucharist is thus not only a participation in the life of Christ but also a deepening of membership in the cult that celebrates and grows into that life. Like baptism, eucharist is a universal rite, though it has many forms. To participate in it is not just to deepen participation in one's local congregation, but in the Church universal. The participation affirms and solidifies connection with Christians in all times and areas, and with all polities and interpretations of what it means to be a disciple of Christ. Participation in the eucharist rehearses us individually for our own ultimate things, and it binds us to understand that it is the covenant, not individuals alone, that is renewed.

The word "rehearse" picks up a special meaning of religious "rite" or "liturgy." A rite is a symbolic action that through repetition shapes the imagination of the participants.[2] The kinds of symbolic actions that get enshrined in religious rites are basic ones that define the relation of people to the cosmos. In Christian theology, rites have to do with the covenant and its rescue. But Christianity rests on rituals far deeper in history than its own special forms.

In paleolothic times the fundamental problematic relation of people to the cosmos had to do with hunting and protection from beasts, hence the hunting rites and those having to do with appropriation of the power of the hunter and protector, expressed sometimes in cannibalism. In neolithic times of cultivated fields, the rites had to do with sacrifices for seasonal fertility. With the rise of civilization and hierarchically organized society, the rites had to do with the establishment of political order, and gods were called kings and lords; piety took on a dimension of obedience. By the time of the rise of Christianity and rabbinic Judaism in the Near East, of Mahayana Buddhism in India, and Confucianism and Taoism in China, the great empires encompassing vast areas had moved people from the ancestral homes that gave them identity and had taught them a second, cosmopolitan language such as Koine Greek. The liturgical "actions" sought during this so-called "Axial Age" had to do with people defining identity both as individuals personally facing the divine and as communities constructed either voluntarily, as in the case of Christianity and Buddhism, or as alien and problematic remnants surviving in a potentially hostile environment, as in the case of Judaism and Confucianism.

In the development of liturgical consciousness, these historically different needs for deep symbolic action to form imagination are not so much displaced in succession as layered on top of one another. The rites of Christianity, especially the eucharist, are vastly dense in symbolic layering. The very cannibalistic act of symbolically eating the flesh and blood of Jesus, advocated by him explicitly according to the New Testament, sets to vibrating the deep chords of the hunting society mentality, seeking to incorporate the virtue or power of the Great Hunter who brings the food of life despite the depredations of monstrous Satan and his beastly minions. At the same time the eucharist brings us to the bosom of the one who dies each year and rises again at Easter, the Shepherd of the spring lambs, our Mother of Salvation. Then again, through the eucharist we participate in the death of Christ and his resurrection to reign as King in his Kingdom. And, though a communal act, the efficacy of the eucharist is such that even if there is no truly faithful person in participation, the grace of God is effective, for God loves each and every one, particularly the lost sheep.

As mentioned earlier, Paul Tillich (1952) pointed out that, for historical reasons, moral righteousness or retributive justice in a reward and punishment system became the preoccupation of the late medieval European culture, and the Protestant reformation controversies added ritual dimensions of atonement and forgiveness. In the twentieth century, the very meaningfulness of life became problematic, and Tillich highlighted the existentialist dimensions of mid-century worship and thinking.

At the end of the twentieth century, when the Christian community is clearly seen to be worldwide, not merely European and North American, and the world society itself is seen to be rather much of a piece, the problematic relation of human beings to the cosmos seems to be that of the achievement of distributive justice. Rituals that add distributive justice to our fundamental consciousness are our current need, and as much in Buddhism, Hinduism and the other world religions as in Christianity. A covenant theology such as presented here, which would have been impossible only as short a time ago as 1950, formulates much of the character of sanctification in terms of renewing the covenant through establishing just institutions and recognizing the justice due suppressed groups. Current trends in worship, as well as in much else of church life, have to do with adding the dimension of distributive justice to the already dense and complex layers of liturgy.

The word "sacrament" has often been restricted to those rites of grace that are specifically authorized as sacraments by tradition or scripture. Most Protestants recognize only baptism and the eucharist, whereas other communions expand the list, a list which has varied considerably over time. Nevertheless, many other rites of worship, and activities of cultivation and service in the Church, are also bearers of Christ-making grace and are called sacramental by many. Indeed, the whole Church can be viewed as a sacrament, a line of metaphoric development more common in Orthodox and Roman Catholic thinkers than Protestant. Some thinkers (e.g. Teilhard de Chardin, Bowman) have gone so far as to say the entire world is a sacrament of God and that the Cosmic Christ is to be found everywhere in all people and all religions. The development in this book of the notion of covenant to encompass the entire universe, insofar as human beings can relate to it, is an attempt to recognize the universality of grace without running the danger of diluting the specifically Christian notions and practices properly unique to the cult of Jesus Christ.

The discussion of the sacramental life of the Church is curiously incomplete without its concrete historical dimension. From the historical standpoint, the Church, unified by its sacramental embodiment of the mind of Christ, is the Body of Christ. Before that can be discussed in detail, however, it is necessary to examine the relation of the cultic community of disciples of Jesus Christ to the world.

II. MISSION, TEACHING, PREACHING, AND ACTION

The purpose of Christian mission is to renew the covenant, starting with the means of grace Christians have through Jesus Christ, and extending to all means of grace whatsoever. This understanding of mission is quite different from that which says its purpose is to make Christians of everyone. To make Christians of everyone is simply to insist that everyone belong to the same cult. Yet the meaning of cultic symbols is always specific to cultures, and the Christian cult requires a context of messianic expectation. Besides, the point of Christianity is not membership but salvation, the restoration of the covenant individually and across the whole of creation. The Church as the cult of Jesus Christ presents itself as *a* valid way of salvation and additionally as having a special mission among the other cultures of the world; in both of these points, Christianity borrows from Judaism. The special mission is to bring all people to renew the covenant in whatever terms are appropriate for the diverse situations; this might include conversion to the cult of Jesus, but does not require it.

Against this understanding of mission, Matthew 28:18a–20 is often
cited, and it is worth quoting in full:

> All authority in heaven and on earth has been given to me. Go
> therefore and make disciples of all nations, baptizing them in the name of
> the Father and of the Son and of the Holy Spirit, and teaching them to
> obey everything that I have commanded you. And remember, I am with
> you always, to the end of the age.

A surface reading of this passage is that Jesus was enjoining his disciples
to extend the cult universally, especially in its reference to baptism; surely it has often been interpreted this way. The surface reading to the contrary, a different interpretation seems more persuasive. The command
surely does mean to extend the community of baptized Christians.
Whereas before, Matthew 15:24, Jesus' ministry was supposed to be
limited to Israel (actually it was not, even when Jesus said it was), now
the mission is extended to all peoples. The purpose of this is not only to
have people in all nations able to join the cult as Jesus' disciples, but also
to have branches of the cult everywhere to carry out the larger dimensions of the mission, the renewal of the covenant and establishment of
the reign of God.

There is no sense that the entire covenant and reign of God is to be
construed as discipleship alone. The disciples serve a larger world. There
is, to be sure, a reference in language and tone to Daniel 7:14, in which
one "like a son of man" is given everlasting dominion over "all peoples,
nations, and languages," a dominion "which shall not pass away." But
this is to be read against Jesus' own teaching of the Kingdom, which is
not political in Daniel's sense, but a rule by love. Furthermore, the
character of kingly rule in Jesus' sense includes crucifixion, a strange
transmogrification of glory but one at the heart of Christianity. Jesus'
claim in the quotation from Matthew that all authority is given to him,
asserts this paradoxical kingship of the cross and resurrection. Jesus'
assertion is the incarnational claim that the Logos, defining the ideals of
the covenant, is embodied in him with his kenotic life, persecution in
death, and resurrection.

Therefore, the way to restore the covenantal expression of the
Logos is by means of the cultic mission of discipleship to Jesus. The outcome of that mission is simply to be the renewal of the covenant. There is
no authority for recovering the covenant that Jesus does not have and extend through discipleship. But Jesus' life, and by analogy the life of the
Church through discipleship, is the kenotic one of sacrifice. The work of
discipleship is to renew the people and institutions of the world so as to
express the ideals of righteousness, piety, faith, and hope, combined in
love. But this does not require that the world so renewed share the

kenotic ministry of Christians. Indeed, the cross is *not* appropriate for the condition of *shālōm*. When Jewish theologians, for instance, take a dim view of Christian kenotic ideals such as poverty and martyrdom, this is because they rightly apprehend the ideals of the restored covenant, the Kingdom of God, and because they do not adopt the ministry of Jesus as the way to achieve that.

The Church then has a mission very like that of the Suffering Servant of Israel, to devote itself to the saving of the world. The last thing this should mean is the reduction of the world to the form of the Church, the opposite of the suffering motif. Rather, the Church will disappear with the restoration of the covenant, its mission of sacrifice completed, and only the resurrected life of all things in God will remain.

The teaching of the Church thus is extremely complex. It must begin with the life of Jesus and carry that paradoxical cross and resurrection through all else. This is the teaching for the Christian community. But for the world beyond, the teaching must be the proclamation of righteousness, piety, faith, and hope, summed up in the Great Commandment. Although the language of covenant arises from the biblical tradition, a tradition not always meaningful abroad, the point expressed in the biblical language can be translated because it has universal reference. Not everyone needs to be of the cult of Jesus, but everyone needs righteousness, piety, faith, hope, and love, however these are named.

A further complication of Christian teaching is that it must be responsive to questions that arise, questions coming from cultures wholly alien to the Christian cult, from situations unimaginable in biblical times, as well as from Christians within the cult attempting to live out their discipleship in confusing conditions. Therefore Christian teaching must be responsive and extend itself with imagination, creativity, and yet faithfulness.

Theology thus can be thought of in the terms mentioned in chapter 2: it is historical, systematic and evangelical. Historical, because Christian teachings must carefully track how they have been developed, extended, and sometimes corrupted by new applications and new cultural embodiments. Systematic, because questioning situations need answers that are not only immediately relevant but that also focus how the whole of the gospel of renewal bears on the situation. Evangelical, because theology and Christian teachings must think through new conditions of experience and say a new saving word, based on the original and intermediate words but new in addressing a new situation. System and evangelism prevent history from making Christian teachings a dead letter. History and evangelism prevent systematic theology from becoming fixed or dogmatic in the sense of being doctrinaire and graceless. History and system prevent evangelical theology from becoming idiosyncratic and disconnected from the historical work of Christ. The point of Christian teachings, to reiterate, is principally to address the reconstruction of the covenant which includes, as an instrumental part, the ordering of special life within the Church.

Christian preaching is based on Christian teachings, but is not reducible to it. Like the Word through which the world was created, according to Genesis 1, and like the Word John proclaimed to be incarnate in Jesus, the preached word is intended to create a new reality. The reality, of course, is a new orientation of imagination, belief, discipline, and commitment in the hearts and minds of the hearers. The intention of the preached word is as often for the hearers collectively as for them individually. The hearers are both those in the Church and those without.

There are obviously many styles of preaching, arising from different traditions and addressing different conditions. Each preacher needs to develop one or more styles that are integral to the preacher's personality, experience, and age. Yet all styles need to be able to embody a variety of elements over a relatively short course of preaching.

The first element is to be able to express the love of God, especially as found in Jesus, love addressed to the world as a whole and to the individual hearers. To accomplish this it is absolutely necessary to be able to make the biblical language and stories live in contemporary consciousness, and to interpret how they tie in to contemporary consciousness. The bridge between the scriptural symbols and contemporary consciousness is crucial because the loss of either end is an abandonment of the gospel. Scriptural language by itself reduces to a kind of psychological fundamentalism that depends on barricading the "religious" part of life from the texture of actual contemporary living. The language of contemporary consciousness by itself is at base secular and quickly loses the transformative power of the gospel, as has so sadly happened with much current Christian social thinking.

In addition to proclamation—presentation, vivification—of the love of God in Christ, preaching must weave for imagination and understanding a Christian conception of the human condition; the notion of covenant is one such way to do this, though many preaching traditions have other valuable ways.

Upon the base of proclamation of the love of God, and the urging of a Christian interpretation of the human condition, preaching needs to build in people the heart for repentance, acceptance of justification, and commitment to sanctification. Many elements of experience, for instance personal difficulties and the example of other persons, contribute to the changing of the heart and building up of Christian sanctification. But the human person is hardwired for words and ideas. The word is the mighty lever that changes the heart. For human beings, the preached word is the most integral means of cultivation.

Finally, preaching needs to provide leadership in addressing the directions of spiritual growth, both in terms of the reformation of society and direct charitable actions, and in terms of individual spiritual development. In this last mode, preaching must be sensitive to the particularities of individual and historical situations, including the transformative development of Christian institutions themselves in new or changing cultural conditions. In all these dimensions of preaching, most of which are present in any one sermon or homiletical address or writing, the connection between the scriptural roots of Christian language and the contemporary situation must be maintained. At the present time, many preachers are following the lectionary for the purpose of maintaining that connection, as well as for various purposes of exercising unity across the many cultural conditions of the churches. Lectionary preaching, however, is not the only homiletical way of building the bridge from the tradition to the local situation.

The audience for Christian preaching, as mentioned above, cannot be only those within the Church. Christians themselves need the constant nurture of the preached word, to be sure. And the only standard role for the preacher in European and North American Christianity today is pulpit preaching. Nevertheless, the gospel is needed as much by those outside the Church as by those within it, by any who hunger for spiritual sustenance or languish in pain without knowing the pain to be a spiritual malaise. Furthermore, the gospel contains direct words about evils in society and what ought to be done to correct them, words that should be heard by everyone.

Perhaps it is not to the point to direct Christian preaching at committed followers of other deep religious traditions, although they seem to welcome it. But for everyone else, the gospel is a necessity. That Christian preaching in the European and North American context seems to have abdicated its responsibility to the secular world, after a century of trying to mimic that world, is a special problem for the Church in this context. Asian, African, and Latin American forms of preaching do not have this problem (yet), whatever other problems they face; furthermore, these preachers are not limited to pulpit preaching.

Preaching should lead those in the Church to take action to restore the covenant. In its most obvious forms, this means addressing problems of injustice, both in particular situations and in social institutions. Christians join with many others in the pursuit of justice.

The special contributions of Christianity regarding social action have to do with spreading irony over the self-righteousness that so easily attends the social justice movement. Christians must continually point out that the God whose love we are supposed to emulate loves bad people. For Christians, it is more important to love the enemy, the one who embodies injustice, before destroying the enemy, although that destruction may well be entailed by the needs to restore the covenant. Christians also need to direct action in ways that acknowledge the limits of morality and the importance of piety, historical faithfulness, and hope beyond reason. Although this might seem to some to be a muting of Christian participation in the social justice movements in various parts of the world, in fact it is a recognition that Christian involvement in social action to renew the covenant is immensely complex, with a density of obligation that far outstrips the sense of morality so often expressed in the language of power and struggle.

III. THE CHURCH AS THE BODY OF CHRIST

The Church as the cult of Jesus Christ, formed around gracious sacraments, and the Church as a mission to the world, combine to form the overall identity of the Church which is taken from its relation to God. The history of its sacramental life and of its mission in the world to restore the covenant provide its historical content and identity. But the full identity of this can only be conceived in relation to God: loving neighbor is essentially tied to loving God; the Christians' love of the covenanted world is essentially tied to God's creating love in creation.

The metaphor of "the Body of Christ" as a description of the Church is extremely complex, depending on an effective interpretation of the spirit/body unity. Most attempts to render that unity suppose that the unit under consideration is based on the analogy of a human individual. The nonindividualistic covenant theology suggests a different, though no less complicated, analogy.

Let us assume, for the analogy, that the body side consists of various individuals and institutions that perform, or can perform, functions that contribute to a working organism. When the body is dead, those interrelated organic functions are not performed, whatever the individuals and institutions might be doing on their own. So it was with Jesus' body after the crucifixion and before Easter. In the quickened or resurrected body, those parts are set to functioning together to carry out the sacramental and missional life of the Church. Paul in various places (I Corinthians 12, Ephesians 4) discusses different talents, offices, and tasks according to the analogy of the parts of the body.

The analogy for the spirit side is the mind of Christ, graspable by the people and incorporable into the institutions that make up the body of Christ. The mind of Christ is not a substantial soul of the sort

popularly believed in some religions of the first century, but the mind of
Jesus represented and proclaimed by the gospel witnesses from the first
down to the present day. That "mind" on the one hand is the Logos of
creation, but as fixed historically in the personal life of Jesus. The mind
of Christ contains both divine and human natures, and is the animating
spirit of the Church in two senses: insofar as it is the norm for the
multitude of ecclesiastical efforts and insofar as it is actually embodied in
the Church's life. (The mind of Christ is present in the Church by virtue
of the Holy Spirit. It is crucial to acknowledge the ascension in order to
guard against easy Jesusology. With Christ ascended, the spirit of Christ
is present in the Holy Spirit, guiding the witnesses both early and late.)

Three misinterpretations of the "Body of Christ" description of
the Church need to be highlighted.

First, a distinction needs to be observed between the way in which
the mind of Christ unifies the various persons and institutions in the
Church and the ways in which they are culturally organized. The means
of unity through the mind of Christ are the ways in which that mind
takes over the thinking and feeling of individuals and Church institutions; to understand how this is so in any particular situation requires a
spiritual analysis.

Their cultural organization, by contrast, is a matter for sociological
or political analysis, an analysis of the ways in which individuals and institutions function regarding one another. The Church always has an
organizational pattern, and sometimes that pattern is highly unified in
ways that justify the metaphors of organicism. At other times, however,
the Church is greatly divided in organization, split into noncom-
municating groups, separated by language, culture, social class, and by
other distinctions. At these times the organicist metaphors are inappropriate for the Church as such, and usually are offensively appropriated by some one segment of the Church, as in the pre-Vatican II
claims of the Roman Catholic Church or in the title "United Methodist"
used to distinguish one Methodist church organization from the AME,
AME Zion, Nazerene, Cambellite, and other Wesleyan churches and
sects.

Because both unified and diversified church organizations have had
good times and bad times, church organization is not altogether relevant
to the spiritual unity of the Church in the mind of Christ. That spiritual
unity has to do rather with the ways in which individuals and particular
institutions within the Church relate themselves to the sacramental and
missional activities of the Church at large, conceived as stemming from
Jesus and the disciples at Pentecost and branching into all the cultures affected by the gospel. Organizational unity does not at all guarantee

spiritual unity; nor does spiritual unity, in which all the parts of the Church are doing their job for the sacramental and missional life of the gospel, require organizational unity.

Second, the mind of Christ, whose body is the Church, is the Jesus with the specific mission which is the norm for the Church to continue to carry out. Although itself a way of salvation, life in the Church has the specific task of bringing the whole broken covenant to renewal. The Church is servant to the larger world, not to engulf it, but in the way Christ was servant to the divine will of redemption for the world. It has been tempting to think of the whole world as being Christ's body, and the mind of Christ being the spirit of the world as a whole. This kind of thinking has been manifest in conceptions of the Cosmic Christ. Yet this loses the historical character of Jesus and the speciality of the identity of the Christian Church with its special mission. Other religions might have missions related to the Christian, or perhaps not so related. The scheme of each in the overall plan of salvation is not for Christians to determine, although Christians have their own view, as in the covenant theology, of what salvation consists in. As particularly quickened by the mind of Christ, the Christian Church is partial and particular within the world, however much it has a mission regarding the whole.

Third, the Church takes its identity as the Body of Christ from the divine initiative, to be understood in terms of all Persons of the Trinity. Yet it is also a human institution. Paul Tillich, anxious to distinguish the true "spiritual community" of the new being created in the Holy Spirit from the historical institutions of the Church, in fact separated them and named them separately. In this he reflected the concerns of mid-twentieth-century theologians to distinguish true Christianity from the German Christians who had taken over the Church organization. Though understandable, Tillich's distinction and separation was a mistake. It introduces a dualism that prohibits an incarnational view of divine work. The Church, like the Christ, is the incarnation of the saving work of God in human personal and institutional forms. But whereas Jesus on the human level is sometimes said to be perfect, the Church is not perfect on its actual level. The Church, like its members, is a body full of sin but not in bondage to it, filled with erring individuals and flawed institutions, but forgiven and on the way to holiness. The Church is like the rest of the world in the broken covenant, filled with the power of renewal but not fully renewed. Judged from the standpoint of actual performance, the Church is better than some historical institutions, worse than others. Its mission, however, is unique.

IV. CHRISTIANITY AND OTHER RELIGIONS

The theme of Christianity and other religions has been developed at many places through the discussion in this and earlier chapters. To summarize the main contention, several points can be made.

First, on its own terms, Christianity is a way of salvation irrespective of whether other religions are similar ways of salvation with only minor differences, valid ways to other senses of salvation, invalid ways to the Christian sense of salvation, or just plain invalid. To say anything normative about the other religions involves examining them on their own terms, and participating in their life to the same degree one would have to participate in Christianity in order to understand it. For its part, Christianity is a way of salvation.

Second, Christianity has an understanding, based on its own history and special metaphors, of the nature of the human condition and what is wrong with it. The covenant theory presented here is a central line of exposition of the Christian position. In light of the Christian understanding of the human condition, it is possible to examine other religions to see whether they have similar understandings, expressed in different terms. Those who have engaged in serious dialogue with representatives of other living faiths have usually come to the conclusion that there is great spiritual unanimity beneath the rhetoric. On the other hand, perhaps the conceptions of the human condition cannot be reconciled. Perhaps they simply disagree, and none can learn from another without abandoning its own central symbols. If so, there may be several versions of the human condition, and different religions are structurally different in order to be responsive to this fact.

Third, Christianity is a particular response to the brokenness in the human condition, a response based on the cultic following of Jesus Christ. Other religions have other cults with similarities and differences. Perhaps all the cults serve the same end. Or perhaps each has something special to contribute, as Christianity practices the sacrificial loving servanthood of Jesus, Buddhism and Hinduism are the various cults of enlightenment, Confucianism and Taoism the cults of personal and social relations, Judaism and Islam the cults of encultured law. We Christians see ourselves as having a special mission to restore the whole covenant; perhaps other religions have an analogous sense of self-identity.

Fourth, the practice of dialogue among living faiths is itself a religious act, transforming the traditions of the faiths as it takes place.

Genuine dialogue does not require any living faith to separate itself from
its roots, including both its metaphoric and scriptural roots and its
historic roots. It does, however, require further growth from those roots,
because the mutual influences worked out in previous ecumenical encounters are not sufficient for the situation of today. Today, the world
situation threatens the inertia of each major religion's self-
understanding, and the encounter of the religions with each other and
with the quasi-religions of secular modernity requires both a reappraisal
and reappropriation of roots and their extension.

As a final observation on the *Primer's* theology, Christianity cannot understand itself by self-reflection alone but must see itself from the
standpoint of the other religious options in our world. Only by trying to
express Christian identity in dialogue with representatives of other living
faiths are we drawn to see what is truly distinctive about the Christian
faith, as opposed to its being merely a way of speech and culture. This
need for self-understanding by reflection from other religious options
was the norm for Christianity during its first four centuries in Europe,
and it has always been the norm in India, East Asia, and Africa. It re-
curred in the thirteenth century in Europe, and now is a requirement for
Christianity anywhere. Although not often explicitly thematized, the
definition of Christianity as distinct in comparison with its options has
guided the discussion in the *Primer.*

We live now in an age and place at which Christendom is dead, and
many have not yet noticed. To be a Christian cannot be an act of inertia,
but must result from special work. We are again a small remnant, and
perhaps better for that. Instead of believing that we shall encompass the
world, saving everyone by making them Christians, we can now look to
the particular work Christians have for restoring the covenant. Our hope
is that we can extend the ministry of Jesus until the covenant is indeed
renewed. Our faith is that, given our historical limitations, there is
nothing we can fail that God cannot fulfill.

Readings in Key Texts:

1. Aquinas, *SCG*, Book 4, chaps. 56–78.
2. Aquinas, *ST*, no reading.
3. Augustine, no reading.
4. Barth, *Credo*, chap. 14.
5. Calvin, *Inst.*, Book 4, chaps. 1–5, 13–19.
6. Cobb and Griffin, *PT*, chap. 8.
7. Ferm, *TWLT*, chaps. 17 (by Appiah-Kubi), 9
   (by Assmann), 11 (by Miranda).

8. Hildegard, *Sci.*, Book 2, Visions 3-6; Book 3, Vision 9.
9. Luther, *TT*, "The Babylonian Captivity of the Church."
10. Rahner, *Found.*, chap 7; chap. 8, section 2.
11. Ruether, *Sexism*, chaps. 6, 8.
12. Schleiermacher, *CF*, pp. 532-536, 560-591, 611-692.
13. Tillich, *Sys.*, Vol. 3, pt. 4, section 3: A; pt. 5, section 2.

Appendix A

A Brief Bibliography of Liberation Theology

Aptheker, Herbert

1968 *Marxism and Christianity.* New York: Humanities Press.

Baum, Gregory

1975 *Religion and Alienation.* New York: Paulist Press.

Boff, Clodovis, and Leonardo Boff

1987 *Introducing Liberation Theology.* Maryknoll, N.Y.: Orbis Press.

Boff, Leonardo

1987 *The Maternal Face of God.* Maryknoll, N.Y.: Orbis Press.

Bonino, Miguez

1984 *Faces of Jesus: Latin American Christologies.* Maryknoll, N.Y.: Orbis Press.

Brown, Robert McAfee

1978 *Theology in the New Key.* Philadelphia: The Westminster Press.

1982 *Process Theology as Political Theology.* Philadelphia: The Westminster Press.

Cone, James H.

    1970 *A Black Theology of Liberation*. New York: Lippincott.

    1975 *God of the Oppressed*. New York: The Seabury Press.

Evans, M. Stanton

    1965 *The Liberal Establishment*. New York: Devin-Adair, Co.

Ferm, Deane William, editor

    1986 *Third World Liberation Theologies: A Reader*. Maryknoll, N.Y.: Orbis Books.

Fetscher, Irving

    1971 *Marx and Marxism*. New York: Herder and Herder.

Gottwald, Norman

    1983 *The Bible and Liberation*. Maryknoll, N.Y.: Orbis Press.

Gutierrez, Gustavo

    1973 *A Theology of Liberation: History, Politics, and Salvation*. Maryknoll, N.Y.: Orbis Press.

    1983 *The Power of the Poor in History: Selected Writings*. Maryknoll, N.Y.: Orbis Press.

    1987 *On Job: God Talk and the Suffering of the Innocent*. Maryknoll, N.Y.: Orbis Press.

Harrington, Michael

    1972 *Socialism*. New York: Saturday Review Press.

Kalokoski, Leszek

    1968 *Toward A Marxist Humanism*. New York: Grove Press.

Lochman, John

    1977 *Encountering Marx*. Philadelphia: Fortress Press.

McCann, Dennis P.

    1981 *Christian Realism and Liberation Theolgy: Practical Theologies in Creative Conflict*. Maryknoll, N.Y.: Orbis Books.

Machovec, Milan

   1976 *A Marxist Looks at Jesus.* Philadelphia: Fortress Press.

Migliore, Daniel L.

   1980 *Called to Freedom: Liberation Theology and the Future of Christian Doctrine.* Philadelphia: The Westminster Press.

Miranda, Hosea

   1974 *Marx and the Bible.* Maryknoll, N.Y.: Orbis Press.

Myers, Ched

   1988 *Binding the Strong Man: A Political Reading of Mark's Story of Jesus.* Maryknoll, N.Y.: Orbis Books.

Segundo, Juan Luis

   1976 *The Liberation of Theology.* Maryknoll, N.Y.: Orbis Books.

   1984 *Faith and Ideologies.* Vol. 1 of *Jesus of Nazareth Yesterday and Today.* Translated by John Drury. Maryknoll, N.Y.: Orbis Books.

Sobrino, Jon

   1978 *Christology at the Crossroads.* Maryknoll, N.Y.: Orbis Books.

Song, C. S.

   1979 *Third-Eye Theology.* Maryknoll, N.Y.: Orbis Books.

Watkins, Frederick

   1984 *The Political Traditions of the West.* Cambridge: Harvard University Press.

West, Cornel

   1982 *Prophesy Deliverance!: An Afro-American Revolutionary Christianity.* Philadelphia: The Westminster Press.

Wolf, Robert Paul

   1968 *The Poverty of Liberalism.* Boston: Beacon Press.

Appendix B

A Brief Bibliography of Feminist Theology

Bachofen, J. J.

1967 *Myth, Religion, and Mother Right: Selected Writings of J. J. Bachofen.* Translated by Ralph Manheim, with a preface by George Boas and an introduction by Joseph Campbell. Princeton: Bollingen/Princeton University Press.

Berger, Pamela

1985 *The Goddess Obscured: Transformation of the Grain Protectress from Goddess to Saint.* Boston: Beacon.

Bordo, Susan R.
1987 *The Flight to Objectivity.* Albany: State University of New York Press.

Brown, Joanne Carlson, and Carole R. Bohn, editors

1989 *Christianity, Patriarchy, and Abuse: A Feminist Critique.* New York: Pilgrim Press.

Cady, Susan, Marian Ronan, and Hal Taussig

1986 *Sophia: The Future of Feminist Spirituality.* San Francisco: Harper and Row.

Carr, Anne E.

> 1988 *Transforming Grace: Christian Tradition and Women's Experience.* San Francisco: Harper and Row.

Christ, Carol P.

> 1980 *Diving Deep and Surfacing: Women Writers on Spiritual Quest.* Boston: Beacon.

Christ, Carol P., and Judith Plaskow

> 1979 *Womanspirit Rising: A Feminist Reader in Religion.* San Francisco: Harper and Row.

> 1989 *Weaving the Visions: New Patterns in Feminist Spirituality.* San Francisco: Harper and Row.

Daly, Mary

> 1973 *Beyond God the Father.* Boston: Beacon.

> 1984 *Pure Lust: Elemental Feminist Philosophy.* Boston: Beacon.

Darr, Katheryn Pfisterer

> 1991 *"Far More Precious than Jewels": Critical, Rabbinical, and Feminist Perspectives on Biblical Women.* Philadelphia: The Westminster Press.

Dexter, Miriam Robbins

> 1990 *Whence the Goddesses: A Source Book.* New York: Pergamon.

Evans, Arthur

> 1988 *The God of Ecstasy: Sex-Roles and the Madness of Dionysos.* New York: St. Martin's Press.

Fiorenza, Elisabeth Schuessler

> 1984 *Bread Not Stone: The Challenge of Feminist Biblical Interpretation.* Boston: Beacon.

> 1985 *In Memory of Her: A Feminist Theological Reconstruction of Christian Origins.* New York: Crossroad.

Harrison, Beverly Wildung

1983 *Our Right to Choose: Toward a New Ethic of Abortion.* Boston: Beacon.

Heyward, Carter

1989a *Touching Our Strength: The Erotic as Power and the Love of God.* San Francisco: Harper and Row.

1989b *Speaking of Christ: A Lesbian Feminist Voice.* Edited by Ellen C. Davis. New York: Pilgrim Press.

Keller, Catherine

1986 *From a Broken Web: Separation, Sexism, and Self.* Boston: Beacon.

Kingsley, David

1989 *The Goddesses' Mirror: Visions of the Divine from East and West.* Albany: State University of New York Press.

Kristeva, Julia

1980 *Desire in Language: A Semiotic Approach to Literature and Art.* Edited by Leon S. Roudiez. New York: Columbia University Press.

McFague, Sallie

1987 *Models of God: Theology for an Ecological, Nuclear Age.* Philadelphia: Fortress Press.

Mollenkott, Virginia Ramey

1988 *The Divine Feminine: The Biblical Imagery of God as Female.* New York: Crossroad.

Neumann, Erich

1955 *The Great Mother: An Analysis of the Archetype.* Translated By Ralph Manheim. Princeton: Princeton University Press/ Bollingen.

Ochs, Carol

1977 *Behind the Sex of God.* Boston: Beacon.

Pagels, Elaine

    1979 *The Gnostic Gospels.* New York: Random House.

    1988 *Adam, Eve, and the Serpent.* New York: Random House.

Ruether, Rosemary Radford

    1983 *Sexism and God-Talk: Toward a Feminist Theology.* Boston: Beacon.

    1985 *Womanguides: Readings Toward a Feminist Theology.* Boston: Beacon.

Sharma, Arvind, editor

    1987 *Women in World Religions.* Albany: State University of New York Press.

Soelle, Dorothee

    1984 *To Work and To Love: A Theology of Creation.* Philadelphia: Fortress.

Suchocki, Marjorie Hewitt

    1986 *God, Christ, Church: A Practical Guide to Process Theology.* New York: Crossroad.

    1988 *The End of Evil: Process Eschatology in Historical Context.* Albany: State University of New York Press.

Trible, Phyllis

    1978 *God and the Rhetoric of Sexuality.* Philadelphia: Fortress.

Notes

INTRODUCTION

1. Distinguished leaders of this movement include Hans Frei (1974), Stanley Hauerwas (1988), and George Lindbeck (1984).

2. I have defended not only abstract concepts but abstract metaphysics in *The Cosmology of Freedom* (1974), chapter 2, *The Tao and the Daimon* (1982), chapters 3 and 4, and *Recovery of the Measure* (1989).

3. This temptation is pursued by Thomas Oden, 1987.

4. This is the ambition, brilliantly carried out, of David Tracy in *Blessed Rage for Order*, 1975.

CHAPTER 1   THE NATURE OF THEOLOGY

1. The existentialist movement brought with it the invention of a subdiscipline known as "theology of culture," whose premier protagonist was Paul Tillich (see Tillich, 1932, 1948, and 1959). Theology had long been involved with political criticism, as illustrated so superbly in Reinhold Niebuhr (1937, 1949, 1953, and 1959). The idea of theology of culture is by no means universally accepted, however; Karl Barth (1921), attacked the very notion that theology should investigate and assess the religious dimensions of culture, on the ground that theology should express the Word of God which always stands in judgment on culture. In making that point, however, he engaged with considerable brilliance in the enterprise Tillich and others later took up. See Reinhold Niebuhr, 1959: part 3, for a critique of Barth on these issues.

2. Some theologians would go so far as to say that every description of the divine, though partly true, is ultimately false and must be transcended; this is sometimes called apophatic theology, or the *via negativa*. Other theologians

would allow that some descriptions are true of the divine without reservation, such as that the divine is Being itself; but none of these descriptions is more than partial and still is in need of supplementation by other descriptions.

3. The problem of finding a common language to compare different religions is very deep, and surface similarities and differences often turn out not to be sustained upon thorough examination. For methodologically oriented discussions of this, see Barth, 1921; Hick, 1985; Neville, 1991; Smart, 1987; and Wilfrid Cantwell Smith, 1981.

4. Theology in the *Primer* makes unashamed use of philosophical, indeed metaphysical, ideas. Every claim about the world presupposes metaphysical notions of location in space and time, of causation, of order, plurality, unity, actuality, possibility, value, and a host of other ideas. We cannot be non-metaphysical; we can only be badly metaphysical by not taking responsibility for presupposed philosophy and correcting it as much as possible. Nevertheless, much Christian theology in the century since Ritschl has sought to separate itself from philosophy, believing that the theology deriving from classical Greek culture was a corruption of the somehow philosophically empty Hebrew culture that was supposed to be the pure source of Christianity. This belief about the so-called "conflict between Athens and Jerusalem" is historically false; Judaism was Hellenized over a century before the rise of Christianity, and both Christianity and pharisaic Judaism—what we know as Judaism today—arose as Hellenistic religions. The deeper root of the desire to free theology from philosophy and metaphysics was the wholly modern belief that metaphysics itself is impossible. This was claimed by Kant in the eighteenth century, by Nietzsche in the nineteenth, and then again by positivists, phenomenologists, Heideggerians, and now literary theorists in the twentieth. Although this is not the place to review these arguments (see Neville, 1981), they are not valid, and are ceasing to be persuasive to nervous theologians. Wolfhard Pannenberg, one of the preeminent theologians of the classic German tradition in our time, has recently written:

> More than anything else, theological discourse about God requires a relationship to metaphysical reflection if its claim to truth is to be valid. For talk of God is dependent on a concept of the world, which can be established only through metaphysical reflection. Christian theology must therefore wish for and welcome the fact that philosophy should begin, once again, to take its great metaphysical tradition serously as a task for contemporary thought. Unfortunately, theologians today rarely concede this dependence upon metaphysics. Nevertheless, the dependence is only too clear: a theological doctrine of God that lacks metaphysics as its discussion partner falls into either a kerygmatic subjectivism or a thoroughgoing demythologization—and frequently both at the same time! (1990: 6)

5. The interpretation of concepts as rules was first presented by Immanuel Kant. In the twentieth century the discipline of hermeneutics (theory of interpretation) has been developed with great sophistication. For the theory of interpretation elaborating the discussion of concepts employed in the *Primer*, see Neville, 1989.

6. For a more extended discussion of both the strong and weak senses of analogy, see Neville, 1992, chaps. 1, 6.

CHAPTER 2   REVELATION: SOURCES AND USES OF THEOLOGY

1. For a general historical survey of this period, emphasizing the conundrums of authority, see Pelikan, 1989. In many respects, Ferdinand Christian Baur, one of the founders of the historical method in Biblical studies and theology, was a test case for the issues. See the fine monographic study of him by Hodgson, 1966. For an approach to introductory theology that turns around the nineteenth century debates about authority and modernity far more than this *Primer* does, see the excellent collection edited by Hodgson and King, 1985; this *Primer* reflects these debates but is more deeply oriented by consideration of non-European forms of Christianity, by the encounter of Christianity with cultures formed by other religions, and by liberation movements that displace the importance of European modernism without explicitly attempting to refute it.

2. "Making a case" is a phrase popularized by Stephen Toulmin (1958) and applied to theology by Van A. Harvey (1966). It notes that powerful arguments rarely take a logical deductive form alone but rather come in from many angles. A good argument, according to the American pragmatist Charles Peirce, is not like a chain attached to an authoritative anchor but instead like a rope made of many strands reaching to many sources.

3. Hermeneutics as the interpretation of scripture and other theological sources was begun as a discipline by the philosopher Spinoza in the seventeenth century and developed clearly by the theologian Schleiermacher in the nineteenth. Contemporary hermeneutics has been deeply formed by Gadamer, 1975; Ricoeur, 1967, 1974; Habermas, 1968; Foucault; and Derrida, 1976. For analytical accounts of the hermeneutical turns, see Bleicher, 1980; Caputo, 1987; and Lentricchia, 1980.

4. This pragmatic theory of interpretation is developed in great detail in Neville, 1989.

5. For an elaboration and defense of this view of truth as the carryover of value, see Neville, 1989, ch. 3.

CHAPTER 3   GOD THE CREATOR

1. "Modernity" is an historical concept whose definition has generated a vast literature. For most thinkers, it arose in the European Renaissance as a function of the development of mathematical physics. Among the best accounts from this angle are Burtt, 1932 (still the best!) and Klaaren, 1977. See also, for a thorough philosophical discussion, Cahoone, 1988.

2. For Brightman, God is not in all respects infinite, being limited by intractable stuff that causes evil; God, for him, is nevertheless to be understood as mind.

3. This metaphysical theory has been worked out in great detail in my book *God the Creator*, 1992. It has been related to cosmological issues in *Recovery of the Measure* (1989), chapters 5–12, and to moral issues in *The Puritan Smile* (1987). Each one of those works expands on the notion of essential and conditional features. That a harmony has value because of its essential and conditional features is argued at length in *the Cosmology of Freedom* (1974), chapter 3.

4. Throughout *Process and Reality* (1929), Whitehead affirmed what he called the "ontological principle," namely, that any complex thing (and every "thing" is complex) is to be explained by the decisions either internal to itself in its own coming to be or those in prior conditions that affect it. He did not, however, extend the principle that every complexity requires explanation in a decision or set of decisions to the complex metaphysical conditions of existence. Had he done so, he would have affirmed creation *ex nihilo*. That he did not is arbitrary. See Neville, 1980.

5. This point is the conclusion of a long argument that examines other candidate ways of accounting for ontological togetherness. See Neville, 1992: chaps. 1–3.

CHAPTER 4   GOD AS TRINITY

1. For a splendid account of both the historical and conceptual problems in the early controversies concerning the Trinity, see Richardson, 1958. Because most of the Trinitarian controversies were motivated by Christological concerns, see Grillmeier, 1965. For excellent analytical surveys of the Trinitarian problems, see Kelly, 1960, and Lohse, 1963. For recent translations of the relevant texts, see Rusch, 1980, and Norris, 1980. Many of the classical problems calling forth the doctrine of the Trinity will be discussed in the Christological chapters, 11 and 12, below.

2. For an explicit treatment of the classic problems of Trinitarian theology in contemporary terms connected to the categories of the *Primer*, see Neville, 1982, chap. 4.

3. For a detailed analysis of how the creator is revealed in the contingency of the world, described as the contingency of essential and conditional features and of their harmony, see Neville, 1992, chap. 8.

4. For some thinkers, for instance Paul Weiss (1958: chap. 3), time and space are large containers in which things come to be; as such, they are somewhat independent in reality and properties of the things contained. For others, for instance Alfred North Whitehead (1929: part 4) and Neville (1989: div. 4), it is the things that are spatial and temporal, and hence space and time are functions of the things.

5. For a detailed analysis of temporality as embracing past, present, and future together, see Neville, 1989: chaps. 9–10.

6. These four elements, form, components, the actual mixture of the two, and value as the cause of mixture, are conceived by extension of categories found in Plato's *Philebus*. They have been discussed at length in Neville, 1989 and 1991.

CHAPTER 5   THE HUMAN CONDITION: COVENANT

1. Feminists have argued that "pride" is a peculiarly masculine form of sin, stemming from the overassertiveness and arrogance so tempting to men who are raised to have to prove themselves continually. Women, by contrast, can have sexual identity passively, and tend by contrast to become dependent and trivialize themselves. See Valerie Saiving's "The Human Situation: A Feminine View," in Christ and Plaskow, 1979.

2. The Psalms are among the many places in the Bible in which the transhuman magnitude of the creation is expressed, over against which the moral economy of the human scale must find a place. Lao Tze's *Tao Teh Ching*, however, is almost exclusively devoted to this theme; the metaphor of "straw dogs" comes from chapter 5.

3. Scholarly interest in the Earth Mother as a counterpoint to the Western Sky god (Yahweh, Zeus, Jupiter) received great stimulation from the nineteenth-century writings of J. J. Bachofen (1967); his specific theories have been brought into considerable doubt, although his general point has been accepted. The most recent scholarly compendium of information is Dexter, 1990. Consult also the many appropriate titles in the bibliography of feminist writings below, and Neville, 1991.

4. On the point of the limitation of the moral extension of order, see David Hall's defense of the aesthetic dimension in contrast to the moral in *Eros and Irony*, 1982; for an argument defending the moral sphere from reduction to the aesthetic, see Neville, 1987.

CHAPTER 6   THE HUMAN CONDITION: SIN

1. The literature in religious ethics is vast. Perhaps the place to start, following up on the internal references, is James Gustafson's *Ethics from a Theocentric Perspective*, 1983-1984.

2. The ambiguity of moral life, particularly that dealing with the management of institutions, is a major theme of Paul Tillich's work, particularly 1957; see also Neville, 1987.

3. Of course this is by no means the whole of the feminine, and far less a complete expression of the interests of the feminist movement. In fact, insofar as feminism has a civil rights component, insisting on equal job opportunities, self-

determination for women, and most particularly a shift in women's roles from family identity to a merit system, the feminist movement is adopting the ideals usually associated with the more nearly abstract morality of the masculine stereotype. It should be clear that the distinction used here between the feminine and the masculine is a stereotype based on the religious distinction between the Earth Mother and the Sky God.

CHAPTER 7   SALVATION, FREEDOM, AND BONDAGE

1. Because theologians are so preoccupied with problems in the religious dimension of life, it is important to be reminded that every other dimension looks upon religion as but one among many, and that its own characters, say, of the economy, pervade every dimension. See Weiss, 1958, or Neville 1987: chap. 10.

2. For a fine treatment of the limitations of some of the traditional language of justification versus sanctification, and a renewed attempt to make the point, see Pannenberg, 1983.

3. An extensive philosophic treatment of freedom, of which the discussion here is a summary, is in Neville, 1974.

4. A technical philosophic way of saying this is that experience is thoroughly hermeneutical or interpretive. Everything we deal with already bears signs or marks of significance that register in imagination and judgment. See Neville, 1989: chaps. 15–16.

5. "Heart, mind, and will" is a classic trilogy of human faculties. It was the core of Augustine's Trinitarian theology and it was included in Jesus' expression of the Great Commandment, to love God with all one's heart, mind, soul (will) and strength. The first extensive and systematic statement of the division was in Plato's *Republic*. See also Neville, 1978.

CHAPTER 8   JUSTIFICATION, GRACE, AND LOVE

1. The sources for the theology or philosophy in Indian religion are vast. A good place to begin is with Radhakrishnan and Moore, 1957: chaps. 2, 3 , 8, 9, 12, and 15.

2. The best collection of the basic Chinese theological and philosophical texts is Chan, 1963.

3. On the point of the validity of the Torah, see Paul van Buren's three-volume *Theology of the Jewish-Christian Reality*, especially vol. 2, 1983.

CHAPTER 9   SIN AND SOCIETY

1. This theory of identity is laid out in detail in Neville, 1989: chap. 5. It is ap-

plied to individuals generally in Neville, 1974: chaps. 4–7, and to moral and religious life in Neville, 1987: chaps. 3–7, 10.

2. Juan Luis Segundo has argued that "ideology" need not have the pejorative sense Marx gave to it. He defines it rather as the way to understanding things and their connections so as to be effective. In this, ideology contrasts with faith which supplies the values in pursuit of which we aim to be effective. See his *Faith and Ideologies*, 1984.

3. For an analysis of the extent to which Marxism can supply the terms for the Christian liberation movement, see Segundo, 1984.

4. The Western world reacted with horror to the call by the Iranian government for the punitive murder of Salman Rushdie, a British novelist who wrote a book offensive to some Muslims. Part of the horror was at the lack of appreciation of the freedom of writers to say and criticize what they want. A deeper part, however, was reaction against the use of the charge of blasphemy. Secular culture can make nothing of a charge of blasphemy except that it seems to assert a kind of idolatry. How like the Western reaction to Iran was Iran's reaction to Rushdie! Perhaps the West has its own idols, among them freedom of speech. Or perhaps blasphemy is not a function of mere idolatry but rather of something truly holy.

CHAPTER 10   SANCTIFICATION

1. Jones, Wainwright, and Yarnold (1986) present a comprehensive and illuminating overview of Christian approaches to spirituality. For a fascinating study of the Mediterranean context within which Christian spirituality arose, see Armstrong, 1986. For the main themes that have illuminated the modern period, see Raitt, 1987. The scheme of spirituality presented in the text does not claim to represent a survey but rather the interests and benefits received by the author (Neville, 1978).

CHAPTER 11   CHRISTOLOGY: THE CULT OF JESUS CHRIST

1. Neo-orthodox theologians (e.g. Barth, 1921, 1963), anxious to distinguish Christianity from other religions as being not a religion at all, but utterly unique as the special product of God, did so by making the understanding of Jesus Christ prior to any understanding of creation, the human condition, or culture. Arianism was the ancient position declared a heresy in 326 C.E. at the First Council at Nicea. Although Arius' own works have been lost except for fragments, he was accused of believing that Christ is significantly subordinate to God the Father, not part of a true Trinity (see Kelly, 1960: 223–374).

2. The Christology developed in the *Primer* is oriented toward addressing ideas and problems that are deeply influential in the contemporary world of global

Christianity. Nevertheless, the background for the discussion is the classical Trinitarian and Christological controversies of the second through the fifth centuries. Underlying the discussion is an attempt to meet the criteria of orthodoxy hammered out in the Church of late antiquity, such as the unity in diversity of the Persons of the Trinity, the two natures of Jesus Christ, and the activity of all Persons of the Trinity in the activity of any one Person. The difference between the classical Christology and that of the *Primer* comes from differences in the underlying philosophies or metaphysics and from differences in the things assumed that constitute the context of the discussions. The Christology here is far more classical than those generally popular in the nineteenth and early twentieth centuries arising from either a scholastic or an anthropological base. Those wishing to explore the classical discussions should consult Grillmeier, 1965, Kelly, 1960, and Richardson, 1958; the relevant creeds, with commentary, are in Leith, 1963; relevant collections of the early theological arguments are in Norris, 1980, and Rusch, 1980. For twentieth-century disscussions, see Welch, 1952.

The background is relevant for the next chapter as well as the present one and is, of course, relevant to the Trinitarian discussion in chapter 4.

CHAPTER 12   CHRISTOLOGY: THE DIVINITY OF CHRIST

1. Neo-Platonism derives from the thought of the philosopher Plotinus, who was influential on Augustine. See Armstrong, 1986: chaps. 10, 16. J. N. Findlay was a sophisticated contemporary Neo-Platonist (1974). For a criticism of Neo-Platonism from the standpoint of creation *ex nihilo*, see Neville, 1992: chap 3.

2. See, for instance, discussions of the Cosmic Christ in the writings of Teilhard de Chardin (e.g. 1968) or Raimundo Panikkar (e.g. 1973). Transcendental theologians, such as Karl Rahner, argue that Christ is to be understood as a transcendental condition of human reality as such (Rahner, 1978: chap. 6).

CHAPTER 13   THE HOLY SPIRIT IN THE CHURCH

1. This approach to definition or identity illustrates the thesis that description is always normative. That is, any actual state of affairs achieves some value; if it has alternatives, its relation to the alternative values is part of its description. Furthermore, the better options for a state of affairs are ideal. Thus, things are always to be described with implicit if not explicit reference to their ideals. See Neville, 1987: chap. 4; 1989: div. 2.

2. The nature of imagination, as the basic former of experience, has been discussed in Neville, 1981: pt. 2. Religion shapes imagination at very basic levels, especially those described by Peter Berger, 1967. A similar approach to the role of ritual is taken by George Lindbeck, 1984, in his cultural/linguistic theory. See also Neville, 1978: chap. 1.

Bibliography

Alter, Robert

    1981 *The Art of Biblical Narrative.* New York: Basic Books.

Altizer, Thomas J. J.

    1970 *Descent into Hell.* New York: Lippincott.

    1977 *The Self-Embodiment of God.* New York: Harper and Row.

    1980 *Total Presence: The Language of Jesus and the Language of Today.* New York: The Seabury Press.

    1985 *History as Apocalypse.* Albany: State University of New York Press.

Aquinas, St. Thomas

    1259-1264 *Summa Contra Gentiles: On the Truth of the Catholic Faith.* Garden City, N.Y.: Doubleday Image. Book 1, *God*, translated by Anton C. Pegis, 1955; Book 2, *Creation*, translated by James F. Anderson, 1956; Book 3, *Providence*, Parts 1 and 2, translated by Vernon J. Bourke, 1956; Book 4, *Salvation*, translated by Charles J. O'Neil, 1957.

    1265-1272 *Summa Theologica.* Relevant sections in Anton C. Pegis, translator and editor, *Basic Writings of Saint Thomas Aquinas*, two volumes. New York: Random House, 1945.

Armstrong, A. H., editor

  1986 *Classical Mediterranean Spirituality: Egyptian, Greek, Roman.* Vol. 15 of *World Spirituality: An Encyclopedic History of the Religious Quest.* New York: Crossroad.

Augustine, St.

  398 *Confessions. Translated by Albert C. Outler. Vol. 7 of Library of Christian Classics.* Philadelphia: The Westminster Press, 1955.

  426 *City of God.* Abridged version edited by Vernon J. Bourke. Garden City, N.Y.: Doubleday Image, 1958.

Bachofen, J. J.

  1967 *Myth, Religion, and Mother Right: Selected Writings of J. J. Bachofen.* Translated by Ralph Manheim, with a preface by George Boas and an introduction by Joseph Campbell. Princeton: Bollingen/Princeton University Press.

Barth, Karl

  1921 *The Epistle to the Romans.* Second edition. Translated by Edwyn C. Hoskyns. London: Oxford University Press, 1933.

  1957 *The Word of God and the Word of Man.* Translated by Douglas Horton. New York: Harper and Brothers.

  1962 *Credo.* Translator anonymous. New York: Scribners.

  1963 *Evangelical Theology: An Introduction.* Translated by Grover Foley. New York: Holt, Rinehart and Winston.

Berger, Pamela

  1985 *The Goddess Obscured: Transformation of the Grain Protectress from Goddess to Saint.* Boston: Beacon.

Berger, Peter L.

  1967 *The Sacred Canopy: Elements of a Sociological Theory of Religion.* Garden City, N.Y.: Doubleday.

Bleicher, Josef

  1980 *Contemporary Hermeneutics: Hermeneutics as Method, Philosophy and Critique.* London: Routledge and Kegan Paul.

Bordo, Susan R.

   1987 *The Flight to Objectivity*. Albany: State University of New
   York Press.

Bowne, Borden Parker

   1882 *Metaphysics: A Study in First Principles*. New York: Harper
   and Brothers.

Brightman, Edgar Sheffield

   1940 *A Philosophy of Religion*. Englewood Cliffs, N.J.: Prentice-
   Hall.

Brown, Joanne Carlson, and Carole R. Bohn, editors

   1989 *Christianity, Patriarchy, and Abuse: A Feminist Critique*.
   New York: Pilgrim Press.

Burtt, E. A.

   1932 *The Metaphysical Foundations of Modern Science*. Revised
   edition. New York: The Humanities Press. (Reprint, Garden
   City: Doubleday Anchor, 1954.)

Cady, Susan, Marian Ronan, and Hal Taussig

   1986 *Sophia: The Future of Feminist Spirituality*. San Francisco:
   Harper and Row.

Cahoone, Lawrence E.

   1988 *The Dilemma of Modernity: Philosophy, Culture, and Anti-
   culture*. Albany: State University of New York Press.

Calvin, John

   1559 *The Institutes of the Christian Religion*. Edited by John T.
   McNeill, translated by Ford Lewis Battles. Philadelphia: The
   Westminster Press, 1960. Vols. 20 and 21 of *Library of Chris-
   tian Classics*.

Caputo, John

   1987 *Radical Hermeneutics*. Bloomington: Indiana University
   Press.

Carr, Anne E.

  1988 *Transforming Grace: Christian Tradition and Women's Experience.* San Francisco: Harper and Row.

Chan, Wing-tsit

  1963 *A Source Book in Chinese Philosophy.* Princeton: Princeton University Press.

Christ, Carol P.

  1980 *Diving Deep and Surfacing: Women Writers on Spiritual Quest.* Boston: Beacon.

Christ, Carol P., and Judith Plaskow

  1979 *Womanspirit Rising: A Feminist Reader in Religion.* San Francisco: Harper and Row.

  1989 *Weaving the Visions: New Patterns in Feminist Spirituality.* San Francisco: Harper and Row.

Cobb, John B., Jr.

  1962 *Living Options in Protestant Theology.* Philadelphia: The Westminster Press.

  1965 *A Christian Natural Theology.* Philadelphia: The Westminster Press.

  1967 *The Structure of Christian Existence.* Philadelphia: The Westminster Press.

  1975 *Christ in a Pluralistic Age.* Philadelphia: The Westminster Press.

  1982 *Process Theology as Political Theology.* Philadelphia: The Westminster Press.

Cobb, John B., Jr., and David Ray Griffin

  1976 *Process Theology: An Introductory Exposition.* Philadelphia: The Westminster Press.

Cobb, John B., Jr., Lewis S. Ford, and Charles Hartshorne

  1980 "Three Responses to Neville's *Creativity and God*," in *Process Studies*, 10/3–4 (Fall-Winter).

Cracknell, Kenneth

    1986 *Towards a New Relationship*. London: Epworth Press.

Cullmann, Oscar

    1962 *Christ and Time*. Translated by Floyd V. Filson. London: SCM Press.

Cunliffe-Jones, Hubert, editor, with Benjamin Drewery

    1978 *A History of Christian Doctrine*. Edinburgh: T. and T. Clark.

Daly, Mary

    1973 *Beyond God the Father*. Boston: Beacon.

    1984 *Pure Lust: Elemental Feminist Philosophy*. Boston: Beacon.

Darr, Katheryn Pfisterer

    1991 *"Far More Precious Than Jewels": Critical, Rabbinical, and Feminist Perspectives on Biblical Women*. Philadelphia: Westminster Press.

Dean, William

    1986 *American Religious Empiricism*. Albany: State University of New York Press.

    1988 *History Making History: The New Historicism in American Religious Thought*. Albany: State University of New York Press.

Derrida, Jacques

    1976 *Of Grammatology*. Translated by Gayatri Chakravorty Spivak. Baltimore: The Johns Hopkins University Press.

Dexter, Miriam Robbins

    1990 *Whence the Goddesses: A Source Book*. New York: Pergamon.

Dulles, Avery, S. J.

    1973 *The Survival of Dogma*. New York: Image.

Evans, Arthur

1988 *The God of Ecstasy: Sex-Roles and the Madness of Dionysos.*
New York: St Martin's Press.

Ferm, Deane William, editor

1986 *Third World Liberation Theologies: A Reader.* Maryknoll,
N.Y.: Orbis Books.

Findlay, J. N.

1974 *Plato: The Written and Unwritten Doctrines.* London:
Routledge and Kegan Paul.

Fiorenza, Elisabeth Schussler

1984 *Bread Not Stone: The Challenge of Feminist Biblical Interpretation.* Boston: Beacon.

1985 *In Memory of Her: A Feminist Theological Reconstruction
of Christian Origins.* New York: Crossroad.

Fiorenza, Francis Schussler

1985 *Foundational Theology: Jesus and the Church.* New York:
Crossroad.

Foucault, Michel

1976 *The Archaeology of Knowledge.* Translated by A. M.
Sheridan Smith. New York: Harper and Row.

Frankenberry, Nancy

1987 *Religion and Radical Empiricism.* Albany: State University
of New York Press.

Fredriksen, Paula

1988 *From Jesus to Christ: The Origins of the New Testament
Images of Jesus.* New Haven: Yale University Press.

Frei, Hans

1974 *The Eclipse of Biblical Narrative.* New Haven: Yale University Press.

Gadamer, Hans-Georg

   1975 *Truth and Method.* Edited by Garrett Barden and John Cum-
        ming. New York: The Seabury Press. (Original German publi-
        cation, 1960.)

Gilkey, Langdon

   1959 *Maker of Heaven and Earth: The Christian Doctrine of
        Creation in the Light of Modern Knowledge.* Garden City,
        N.Y.: Doubleday.

   1969 *Naming the Whirlwind: The Renewal of God-Language*
        Indianapolis: Bobbs-Merrill.

   1979 *Message and Existence.* New York: The Seabury Press.

Girardot, Norman

   1983 *Myth and Meaning in Early Taoism.* Berkeley: University of
        California Press.

Griffin, David R.
   1973 *A Process Christology.* Philadelphia: The Westminster
        Press.

Grillmeier, Aloys, S.J.

   1965 *Christ in Christian Tradition: From the Apostolic Age to
        Chalcedon (451).* Translated by J. S. Bowden. New York: Sheed
        and Ward.

Gustafson, James

   1983–1984 *Ethics from a Theocentric Perspective.* Vol. 1, 1983;
        Vol. 2, 1984. Chicago: University of Chicago Press.

Habermas, Jurgen

   1986 *Knowledge and Human Interests.* Translated by Jeremy J.
        Shapiro. Boston: Beacon.

Hall, David L.

   1982 *Eros and Irony: A Prelude to Philosophical Anarchism.*
        Albany: State University of New York Press.

Haller, William

   1938 *The Rise of Puritanism.* New York: Columbia University
   Press.

Harrison, Beverly Wildung

   1983 *Our Right to Choose: Toward a New Ethic of Abortion.*
   Boston: Beacon.

Hart, Ray L.

   1968 *Unfinished Man and the Imagination.* New York: Herder
   and Herder.

Hartshorne, Charles

   1948 *The Divine Relativity.* New Haven: Yale University Press.

Harvey, Van Austin

   1966 *The Historian and the Believer.* New York: Macmillan.

Hauerwas, Stanley

   1985 *Against the Nations: War and Survival in a Liberal Society.*
   New York: Seabury/Winston.

   1988 *Christian Existence Today.* Durham, N.C.: The Labyrinth
   Press.

Hausman, Carl R.

   1984 *A Discourse on Novelty and Creation.* Albany: State
   University of New York Press.

Hegel, Georg Wilhelm Friedrich

   1807 *Phenomenology of Spirit.* Translated by A. V. Miller.
   Oxford: Oxford University Press, 1977.

   1832 *Lectures on the Philosophy of Religion.* Three volumes.
   Translated and edited by E. B. Speirs and J. Burdon Sanderson.
   New York: Humanities Press, 1962.

Heyward, Carter

   1989a *Touching Our Strength: The Erotic as Power and the Love
   of God.* San Francisco: Harper and Row.

1989b *Speaking of Christ: A Lesbian Feminist Voice.* Edited by Ellen C. Davis. New York: Pilgrim Press.

Hick, John

1985 *Problems of Religious Pluralism.* New York: St. Martin's Press.

Hildegard of Bingen

1151 *Scivias.* Translated by Mother Columba Hart and Jane Bishop. New York, Paulist Press, 1990.

Hodgson, Peter C.

1966 *The Formation of Historical Theology: A Study of Ferdinand Christian Baur.* New York: Harper and Row.

1988 *Revisioning the Church: Ecclesial Freedom in the New Paradigm.* Philadelphia: Fortress.

Hodgson, Peter C., and Robert H. King, editors

1985 *Christian Theology: An Introduction to Its Traditions and Tasks.* Second edition, revised. Philadelphia: Fortress Press.

Jonas, Hans

1958 *The Gnostic Religion.* Boston: Beacon.

Jones, Cheslyn, Geoffrey Wainwright, and Edward Yarnold, S.J., editors

1986 *The Study of Spirituality.* New York: Oxford University Press.

Kaufman, Gordon D.

1968 *Systematic Theology: A Historicist Perspective.* New York: Charles Scribner's Sons.

1972 *God the Problem.* Cambridge: Harvard University Press.

1981 *The Theological Imagination: Constructing the Concept of God.* Philadelphia: The Westminster Press.

Kee, Howard Clark

  1980 *Christian Origins in Social Perspective.* Philadelphia: Westminster.

  1983 *Understanding the New Testament.* Fourth edition. Englewood Cliffs, N.J.: Prentice-Hall.

Kelber, Werner

  1979 *Mark's Story of Jesus.* Philadelphia: Fortress Press.

Keller, Catherine

  1986 *From a Broken Web: Separation, Sexism, and Self.* Boston:
  Beacon.

Kelly, J. N. D.

  1960 *Early Christian Doctrines.* Second edition. New York:
  Harper and Row.

Kieckhefer, Richard, and George D. Bond, editors

  1988 *Sainthood: Its Manifestations in World Religions.* Berkeley:
  University of California Press.

Kierkegaard, Soren

  1849 *The Sickness Unto Death.* In *Fear and Trembling and The
  Sickness Unto Death.* Translated by Walter Lowrie. Garden
  City, N.Y.: Doubleday Anchor, 1954.

Kingsley, David

  1989 *The Goddesses' Mirror: Visions of the Divine from East and
  West.* Albany: State University of New York Press.

Klaaren, Eugene M.

  1977 *The Religious Origins of Modern Science.* Grand Rapids:
  Eerdmans.

Knudson, Albert C.

  1927 *The Philosophy of Personalism.* New York: Abingdon Press.

Koester, Helmut

   1982 *Introduction to the New Testament.* Vol. 1, *History, Culture, and Religion of the Hellenistic Age*; Vol. 2, *History and Literature of Early Christianity.* Translated from the German by the author. Berlin: Walter de Gruyter and Co.

Kung, Hans

   1986 *Christianity and the World Religions.* With Josef van Ess, Heinrich von Stietencron, and Heinz Bechert, and translated by Peter Heinegg. Garden City, N.Y.: Doubleday.

   1988 *Theology for the Third Millennium.* Translated by Peter Heinegg. New York: Doubleday.

Kung, Hans, and Julia Ching

   1989 *Christianity and Chinese Religions.* Chapters by Kung translated by Peter Beyer. New York: Doubleday.

Leites, Edmund

   1986 *The Puritan Conscience and Modern Sexuality.* New Haven: Yale University Press.

Leith, J. H., editor

   1963 *Creeds of the Churches.* Garden City, N.Y.: Doubleday/ Anchor.

Lentricchia, Frank

   1980 *After the New Criticism.* Chicago: University of Chicago Press.

Lindbeck, George A.

   1984 *The Nature of Doctrine: Religion and Theology in a Post-liberal Age.* Philadelphia: The Westminster Press.

Lohse, Bernhard

   1963 *A Short History of Christian Doctrine from the First Century to the Present.* Translated by F. Ernest Stoeffler. Revised American edition. Philadelphia: Fortress Press, 1985.

Lonergan, Bernard J. F., S.J.

　　1957 *Insight: A Study of Human Understanding.* London: Long-
　　mans, Green.

　　1972 *Method in Theology.* New York: Herder and Herder.

Long, Charles H.

　　1986 *Significations: Signs, Symbols, and Images in the Inter-
　　pretation of Religion.* Philadelphia: Fortress.

Luther, Martin

　　1520 *Three Treatises: An Open Letter to the Christian Nobility,
　　A Prelude on the Babylonian Captivity of the Church, and A
　　Treatise on Christian Liberty.* Translated by C. M. Jacobs,
　　A. T. W. Steinhaeuser, and W. A. Lambert, respectively.
　　Philadelphia: Muhlenberg Press, 1943.

McCann, Dennis P.

　　1981 *Christian Realism and Liberation Theology: Practical
　　Theologies in Creative Conflict.* Maryknoll, N.Y.: Orbis
　　Books.

McFague, Sallie

　　1987 *Models of God: Theology for an Ecological, Nuclear Age.*
　　Philadelphia: Fortress Press.

Martinson, Paul Varo

　　1987 *A Theology of World Religions.* Minneapolis: Augsburg.

Migliore, Daniel L.

　　1980 *Called to Freedom: Liberation Theology and the Future of
　　Christian Doctrine.* Philadelphia: The Westminster Press.

Miller, Perry, and Thomas H. Johnson, editors

　　1963 *The Puritans.* Two volumes. Revised edition by George
　　McCandlish. New York: Harper Torchbooks.

Mollenkott, Virginia Ramey

　　1988 *The Divine Feminine: The Biblical Imagery of God as
　　Female.* New York: Crossroad.

Moltmann, Jurgen

   1985 *God in Creation: A New Theology of Creation and the Spirit of God.* Translated by Margaret Kohl. San Francisco: Harper and Row.

Myers, Ched

   1988 *Binding the Strong Man: A Political Reading of Mark's Story of Jesus.* Maryknoll, N.Y.: Orbis Books.

Neumann, Erich

   1955 *The Great Mother: An Analysis of the Archetype.* Translated by Ralph Manheim. Princeton: Princeton University Press/ Bollingen.

Neville, Robert Cummings

   1974 *The Cosmology of Freedom.* New Haven: Yale University Press.

   1978 *Soldier, Sage, Saint.* New York: Fordham University Press.

   1980 *Creativity and God.* New York: The Seabury Press.

   1981 *Reconstruction of Thinking.* Albany: State University of New York Press.

   1982 *The Tao and the Daimon.* Albany: State University of New York Press.

   1987 *The Puritan Smile.* Albany: State University of New York Press.

   1988 "Beyond Production and Class: A Process Project in Economic Theory," in *Economic Life*, edited by W. Widick Schroeder and Franklin I. Gamwell. Chicago: Center for the Scientific Study of Religion.

   1989 *Recovery of the Measure.* Albany: State University of New York Press.

   1991 *Behind the Masks of God.* Albany: State University of New York Press.

   1992 *God the Creator: On the Transcendence and Presence of God.* Reprinted, with a new Introduction. Albany: State University of New York Press. Original, 1968.

Niebuhr, H. Richard

1929 *The Social Sources of Denominationalism.* New York: Henry Holt. (Meridian Books, 1957.)

1963 *The Responsible Self.* Postumously published with an introduction by James Gustafson. San Francisco: Harper and Row.

Niebuhr, Reinhold

1937 *Beyond Tragedy: Essays on the Christian Interpretation of History.* New York: Charles Scribner's Sons.

1949 *The Nature and Destiny of Man: A Christian Interpretation.* A one volume edition of *Human Nature* (1941) and *Human Destiny* (1943). New York: Charles Scribner's Sons.

1953 *Christian Realism and Political Problems.* New York: Charles Scribner's Sons.

1959 *Essays in Applied Christianity.* Selected, edited, and introduced by D. B. Robertson. New York: Meridian.

Nietzsche, Friedrich

1887 *The Genealogy of Morals.* Translated by Francis Golffing. Garden City: Doubleday Anchor, 1956.

Norris, Richard A., Jr., editor

1980 *The Christological Controversy.* Philadelphia: Fortress.

Ochs, Carol

1977 *Behind the Sex of God.* Boston: Beacon.

Oden, Thomas C.

1987 *The Living God: Systematic Theology: Volume One.* San Francisco: Harper and Row.

Ogden, Schubert M.

1973 *The Reality of God.* New York: Harper and Row.

Olson, Alan M., editor.

1980 *Myth, Symbol, and Reality.* Notre Dame, Indiana: University of Notre Dame Press.

Pagels, Elaine

   1979 *The Gnostic Gospels.* New York: Random House.

   1988 *Adam, Eve, and the Serpent.* New York: Random House.

Panikkar, Raimundo

   1973 *The Trinity and the Religious Experience of Man.* London: Darton, Longman and Todd.

   1989 *The Silence of God: The Answer of the Buddha.* Maryknoll, N.Y.: Orbis.

Pannenberg, Wolfhart

   1983 *Christian Spirituality.* Philadelphia: The Westminster Press.

   1990 *Metaphysics and the Idea of God.* Translated by Philip Clayton. Grand Rapids: Willim B. Eerdmans.

Park, Sung-bae

   1983 *Buddhist Faith and Sudden Enlightenment.* Albany: State University of New York Press.

Pegis, Anton C., editor and translator

   1945 *Basic Writings of Saint Thomas Aquinas.* Two Volumes. New York: Random House.

Pelikan, Jaroslav

   1971–1989 *The Christian Tradition: A History of the Development of Doctrine.* Vol. 1, *The Emergence of the Catholic Tradition (100–600)*, 1971; Vol. 2, *The Spirit of Eastern Christendom (600–1700)*, 1974; Vol. 3, *The Growth of Medieval Theology (600–1300)*, 1978; Vol. 4, *Reformation of Church and Dogma (1300–1700)*, 1984; Vol. 5, *Christian Doctrine and Modern Culture (since 1700)*, 1989. Chicago: University of Chicago Press.

Perrin, Norman, and Dennis C. Duling

   1982 *The New Testament: An Introduction.* Second edition; New York: Harcourt Brace Jovanovich.

Phillips, D. Z.

1976 *Religion Without Explanation*. Oxford: Basis Blackwell.

Plantinga, Alvin, and Nicholas Wolterstorff, editors

1983 *Faith and Rationality: Reason and Belief in God*. Notre Dame, Indiana: University of Notre Dame Press.

Radhakrishnan, S. and Charles Moore, editors

1957 *A Sourcebook in Indian Philosophy*. Princeton: Princeton University Press.

Rahner, Karl

1961 ff. *Theological Investigations*, vols. 1. Baltimore: Helocon.

1978 *Foundations of Christian Faith: An Introduction to the Idea of Christianity*. Translated by William V. Dych. New York Crossroad, 1989.

Raitt, Jill

1987 *Christian Spirituality in the High Middle Ages and Reformation*. Vol. 17 of *World Spirituality: An Encyclopedic History of the Religious Quest*. In collaboration with Bernard McGinn and John Meyendorff. New York: Crossroad.

Richardson, Cyril C.

1958 *The Doctrine of the Trinity*. Nashville: Abingdon.

Ricoeur, Paul

1967 *The Symbolism of Evil*. Translated by Emerson Buchanan. Boston: Beacon Paperback, 1969.

1974 *The Conflict of Interpretations*. Edited by Don Ihde, various translators. Evanston: Northwestern University Press.

Royce, Josiah

1899 *The World and the Individual: First Series: The Four Historical Conceptions of Being*. New York: Dover, 1959.

1913 *The Problem of Christianity*. With a new introduction by John E. Smith. Chicago: University of Chicago Press, 1968.

Ruether, Rosemary Radford

1983 *Sexism and God-Talk: Toward a Feminist Theology.* Boston: Beacon.

1985 *Womanguides: Readings Toward a Feminist Theology.* Boston: Beacon.

Rusch, William G., editor

1980 *The Trinitarian Controversy.* Philadelphia: Fortress.

Schleiermacher, Friedrich

1830 *The Christian Faith.* Translation of the second edition by various scholars, edited by H. R. Mackintosh and J. S. Stewart. Edinburgh: T. and T. Clark, 1928.

Searle, John R.

1969 *Speech Acts.* Cambridge: Cambridge University Press.

Segundo, Juan Luis

1984 *Faith and Ideologies.* Vol. 1 of *Jesus of Nazareth Yesterday and Today.* Translated by John Drury. Maryknoll, N.Y.: Orbis Books.

Semmel, Bernard

1973 *The Methodist Revolution.* New York: Basic Books.

Sharma, Arvind, editor

1987 *Women in World Religions.* Albany: State University of New York Press.

Smart, Ninian

1987 *Religion and the Western Mind.* Albany: State University of New York Press.

Smith, Huston

1958 *The Religions of Man.* New York: Harper.

Smith, John E.

  1961 *Reason and God: Encounters of Philosophy with Religion.*
  New Haven: Yale University Press.

  1967 *Religion and Empiricism.* Milwaukee: Marquette University Press.

  1968 *Experience and God.* New York: Oxford University Press.

  1978 *Purpose and Thought.* New Haven: Yale University Press.

Smith, Wilfrid Cantwell

  1981 *Towards of World Theology.* Philadelphia: Westminister Press.

Soelle, Dorothee

  1984 *To Work and To Love: A Theology of Creation.*
  Philadelphia: Fortress.

Stendahl, Krister

  1976 *Paul Among Jews and Gentiles.* Philadelphia: Fortress.

Suchocki, Marjorie Hewitt

  1986 *God, Christ, Church: A Practical Guide to Process Theology.*
  New York: Crossroad.

  1988 *The End of Evil: Process Eschatology in Historical Context.* Albany: State University of New York Press.

Swinburne, Richard

  1977 *The Coherence of Theism.* Oxford: Oxford University Press.

Taylor, Mark C.

  1984 *Erring: A Postmodern A/Theology.* Chicago: University of Chicago Press.

Teilhard de Chardin, Pierre

  1968 *Writings in Time of War.* Translated by Rene Hague. New York: Harper and Row.

Thiemann, Ronald

> 1985 *Revelation and Theology.* Notre Dame: University of Notre Dame Press.

Tillich, Paul

> 1932 *The Religious Situation.* Translated by H. Richard Niebuhr. New York: Henry Holt. (Reprinted New York: Meridian, 1956.)

> 1948 *The Protestant Era.* Chicago: University of Chicago Press. (Abridged edition, 1957.)

> 1951 *Systematic Theology.* Vol. 1. Chicago: University of Chicago Press.

> 1952 *The Courage to Be.* New Haven: Yale University Press.

> 1957 *Systematic Theology.* Vol. 2. Chicago: University of Chicago Press.

> 1957a *Dynamics of Faith.* New York: Harper and Brothers.

> 1959 *Theology of Culture.* Edited by Robert C. Kimball. New York: Oxford University Press.

> 1963 *Christianity and the Encounter of the World Religions.* New York: Columbia University Press.

> 1963a *Systematic Theology.* Vol. 3, Chicago: University of Chicago Press.

Toulmin, Stephen

> 1958 *The Uses of Argument.* Cambridge: Cambridge University Press.

Tracy, David

> 1975 *Blessed Rage for Order: The New Pluralism in Theology.* New York: Seabury/Crossroad.

> 1981 *The Analogical Imagination: Christian Theology and the Culture of Pluralism.* New York: Crossroad.

> 1987 *Plurality and Ambiguity: Hermeneutics, Religion, Hope.* San Francisco: Harper and Row.

Tu, Wei-ming

   1985 *Confucian Thought: Selfhood as Creative Transformation.*
   Albany: State University of New Press.

van Buren, Paul M.

   1980 *Discerning the Way.* Part 1 of *A Theology of the Jewish-
   Christian Reality.* San Francisco: Harper and Row.

   1983 *A Christian Theology of the People Israel.* Part 2 of *A
   Theology of the Jewish-Christian Reality.* San Francisco:
   Harper and Row.

   1988 *Christ in Context.* Part 3 of *A Theology of the Jewish-
   Christian Reality.* San Francisco: Harper and Row.

Vaught, Carl G.

   1982 *The Quest for Wholeness.* Albany: State University of New
   York Press.

   1986 *The Sermon on the Mount: A Theological Interpretation.*
   Albany: State University of New York Press.

von Rad, Gerhard

   1962 *The Theology of Israel's Historical Traditions.* Vol. 1 of
   Old Testament Theology. Translated by D. M. G. Stalker.
   New York: Harper and Row.

   1965 *The Theology of Israel's Prophetic Traditions.* Vol. 2 of
   Old Testament Theology. Translated by D. M. G. Stalker. New
   York: Harper and Row.

Weiss, Paul

   1958 *Modes of Being.* Carbondale: Southern Illinois University
   Press.

Welch, Claude

   1952 *In This Name: The Doctrine of the Trinity in Contemporary
   Theology.* New York: Macmillan.

West, Cornel

   1982 *Prophesy Deliverance!: An Afro-American Revolutionary
   Christianity.* Philadelphia: The Westminister Press.

Whitehead, Alfred North

   1929 *Process and Reality*. New York: Macmillan. (Corrected edition by David Ray Griffin and Donald W. Sherburne, New York:
   The Free Press, 1978).

Winquist, Charles E.

   1972 *The Transcendental Imagination: An Essay in Philosophical Theology*. The Hague: Martinus Nijoff.

   1975 *The Communion of Possibility*. Chico, Calif.: New Horizons
   Press.

Index